Trauma-Informed Practice in Montessori Classrooms

Trauma-Informed Practice in Montessori Classrooms provides important historical and contemporary evidence of the potential for Montessori schools to act as "healing" environments for children and young people. Drawing upon fascinating archival evidence and contemporary trauma theory, it shows how authentic Montessori schools already have the infrastructure to promote and embed trauma-informed practice (TIP) in their classrooms.

The book provides cutting-edge, interdisciplinary knowledge on trauma and highlights its potential to negatively impact the emotional, social, and cognitive functioning of children and young people. It explains clearly and precisely the principles of TIP and how historically, these were woven into the fabric of the early Montessori schools, resulting in their reputation as "Case della Salute" or "Health Homes." The book shows how this almost forgotten "healing" element of Montessori schools can be revived, harnessed, and promoted in ways that would benefit the overall health and well-being of children and young people.

This timely book is highly informative, hugely practical, and reader-friendly. It includes features such as boxed chapter objectives, learner outcomes, vignettes, chapter summaries, and questions for group discussion. It provides an invaluable guide for Montessori teachers and students, for home educators using the Montessori approach, and for non-Montessori educators and parents.

Bernadette Phillips is based at Maynooth University, Ireland, and has authored several titles on Montessori, trauma, and trauma-informed practice (TIP).

Catriona O'Toole is a Chartered Psychologist and Associate Professor at Maynooth University Department of Education.

Sinéad McGilloway is a Professor of Family and Community Mental Health and Founder Director of the Centre for Mental Health and Community Research at Maynooth University in Ireland.

Stephen Phillips is an Independent Researcher who has co-authored four books on Montessori and human development.

Trauma-Informed Practice in Montessori Classrooms
An Essential Guide for Students and Teachers

Bernadette Phillips, Catriona O'Toole, Sinéad McGilloway, and Stephen Phillips

LONDON AND NEW YORK

Designed cover image: © Getty Images

First edition published 2025
by Routledge
4 Park Square, Milton Park, Abingdon, Oxon, OX14 4RN

and by Routledge
605 Third Avenue, New York, NY 10158

Routledge is an imprint of the Taylor & Francis Group, an informa business

© 2025 Bernadette Phillips, Catriona O'Toole, Sinéad McGilloway and Stephen Phillips

The right of Bernadette Phillips, Catriona O'Toole, Sinéad McGilloway and Stephen Phillips to be identified as authors of this work has been asserted in accordance with sections 77 and 78 of the Copyright, Designs and Patents Act 1988.

All rights reserved. No part of this book may be reprinted or reproduced or utilised in any form or by any electronic, mechanical, or other means, now known or hereafter invented, including photocopying and recording, or in any information storage or retrieval system, without permission in writing from the publishers.

Trademark notice: Product or corporate names may be trademarks or registered trademarks, and are used only for identification and explanation without intent to infringe.

British Library Cataloguing-in-Publication Data
A catalogue record for this book is available from the British Library

ISBN: 978-1-032-57144-7 (hbk)
ISBN: 978-1-032-57145-4 (pbk)
ISBN: 978-1-003-43802-1 (ebk)

DOI: 10.4324/9781003438021

Typeset in Times New Roman
by KnowledgeWorks Global Ltd.

Dedication

Bernadette Phillips and Stephen Phillips

We dedicate this book to everyone at Bright Sparks Montessori School in Dublin, Ireland, who welcomed us into their beautiful setting, as we introduced our newly developed program of professional development on Montessori-attuned, trauma-informed practice. We had both a meeting of the minds and a meeting of the hearts, and it was an experience we will always cherish.

Go raibh míle maith agaibh!

Catriona O'Toole

For the children who have survived trauma and continually inspire and motivate my work, I dedicate this book to your strength and courage.

Sinéad McGilloway

To all the brave children who experience trauma in their lives and to the dedicated teachers and caregivers who support them – this book is for you – and may it be a source of hope and inspiration.

Contents

About the authors   xii
Acknowledgments   xiii

Introduction   1

Aims of this book 3
How this book is organized 3
Chapter outlines 4

PART I
Montessori's early "healing" schools   9

1 Maria Montessori: a pioneer in child mental health and trauma-informed pedagogy   11

Chapter objectives and Learning outcomes 11
Introducing Dr. Maria Montessori (1870–1952) 11
Becoming an expert in child mental health 13
Working with trauma-affected children 14
Campaigning for trauma-informed care 19
Summary of Chapter 1 21
Questions for group discussion 22

2 Devising a "healing" approach   24

Chapter objectives and Learning outcomes 24
Ensuring children feel valued and loved 24
Observing children through a "trauma-informed lens" 26
Helping children to "feel" safe and "be" safe 26

Providing children with regulating tasks – practical life activities 29
Re-organizing disorganized minds – sensorial activities 30
Preventing mental strain by using "muscle memory" – language and math activities 31
Re-wiring the brain – cultural activities, music, movement, art, and drama 32
Empowering children by building on their strengths 33
Summary of Chapter 2 34
Questions for group discussion 34

PART II
Trauma 37

3 What is trauma? 39

Chapter objectives and Learning outcomes 39
Defining the term "trauma" and looking at types of trauma 40
Examining types of stress and explaining the stress response system 42
Explaining the stress response system 44
Understanding "hyper-arousal" and "hypo-arousal" 48
Recognizing signs and symptoms (which may be indicative) of traumatic stress 49
Understanding the concept of "state-dependent functioning" 52
Exploring the concept of a "window of tolerance" 53
Examining the polyvagal theory (PVT) 54
Explaining the PACE model 55
Summary of Chapter 3 56
Questions for group discussion 57

4 The effects of trauma on emotional, social, and cognitive functioning 59

Chapter objectives and Learning outcomes 59
Looking at the impact of trauma on children's emotional functioning 60
Examining the impact of trauma on children's social functioning 64
Understanding the impact of trauma on children's cognitive functioning 68
Summary of Chapter 4 74
Questions for group discussion 75

Contents ix

5 The prevalence and causes of trauma – the ACE study 77

*Chapter objectives and Learning outcomes 77
Revisiting the original ACE study 77
Examining the findings of the ACE study 80
Looking at the limitations and on-going influence of the ACE study 82
Addressing the social determinants of physical and mental ill-health 86
Summary of Chapter 5 87
Questions for group discussion 88*

PART III
Trauma-informed practice
91

6 What is trauma-informed practice? 93

*Chapter objectives and Learning outcomes 93
Defining the term "trauma-informed practice" 93
Outlining the key principles and assumptions of trauma-informed practice 96
Summary of Chapter 6 102
Questions for group discussion 103*

7 Trauma-informed practice in education 104

*Chapter objectives and Learning outcomes 104
Looking at trauma-informed practice in education 105
Shifting the perspective from a deficit lens to a trauma-informed lens 106
Explaining TIP as a relationship-based approach 107
Explaining TIP as a strengths-based approach 109
Explaining TIP as a "whole-school" approach 112
Discussing how TIP promotes a culture of safety, collaboration, and empowerment 112
Outlining the benefits of TIP for children, teachers, and families 113
Promoting the health of educators by highlighting self-care in TIP 114
Explaining the steps in the journey to becoming a trauma-informed school 117
Summary of Chapter 7 117
Questions for group discussion 118*

PART IV
Contemporary Montessori schools and trauma-informed practice   121

8   How the six TIP principles are incorporated into Montessori schools   123

Chapter objectives and Learning outcomes 123
Looking at factors that promote safety in Montessori schools 124
Considering how trustworthiness and transparency are promoted in Montessori schools 130
Showing how peer support can be promoted in Montessori schools 131
Looking at how collaboration and mutuality are promoted in Montessori schools 132
Examining how empowerment, voice, and choice are promoted in Montessori schools 138
How cultural, historical, and gender issues can be responded to in Montessori schools 141
How DEI and ABAR principles can be responded to in Montessori schools 143
Summary of Chapter 8 145
Questions for group discussion 146

9   How the four TIP assumptions can be incorporated into Montessori schools   149

Chapter objectives and Learning outcomes 149
Considering how Montessori schools can realize the widespread impact of trauma 150
Outlining how Montessori schools can recognize the signs/symptoms of trauma 150
Examining how Montessori schools respond to trauma in their policies and practices 153
Looking at how Montessori schools can resist re-traumatization of students and families 155
Summary of Chapter 9 157
Questions for group discussion 157

10   How contemporary Montessori schools can help trauma-affected children   159

Chapter objectives and Learning outcomes 159
Examining sequential memory and how Montessori schools aid its development 160

Prioritizing activities that are regulating for children and young people 163
Creating environments that are relationally rich and promote belonging 169
Maintaining environments that promote deep engagement – how "flow" heals trauma 171
Summary of Chapter 10 174
Questions for group discussion 175

Conclusion 178

Index 182

About the authors

Bernadette Phillips MA (UCD), Mont. Dip. (London Montessori Centre), has recently completed her PhD at Maynooth University, Ireland. An internationally recognized author on Montessori, trauma, and trauma-informed practice (TIP), Bernadette brings 30 years' experience as a practitioner and course developer to advancing the Montessori approach to TIP.

Catriona O'Toole is a Chartered Psychologist and Associate Professor at Maynooth University Department of Education. She specializes in trauma-informed practice and student well-being in educational contexts. An experienced educator, practitioner, and internationally award-winning author, she is recognized for her contributions to both research and practice.

Sinéad McGilloway PhD, CPsychol, CSci, AFBPS, is a Professor of Family and Community Mental Health and Founder Director of the Centre for Mental Health and Community Research at Maynooth University, Ireland. She is an internationally recognized and prizewinning academic specializing in early intervention and prevention, and service evaluation.

Stephen Phillips brings over 30 years of experience as a practitioner, owner, and manager of Montessori schools in Ireland and the UK. He is an independent researcher who has co-authored four books on Montessori and human development and designed and delivered Montessori courses up to University level.

Acknowledgments

Stephen Phillips and Bernadette Phillips

As always, we are grateful to our three beautiful children who enriched our lives, filled us with joy, and occasionally gave us sleepless nights. You changed our lives for the better, and we love you more than words can say.

We wish to acknowledge the early Montessori advocates – Maccheroni, Tozier, George, Canfield Fisher, Stevens, Bailey, White, and Cromwell, to name but a few, who faithfully recorded what they witnessed, leaving us a record of a moment in history that resonates to this day.

We also acknowledge the later Montessorians who faithfully and courageously took Dr. Montessori's principles and either put them into practice, disseminated them, or both –including Paula Polk Lillard, Lynn Lillard Jessen, Angeline Lillard, Paula Lillard Preschlack, John Chattin-McNichols, Tim Seldin, Donna Bryant Goertz, Angela Murray, and many others.

To all of these scholars and practitioners, whose work we stand on, we are deeply indebted.

Bernadette Phillips

I wish to acknowledge the support of the Irish Research Council (IRC).
Go raibh míle maith agaibh go léir.

We would also like to thank the staff of Routledge for their enthusiasm, encouragement, and support throughout the publication process.

Introduction

When 12 year old Jasmin's mom passed away following a month long battle with COVID 19, Jasmin was bereft. She felt numb, terrified and totally overwhelmed. Her mom was the only family she had. Everything felt surreal. In just a few hours, she felt like she had become another person. Now, there was just the memory of the Jasmin who had lived a happy and care-free life for 12 whole years. The ordinary middle school kid whose only worry was getting her homework done in time to sit next to Billy at the ball game sharing popcorn and jokes, was now just a painful memory. Overnight, she had become an orphan. Suddenly strangers were deciding her fate, where she would live and who she would live with. Right now, she wasn't sure she actually wanted to live.

When Bruno was a little fellow, his mother and father were killed in the Messina earthquake. Because he was one of so many left-behind babies, he was quite neglected, and he grew up to four years as a weed grows. Sometimes one madre of the tenement mothered him, sometimes not. At times he was fed, at other times he starved. Because of the great fear that came to him with the blinding smoke and the twisting red river of molten lava and the death cry of his girl mother that day of the earthquake, Bruno's mind seemed a bit dulled. He was often confused by the commands of people who tried to take care of him and so could not obey. Then they would strike him. And he heard very vile language spoken and he saw very evil things done during his babyhood in the tenement.

When Bruno wandered across the threshold of the Via Guisti Children's House in Rome, he seemed like a little alien among the other happy little

DOI: 10.4324/9781003438021-1

> ones who were so carefully watched over, so gently led. For days he sat in silence, his great, frightened blue eyes watching to help him dodge the blow that he expected but never felt; his lips ready to imitate the vile speech that he had known before, but which he never heard here. His timid fingers fumbled with the big pink and blue letters that the other children used in making long sentences on the floor; they tried to button, to lace, to match colors, but not very effectually. It was as if the great fear of his babyhood had shadowed his whole mental life and left him powerless.
>
> (Carolyn Bailey, 1915, *Montessori Children*, p. 36)

There is nothing new about trauma. It has been with us since the beginning of time. Humans have always been prey to natural traumatic events such as floods, earthquakes, storms, as well as personal traumatic events such as adversity, neglect, and abuse. What is new however, is that we now have the knowledge, through interdisciplinary research (in fields as diverse as medicine, psychology, neuroscience and anthropology), to understand the neurobiological mechanisms of trauma, i.e. how it gets under the skin (van Zomeren-Dohm et al., 2013), how it impacts the mind and the body, and how it affects a child's emotional, social and cognitive functioning (Levine & Kline 2007/2019; Perry, 2009; Perry & Szalavitz, 2017; Perry et al., 1995; van der Kolk, 2014). This knowledge explains why children who have been exposed to trauma often have difficulty controlling their emotions, making and maintaining friendships, concentrating, memorizing, and ultimately learning, especially in school settings (Cole et al., 2005; Craig, 2016). Most importantly, understanding the neurobiology of trauma opens the door for us to find ways to heal trauma and prevent re-traumatization. Consequently, over the last two decades, there has been a move to make schools trauma-aware and trauma-informed (i.e., able to recognize and respond to the potentially long-term negative impact of trauma on children) (Alexander, 2019; Brooks, 2020; Brummer, 2021; Brunzell & Norrish, 2021; Cole et al., 2005; Craig, 2016, p. 2013; Jennings, 2019; Nicholson et al., 2023; Thomas et al., 2019; Venet, 2021, Wolpow et al., 2016; Wright, 2023).

Historical evidence shows that early in her career, Maria Montessori, a practicing physician specializing in psychology, and a professor of pedagogical anthropology in the Faculty of Natural Sciences and Medicine, at the University of Rome, recognized the pervasiveness of trauma. She later wrote, "Children have many kinds of sensitiveness, but they are all alike in their sensitiveness to *trauma*" (Montessori, 1967, p. 131). The Montessori Method, as practiced in Montessori's early schools (circa 1907–1917), was by its very nature both trauma-sensitive and trauma-responsive. The combination of years of research, and intensive work with trauma-affected children, aided Professor Montessori in the creation of environments in which children who had been harmed by adversity or trauma could benefit therapeutically. Psychological healing was achieved through the children's daily engagement in a range of practical, sensorial, academic, and mindfulness-based activities that were repetitive and rhythmic (Lillard, 2011; Phillips et al., 2022). These activities included music, movement, dance, art, and horticultural pursuits. The children were free to engage in these activities at their own pace, and these activities had a positive impact on their emotional, social, and cognitive functioning, as well as their overall well-being. A central element of the Montessori approach appeared to be the freedom the children were given to select their own activities and materials, and engage with them and repeat them for as long as they wanted to. Since repetitive, rhythmic activities have been shown to promote healing from trauma (Perry, 2009), these children were essentially selecting their own therapy, and controlling their own dosage. In addition, Montessori recognized the importance of positive relational interactions in the healing of trauma and facilitated this in her schools. In this respect, she anticipated current research in relational neurobiology which points toward the centrality of attuned, responsive relationships in the healing of trauma-affected children (Ludy-Dobson & Perry, 2010). This reduction in the children's anxiety and stress, appeared to lead directly to enhanced academic performance, as well as other aspects of overall well-being, including improved self-esteem and independence (De Stefano, 2022; Kramer, 1976). In the decades to come, Montessori was relentless in creating and advocating for schools that promote and support psychological well-being in children so that they might be able to flourish, whatever their circumstances.

Aims of this book

1 To provide the learner with a knowledge of Montessori's expertise in, and involvement with, trauma and trauma-affected children and her approach to helping them to heal. It also aims to demonstrate how contemporary Montessori teachers can apply trauma-informed principles in their schools with children of all ages, and how Montessori parents and home-schooling families, can use this knowledge about trauma and trauma-informed practice to help children.
2 To provide the reader with a thorough knowledge of the nature and impact of trauma on children of varying ages.
3 To provide the reader with an understanding of what "trauma-informed practice" is and how a school can begin their journey toward becoming "trauma aware," "trauma sensitive," "trauma responsive" and then, becoming equipped with the necessary knowledge, perspective-change and understanding finally commit, as a whole school, to embracing true "trauma-informed practice."

How this book is organized

Part I: Montessori's early "healing" schools

The first part of the book focuses on Montessori's early "healing" schools. It shows how the early Montessori schools were "trauma-sensitive" by their very nature and demonstrates how "trauma-responsive" practices were woven into the very fabric of the schools. It also highlights Montessori's efforts to establish trauma-informed training courses for teachers and nurses working with children who were traumatized by wars and natural disasters.

Part II: Trauma

The second part of the book focuses on trauma. It presents definitions of trauma and outlines the various types of trauma. It discusses stress, categories of stress, and the stress response system. It explains the potential impact of childhood trauma on the developing brain and subsequently on the emotional, social, and cognitive functioning of children. It discusses the prevalence and causes of trauma as demonstrated through the original ACE study.

Part III: Trauma-informed practice (TIP)

Part III focuses on trauma-informed practice (TIP) in general, and trauma-informed practice specifically as applied in educational settings. It outlines the six key principles and four underlying assumptions of TIP and describes what it should look like and feel like for the children/young people/staff in an educational setting. It outlines the steps necessary for a school to commit to and engage in true "trauma-informed practice."

Part IV: Contemporary Montessori schools and trauma-informed practice

The fourth part of the book focuses on contemporary Montessori schools. It suggests that contemporary Montessori schools could learn from and build upon Montessori's early work. It examines to what extent contemporary Montessori schools are already trauma-informed by design, and it addresses the question of how they can better incorporate trauma-informed principles into their daily routines.

Chapter outlines

Chapter 1: Montessori: a pioneer in mental health and TIP pedagogy

The first chapter highlights Dr. Montessori's expertise and recognition as an expert in the area of child mental health. It focuses on her direct involvement with children who were exposed to adversity and trauma. It describes her work with diverse groups of trauma-impacted children. It also describes her efforts to establish an organization to be called the White Cross, which would focus on bringing psychological healing to children who had been traumatized by wars and natural disasters. It also reveals how her early schools were known as *Case della Salute* (Health Houses), because significant numbers of trauma-affected children who attended them began to show signs of psychological healing.

Chapter 2: Devising a "healing" approach

The second chapter outlines what Dr. Montessori did to help children to feel safe, loved, and empowered. It outlines in detail the relational and pedagogical approaches she promoted which brought psychological healing to these children. It also explains how she used Practical Life, Sensorial, Language, Mathematical, and Cultural activities to meet the needs of the trauma-affected children who attended her schools.

Chapter 3: What is trauma?

The third chapter introduces the concept of trauma. It examines definitions of trauma and gives examples of the three main types of trauma. It distinguishes between the different types of stress, and it explains the operation of the stress response system and how repeated activation of the stress response system can lead to toxic stress which can cause serious harm to children both physically and psychologically. It explains what is meant by "adaptive responses" and "hyper and hypo-arousal." It lists common signs and symptoms of trauma, and it explains terms such as "state dependent" functioning, the concept of a "window of tolerance," the "polvagal" theory, and the PACE model.

Chapter 4: The effects of trauma on emotional, social, and cognitive functioning

The fourth chapter explains the effects of trauma on the child's emotional, social, and cognitive functioning. It examines the effect of traumatic experience on the child's ability to control emotions, relate to others, make friendships, concentrate, use language, and develop memory.

Chapter 5: The prevalence and causes of trauma – the ACE study

The fifth chapter highlights the prevalence and causes of trauma. It revisits the original adverse childhood experiences (ACE) study and explains its findings and on-going influence. It discusses the limitations, misapplications, and extensions of the original study. The chapter also discusses some of the social determinants of adversity and trauma such as poverty, discrimination, oppression, as well as racism, refugee status, and SES background.

Chapter 6: What is trauma-informed practice?

The sixth chapter introduces the concept of trauma-informed practice (TIP) in general. It explains clearly and succinctly what TIP is. It outlines the four assumptions, and six key principles of TIP which are – *Safety; Trustworthiness and transparency; Peer support; Empowerment, voice, and choice; Collaboration and mutuality;* and *Cultural, historical, and gender issues* (SAMHSA, 2014).

Chapter 7: Trauma-informed practice in education

The seventh chapter introduces the reader to trauma-informed practice in education. It explains how a TIP approach shifts the perspective of educators away from a deficit lens which focuses on what is wrong with the child toward a trauma-informed lens which focuses on what has happened to the child. It presents TIP as a relationship-based, strengths-based, whole-school approach, which promotes a culture of safety, collaboration, and empowerment. It explains how a TIP approach promotes the health of educators by teaching them about their vulnerability to vicarious trauma and their vital need for self-care. It outlines the steps toward becoming a trauma-informed school.

Chapter 8: How the 6 TIP principles are incorporated into Montessori schools

The eighth chapter outlines how the six key principles of TIP: *Safety; Trustworthiness and transparency; Peer support; Empowerment, voice, and choice; Collaboration and mutuality; and Cultural, historical, and gender issues* are naturally incorporated into genuine Montessori schools. It also discusses how DEI and ABAR principles can be responded to in contemporary Montessori schools.

Chapter 9: How the four TIP assumptions can be incorporated into Montessori schools

The ninth chapter outlines how the four assumptions of TIP; *realize, recognize, respond, and resist-retraumatization,* can be incorporated into Montessori schools.

Chapter 10: How contemporary Montessori schools can help trauma-affected children

The tenth chapter outlines how contemporary Montessori schools can help children affected by trauma. Specifically, it discusses sequential memory and explains clearly and concisely what it is and why it is impaired or slow to develop in trauma-affected children. It explains why it is so necessary for learning and demonstrates how sequential memory problems are circumvented in the Montessori school. It also explains how the structured activities and the structured layout of the Montessori-prepared environment aid the development of sequential memory. It then examines how Montessori environments prioritize exercises and activities that have a *regulating* effect on children and young people, how Montessori environments are *relationally* rich because they emphasize mixed age groups and peer teaching, and how Montessori environments promote *deep engagement* and facilitate the "flow" experience which has been shown to be healing for trauma-affected individuals.

Conclusion

The conclusion synthesizes the information presented in the previous chapters and discusses the unique contribution the Montessori approach can make to the lives of trauma-affected children and young people.

References

Alexander, J. (2019). *Building trauma-sensitive schools: Your guide to creating safe, supportive learning environments for all students.* Brookes.

Bailey, C. S. (1915). *Montessori children.* Holt

Brooks, R. (2020). *The trauma and attachment aware classroom: A practical guide to supporting children who have encountered trauma and adverse childhood experiences.* Jessica Kingsley Publishers.

Brummer, J. (2021). *Building a trauma-informed restorative school: Skills and approaches for improving culture and behaviour.* Jessica Kingsley Publishers.

Brunzell, T., & Norrish, J. (2021). *Creating trauma informed, strengths-based classrooms: Teacher strategies for nurturing student's healing, growth, and learning.* Jessica Kingsley Publishers.

Cole, S. F., Greenwald O'Brien, J., Gadd, M. G., Ristuccia, J., Wallace, D. L., & Gregory, M. (2005). Helping traumatized children learn: Supportive school environments for children traumatized by family violence. *Massachusetts advocates for children, trauma and learning policy initiative.* https://traumasensitiveschools.org/wp-content/uploads/2013/06/Helping-Traumatized-Children-Learn.pdf

Craig, S. E. (2016). *Trauma sensitive schools: Learning communities transforming children's lives.* Teachers College Press.

De Stefano, C. (2022). *The child is the teacher: A life of Maria Montessori.* Other Press.

Jennings, P. A. (2019). *The trauma-sensitive classroom: Building resilience with compassionate teaching.* W. W. Norton & Company.

Kramer, R. (1976). *Maria Montessori: A biography.* Addison-Wesley.

Levine, P. (1997). *Waking the tiger: Healing trauma.* North Atlantic Books.

Levine, P., & Kline, M. (2019). *Trauma through a child's eyes.* North Atlantic Books. (Original work published 2007)

Lillard, A. (2011). Mindfulness practices in education: Montessori's approach. *Mindfulness, 2,* 78–85.https://doi.org/10.1007/s12671-011-0045-6

Ludy-Dobson, C., & Perry, B. (2010). The role of healthy relational interactions in buffering the impact of childhood trauma. In E. Gil (Ed.) *Working with children to heal interpersonal trauma: The power of play.* The Guilford Press.

Montessori, M. (1967). *The absorbent mind* (C. A. Claremont, Trans). Dell. (Original work published 1949)

Nicholson, J., Perez, L., Kurtz, J., Bryant, S., & Giles, D. (2023). *Trauma-informed practices for early childhood educators: Relationship-based approached that reduce stress, build resilience and support healing in young children.* Routledge.

Perry, B. D. (2009). Examining child maltreatment through a neurodevelopment lens: Clinical applications of the neurosequential model of therapeutics. *Journal of Loss and Trauma, 14*(4), 240–245. https://doi.org/10.1080/15325020903004350

Perry, B. D., Pollard, R. A., Blakley, Y. L., Baker, W. L., & Vigilante, D. (1995). Childhood trauma, the neurobiology of adaptation, and use-dependent development of the brain: How states become traits. *Infant Mental Health Journal, 16*(4), 271–291. https://doi.org/10.1002/1097-0355(199524)16:4<271::AID-IMHJ2280160404>3.0.CO;2-B

Perry, B. D., & Szalavitz, M. (2017). *The boy who was raised as a dog: And other stories from a child psychiatrist's notebook—What traumatized children can teach us about loss, love, and healing.* Basic Books.

Phillips, B., O'Toole, C., McGilloway, S., & Phillips, S. (2022). Montessori, the white cross, and trauma-informed practice: Lessons for contemporary education. *Journal of Montessori Research.* 8(1), 13–28.

SAMHSA, (2014). Substance Abuse and Mental Health Services Administration. (2014, July). SAMHSA's concept of trauma and guidance for a trauma-informed approach. Retrieved from https://store.samhsa.gov/shin/content/SMA14-4884/SMA-4884.pdf

Thomas, M. S., Crosby, S., & Vanderhaar, J. (2019). Trauma-informed practices in schools across two decades: An interdisciplinary review of research. *Review of Research in Education, 43*(1), 422–452. https://doi.org/10.3102/0091732X18821123

van der Kolk, B. (2014). *The body keeps the score: Mind, brain and body in the transformation of trauma.* Penguin.

van Zomeren-Dohm, A., Ng, R., Howard, K., Kenney, M., Ritchmeier, L., & Gourneau (2013). *Children's mental health review: How trauma gets under the skin.* University of Minnesota Extension.

Venet, A. S. (2021). *Equity-centered, trauma-informed education.* Norton & co. Inc.

Wolpow, R., Johnson, M. M., Hertel, R., & Kincaid, S. O. (2016). *The heart of learning and teaching: Compassion, resiliency, and academic success.* https://www.k12.wa.us/sites/default/files/public/compassionateschools/pubdocs/theheartoflearningandteaching.pdf

Wright, T. (2023). *Emotionally responsive teaching: Expanding trauma informed practice with young children.* Teachers College Press.

Part I
Montessori's early "healing" schools

1 Maria Montessori: a pioneer in child mental health and trauma-informed pedagogy

Chapter objectives

- To provide a short biography of Dr. Montessori, highlighting her expertise in mental health.
- To describe Montessori's involvement with children affected by adversity/trauma.
- To outline Montessori's campaign to establish trauma-informed care.

Learning outcomes

At the end of this chapter, the learner will have a knowledge of Dr. Montessori's:

- Interest and expertise in child mental health.
- Significant involvement with childhood adversity and trauma.
- Efforts to establish trauma-informed care.

Introducing Dr. Maria Montessori (1870–1952)

Travis Wright, a contemporary author on trauma and trauma-informed practice, states that "the Montessori approach might well be considered the first trauma-informed pedagogy" (2019, p. 136). The *Oxford Handbook of the History of Psychology* (2012) lists Maria Montessori as being among the second generation of scholars who promoted a series of enterprises that included debates, experiments, and laboratories that marked the beginnings of the new science of psychology (Cimino & Foschi, 2012). She is described by her contemporaries and by current Montessori scholars as a "brain specialist" (Radice, 1920, p. 1), "an expert in children's mental illnesses" (Gutek & Gutek, 2016, p. 32),

DOI: 10.4324/9781003438021-3

"a competent clinical psychiatrist" (Povell, 2010, p. 40), and a woman who sculpted out an extraordinary career that embraced both psychiatry and education (Babini, 2000). In the early 1900s, when she directed preschools for young children, she referred to them as *Case della Salute* or "Health Homes" (Montessori, 1966, p. 181), wherein children affected by mental health issues experienced "cures" (Montessori, 1966, p. 181) on a considerable scale. During her lifetime, she won the respect of several famous psychiatrists including Sigmund Freud. She was an esteemed keynote speaker at meetings of the British Psychological Society (BPS). In fact, when Montessori addressed the BPS in 1919, it was recorded that the key theme of the meeting was the question of whether her work in schools would eventually make psychologists redundant (Radice, 1920). The famous Scottish psychiatrist Dr. Hugh Crichton Miller, founder of the Tavistock Mental Health Clinic in London, who translated Montessori's address to the BPS famously stated that when the Montessori method becomes widespread in schools, poorhouses will have to be set up for the psychoanalysts (Radice, 1920). This recognition of Montessori as a mental health expert who promoted psychological health, as well as healing from trauma through her unique pedagogical practice, has been overlooked in contemporary Montessori literature and needs to be highlighted once again so that the full benefits of the Montessori approach can be intentionally utilized in schools to promote positive mental health in children while also helping trauma-affected children and preventing their re-traumatization.

The beginnings

Maria Montessori was born on August 31, 1870, to a middle-class conservative father and a rather more liberal-minded mother. What little records we have of her childhood describe her as a happy, kind child who unfortunately found school to be an oppressive and boring environment in which she initially did not excel (De Stefano, 2022). In her teens, she attended a boy's technical college in order to learn mathematics and science. It was here that she began to distinguish herself in her studies (Kramer, 1976). After a period of interest in engineering, she turned her attention to medicine and applied to the University of Rome to train as a physician. Montessori's tenacious attempts to gain entry to the faculty of medicine at the University of Rome are well documented (De Stefano, 2022; Kramer, 1976). Suffice it to say that in July 1892, following a two-year course in the Faculty of Natural Sciences, studying physics, chemistry, biology, and mathematics, and successfully obtaining the Diploma di Licenza, as well as private tuition in the Classics, Montessori finally gained admission to the Medical Faculty at the University of Rome. She was the only female student to gain acceptance to the medical faculty in that academic year (Povell, 2010). She was a tenacious and disciplined student, and she endured many hardships including being prohibited from attending dissecting classes along with the other students because it was deemed inappropriate for a female to dissect naked bodies in the presence of men (De Stefano, 2022). Despite these hardships, Montessori excelled as a medical student. She also studied and observed patients at the *Clinica Psichiatrica* (Psychiatric Clinic) attached to the University of Rome and chose to write her thesis on a psychiatric subject relating to paranoia (Kramer, 1976). In July 1896, she graduated from the University of Rome with a double honors degree in medicine and surgery (De Stefano, 2022).

Becoming an expert in child mental health

Upon graduation, Montessori continued to carry out research at the Clinica Psichiatrica, where she obtained a position as a voluntary assistant doctor. Her student and life-long friend, Maria Maccheroni, recorded that Montessori spent two years at this clinic, studying mental health issues in children (Maccheroni, 1947,). Specifically, she "specialized in the field of neuropsychiatry" (Quarfood, 2023, p. 7). She worked alongside Dr. Clodomiro Bonfigli, a recognized specialist in mental disabilities in children. His lectures on *social medicine* and what he identified as the common determinants of mental and physical conditions in children – poverty, upbringing, and social inequalities – strongly influenced Montessori's own thinking (Kramer, 1976). She also worked alongside Dr. Guisseppi Montessano, another volunteer physician specializing in psychiatry and just two years older than Montessori, with whom she was to develop a deeply personal as well as professional relationship (Povell, 2010).

As part of her duties at the Clinica Psichiatrica, the young Dr. Montessori was required to go into the Roman psychiatric hospitals to select suitable candidates to take back to the clinic for study. It was during the course of this work that she first became involved with children who because they were unable to function at school or in their homes were taken out of school and placed in these institutions that offered them no opportunities for learning or development (Montessori, 2008). It was believed that they were unteachable, and therefore totally unreceptive to schooling. From the outset, Montessori viewed these children with compassion. She was aware that she was dealing not just with children with developmental difficulties but also with children who had been exposed to adversities such as poverty and neglect, as well as the trauma of being removed from their families and schools. She described these children as being of the poorest classes, neglected even by their own parents, and excluded by the State from education because they were unable to function in traditional schools (Montessori, 2008). Having been told by the children's caretaker that the children were greedy because after their meals they would crawl around the floor searching for breadcrumbs (Kramer, 1976), Montessori observed that the children had no toys or materials of any kind and that the room they spent their days and nights in was completely bare (Standing, 1957). To Montessori, these were not greedy children looking for more bread but were children experiencing neglect, and being starved of intellectual stimulation, they were using the breadcrumbs as playthings or learning materials (Kramer, 1976). She took some of these children back to the psychiatric clinic and began to work with them. She researched everything she could find relating to the education of what were then called "backward" children, and her research led her to the work of two almost forgotten French doctors, Jean-Marc-Gaspard Itard (1774–1838) and

Edouard Seguin (1812–1880). The work of both of these doctors had a profound impact on Montessori's approach to the teaching of children with developmental disabilities (and later, to the teaching of their typically developing peers). Over the next two years, building on the work of Itard and Seguin, Montessori, and her colleague Dr. Montessano established and co-directed a medical-pedagogical institute referred to as the "Orthophrenic School" (Kramer, 1976). In that institute, Montessori improved the emotional, social, and cognitive functioning of these so-called "backward" children to such an extent that she was able to present them at the Italian State Examinations where they were able to pass the same examinations given to children in the primary grades (Montessori, 1912/1964) much to the disbelief of everyone concerned.

At this Institute, Montessori trained teachers in a special method of education for children who were unable to function in traditional schools, as well as children who had been labeled as "unteachable" and sent to live in the psychiatric hospitals (which she referred to as asylums). It was during this short period that Montessori gained both national and international recognition as a knowledgeable clinical psychiatrist and a specialist in mental health difficulties in children. In 1901, Montessori suddenly resigned from the Orthophrenic School. Now in her early 30s, she returned to the University of Rome and immersed herself in research on experimental psychology, educational philosophy, and pedagogical anthropology. She continued her academic work for several years until at the end of 1906, an invitation came her way which was to turn her life in another direction and involve her in work with children who had experienced significant exposure to adversity and trauma (De Stefano, 2022; Kramer, 1976).

Working with trauma-affected children

From 1907 to 1917, Montessori worked with three groups of children who had been harmed by exposure to both chronic and acute experiences of adversity and trauma. These were the impoverished children of San Lorenzo (1907); the traumatized child survivors of the Messina earthquake (1908); and the traumatized French and Belgian war orphans (1916). During these years, Montessori and many of her teacher-directresses witnessed remarkable psychological healing in many of these children through the application of the Montessori Method. Here is a brief account of these three groups of children.

The impoverished children of San Lorenzo (1907)

Toward the end of 1906, Montessori was invited by Edoardo Talamo (the director of the Beni Stabili, a large Italian building society) to undertake the organization of infant schools in its newly refurbished model tenements (Foschi, 2008). Montessori had long wished to experiment with the methods she had used with children with developmental challenges; in a class of children who did not have such challenges, however, she had not considered working with preschool children believing them to be too young for her educational experiment (Montessori, 1964). She said it was pure chance that brought this opportunity to her (Montessori, 1964). Talamo and his organization were seeking to bring social improvements to the extremely impoverished and crime-ridden district of San Lorenzo by improving tenement accommodation that would include a daycare facility for children under six years who were too young to attend the state schools. Montessori who had become well known as an expert in educational matters (Foschi, 2008) was invited to organize and direct the educational aspects of these facilities. On Sunday, January 6, 1907, the first Children's House was officially opened in a large ground floor room in one of these refurbished tenements at 58 Via de Marsi, San Lorenzo, Rome. Montessori vividly describes the children who were enrolled as frightened, fretful children, so shy that they would not even speak (Montessori, 1936). She said they were impoverished, neglected children who had spent their first years in slum tenement buildings with no intellectual stimulation and no care. She said it was obvious to all that they needed better nutrition, sunlight, and a more natural environment (Montessori, 1936). These children had been exposed to chronic neglect and poverty, or what we would today call adverse childhood experiences (Felitti et al., 1998) and Montessori was quick to recognize that their social anxieties and emotional upsets were inextricably linked to their chronic exposure to adversity and psychological healing was needed.

Signs of psychological healing in the San Lorenzo children

Montessori's first biographer, E. M. Standing, records Montessori's statement that her schools, "may be compared in the first place to sanitoria; for the first thing that happens in them is that the children are restored to mental health" (Standing, E. M. *Maria Montessori: Her life and Work.* 1957, p. 178). In her book, *The Secret of Childhood*, Montessori describes how her *experiment* in San Lorenzo resulted in a complete transformation of the children's mental and physical health. Having arrived at the Casa as tearful, frightened children, incapable of following even the simple instructions they were given for the opening ceremony, they were, within a few months, transformed into happy, confident, children who showed indisputable signs of social, emotional, and cognitive flourishing, even learning to write, and then read at four and five years of age. This drew the attention of professors of education from many of the most prestigious universities in the world who traveled to Rome to see these children with their own eyes (Fisher, 1912). The approaches that facilitated this psychological healing in the children will be outlined in Chapter 2.

The traumatized child survivors of the Messina earthquake (1908)

On December 28, 1908, at approximately 5:20 a.m., a violent earthquake (which today would be measured at 7.5 on the Richter scale) struck southern Italy, with devastating force. The cities of Messina and Reggio di Calabria, as well as dozens of other coastal areas at the toe of Italy's geographical boot, were decimated. The quake was followed within minutes by a powerful tsunami that caused tidal waves estimated to be 13 meters (40 feet) high to come crashing down on the coast (Pino et al., 2008). Thousands of men, women, and children were trapped under the debris. Most injuries were fatal, others horrific. The death toll was (conservatively) estimated to be in the region of 80,000. It may have been much higher. Incredibly, there were survivors, many of them children, whose lives within a matter of seconds had changed irrevocably. They were now traumatized, homeless orphans. Some of these child survivors were only found some days after the earthquake. Many were discovered in a state of total shock and trauma, wandering through thick clouds of smoke and sulfur, stepping over the dead and mangled bodies of those who were once their relatives, neighbors, and friends.

In the weeks and months following the earthquake, the Italian Government urgently sought to protect the surviving, mostly orphaned children from further trauma and harm. In the media, the child survivors were referred to as orphans of the nation, and there was a call from the Italian Government for those in a position to help these orphans to step up and do so (Moretti, 2014). However, a year and some months after the earthquake, the needs of many of the child survivors of the disaster were still not being met, and there was a further call for assistance. Responding to this, Montessori stepped up and offered practical help. She had promoted the theory of social motherhood in *Il Metodo* (Montessori, 1909), her first publication on her educational approach, now here was her chance to put the theory into practice (Moretti, 2014).

Montessori states that 60 child survivors of the earthquake were housed in a new Montessori school, located in a Franciscan convent on the Via Giusti in Rome (Montessori, 1936). This school was specially set up to meet the needs of the child survivors of the disaster. The school was directed by Professor Anna Maccheroni, a former music teacher and one of Montessori's first students. Queen Margherita of Italy took a particular interest in these children and became the patron of the school, providing little chairs and tables as well as the didactic materials (Montessori, 1936). In 1910, the nuns attended a training course on the Montessori Method (Kramer, 1976). In her book, *The Secret of Childhood* (1936), Montessori vividly described the traumatized state of the children. She said that they were "numbed," "silent," and "absent-minded," and that it was difficult to get them to eat and difficult to get them to sleep, and she added that during the night, their screams and cries could be widely heard (1936). She said that their names were unknown, and the terrible shock from the earthquake had left them all in the same dazed condition (Montessori, 1936). Today, we would sum it all up by saying that these children were displaying signs of complex post-traumatic stress.

Signs of psychological healing in the Messina orphans

Montessori states that these children, having arrived at the Casa as numbed, emotionally distraught, trauma-affected children, most of them suffering the agony of having lost their parents, their siblings, their homes, their relatives and friends, gradually overcame their sense of sadness and despair and steadily began to experience once more feelings of happiness (1936). The children were observed by eyewitnesses to be slowly but surely overcoming the potentially devastating effects of exposure to trauma (Bailey, 1915; Fisher, 1912). Montessori described the remarkable changes that occurred in the children. She explained how activities involving the repetition of precise and exact movements induced concentration in them and how this concentration, in turn, brought about a state of calm in the children (Montessori, 1936). She gives us a picture of how the nuns, many of whom hailed from the aristocracy, taught the children how to lay out elongated dinner tables with exactitude, placing refined items of cutlery, delicate plates, and beautifully folded serviettes in the correct places paying particular attention to orderliness and precision. She wrote that the meal times that they now had no appetite for interested them as an exercise in order. For example, they appeared to derive some happiness from carefully setting out the long tables with plates, bowls, cutlery, and serviettes, in an exact manner, using controlled and meticulous movements (Montessori, 1936). In a later chapter, we discuss Dr. Bruce Perry's theories on the power of repetitive, activities to regulate the dysregulated brains of trauma-affected children (MacKinnon, 2012). The precise factors that promoted the children's recovery will be examined in Chapter 2.

The traumatized French and Belgian war orphans (1916)

On July 28, 1914, one of the deadliest global conflicts in human history began – World War I (WWI). The conflict lasted four years, leaving vast numbers of soldiers injured or dead. It was a scale of destruction and carnage never before seen. In the summer of 1916, when most of Europe was in the throes of this Great War, Montessori took the brave decision to travel to France to visit some of the Montessori schools there (Montessori, 1917/2013a). On arriving, she found, as she had expected, that almost all of the Montessori schools had been closed, as the teachers had given their services to helping the Red Cross, often acting as nursing assistants in the care of wounded soldiers (Montessori, 1917/2013a). However, one Montessori teacher, the American philanthropist Mary Rebecca Cromwell, who had moved to France in 1902 (and later attended one of Montessori's training courses in Rome), had decided to stay in France during the war. Her plan was not just to keep existing schools running but also to open new ones because of her conviction (from what she had seen in Montessori's schools in San Lorenzo) that the Montessori approach could calm and heal traumatized children (Mayfield, 2006). It was Cromwell's schools, in particular, that Montessori wanted to visit in the summer of 1916.

In the early months of the war, numerous children from Belgium and northern France were taken (often by road in open wooden carts) to Paris in an effort to safeguard them from the German advance into Belgium and northern and eastern France (Moretti, 2021). Many of these children had witnessed the burning of their homes, towns, and villages, and were already in a deep state of shock and trauma. Cromwell witnessed firsthand the devastating effects of war on children, and she responded by making the decision to establish, out of her own funds, schools devoted to the care and remediation of these war-torn children based on Montessori

Methods. As Moretti points out, Cromwell was not entirely alone, she was part of a large number of volunteers from North America, who assisted both civilians and soldiers in Paris, France during the course of WWI (2021).

In a pamphlet Cromwell published in 1916 to raise funds to support the work with these war-torn children, she graphically described the various psychological presentations of the children. She said that some children were in a constant state of hypervigilance and would spend their days building hide-outs and cellars with their small tables and chairs. She said the boys used the wooden counting rods as rifles and guns, rather than mathematical apparatus. She reported that this agitated behavior in the children continued for weeks (Cromwell, 1916/2006). Cromwell described other children as being numb, withdrawn, and disinterested. She reported that they went around in a state of dazed inertia, and they appeared incapable of taking an interest in anything (Cromwell, 1916/2006). When Montessori observed the children herself, she vividly described the kind of psychological effects she witnessed in the children. She wrote that she found that the children presented with a particular type of psychological distress best described as a wound – a psychological wound (Montessori, 1917/2013a). She said that these psychological wounds were like lesions that are as serious as physical wounds in the body (Montessori, 1917/2013a). She wrote that when the children arrived to Miss Cromwell, they were in a trance-like state, they were incapable of comprehending anything, terrified at the approach of anyone, whether it was daylight or night time (Montessori, 1917/2013a). Montessori concluded that these children were now psychologically damaged (Montessori, 1917/2013a). Today, we would say that these French and Belgian children were experiencing the effects of what was initially sudden (acute) trauma but now had become on-going (chronic) trauma as a result of their continued exposure to the horrors of war.

Signs of psychological healing in the French and Belgian refugees

These war-torn children, who were displaying serious signs of psychological distress, slowly began to show signs of psychological healing when they were taken into the Montessori environments created by Ms. Cromwell who went as far as to say that the Montessori environments she created were a true remedy for the children's distress (Montessori, 1917/2013a). In fact, when the Red Cross learned from their own observations that most of the children were starting to become calm by engaging in the simple exercises used in the Montessori method, they began to provide financial aid to Ms. Cromwell's work (Montessori, 1917/2013a). Photographs preserved from the period depict the French and Belgian children happily engaged in meaningful outdoor and indoor activities such as digging, planting, transporting soil in wheelbarrows, and helping in the workshop where the wounded soldiers were engaged in making wooden Montessori materials for the schools. Montessori stated that the depressed young children were starting to return once again to the happiness and carefreeness of childhood (Montessori, 1917/2013a). The factors which appear to have promoted this recovery will be examined in Chapter 2.

Campaigning for trauma-informed care

The transformation of the socially deprived San Lorenzo children, the restoration of the trauma-affected Messina orphans, and the healing of the traumatized Franco-Belgian children provided compelling evidence that children who are adversely affected by adversity and trauma can be supported and brought back to good mental health by the Montessori approach. Additional confirmation of this came from Milan, in Italy, where the Umanitaria opened Case dei Bambini to offer care and education exclusively to children whose fathers were fighting in the war. It was recorded by one of the directresses of these Case that some children showed signs of psychological distress. She said that the children's nervous systems had altered because of being exposed to domestic rows when their fathers returned and showed signs of psychological distress themselves from the impact of the war. The teacher wrote that although the children were being affected by this domestic violence, they found psychological stability and tranquility in the Casa (Trabalzini, 2013). The directress who recorded these comments in her annual reports for 1917 and 1919 (named Lola Condulmari), added that the reason for this psychological stability lay chiefly with the Montessori method which she and her co-teachers found to be so effective with happy, carefree children, but even more effective with these war-torn children who were traumatized by the harsh life changes imposed upon them by the war (Trabalzini, 2013). This directress clearly observed both the effects of trauma on the children and the psychological healing that subsequently arose from attendance at the Casa.

Around 1916/1917, Montessori became convinced that in order to better support children who have suffered trauma, it would be extremely beneficial and perhaps even crucial for teachers and nurses to be provided with an interdisciplinary training course with a focus on addressing the particular psychological characteristics and needs of children who have been exposed to trauma in any of its many forms. She envisioned creating such a course in collaboration with specialists from multiple disciplines such as medicine, psychiatry, social work, and education (Trabalzini, 2013). She also envisioned carrying out this ambitious task by first creating an organization to be called the White Cross, which would work alongside the Red Cross for the purpose of supporting children who had been traumatized by wars or natural disasters (Montessori, 1917/2013a). The aim of the White Cross would be to help to restore children to good mental health following exposure to psychologically harmful traumatic events, just as the Red Cross aims to restore children to good physical health following exposure to physically harmful traumatic events. These psychological trauma courses would form part of the work of the White Cross organization and would be free of charge to the participants (Montessori, 1917/2013a).

Montessori had very clear ideas about what was needed. Her insights into the necessity of understanding the impact of trauma on the body and the mind were ahead of her time and anticipated much of contemporary trauma theory. She said that the first essential was that people planning to help children traumatized by war should initially undertake a comprehensive study of the child, focusing on the diverse psychological characteristics that present in war-torn children (Montessori, 1917/2013a). She believed that this essential preparatory work should be carried out by physicians and psychologists (Montessori, 1917/2013a). The next step would be the dissemination of the knowledge gained by the doctors' observations of the war-torn children to the teachers and nurses who would dedicate themselves to carrying out the actual work of helping to support the children (Montessori, 1917/2013a). She recommended that the teachers and nurses themselves should be trained by psychologists who would provide them with interdisciplinary knowledge so that they might be equipped to care for and support the healing of these trauma-affected children (Montessori, 1917/2013a). In addition, she recommended that the participants should learn a special method of education suited to trauma-affected children, by which she meant the Montessori method (Montessori, 1917/2013a).

Montessori was tireless in her efforts to gain support for the establishment of the White Cross. In August 1917, while delivering a Montessori teacher training course in San Diego, California, she wrote to Professor Giulio Ferrari one of the most prominent Italian psychologists of the early 20th century, urging him to support the setting up of the White Cross, telling him that there was an urgent need for doctors to gather psychological evaluations of war-torn children and conduct scientific research on them, so that the psychological characteristics particular to war-torn children would become part of the recognized body of scientific knowledge and would therefore reveal the possible risks of unaddressed childhood trauma for humankind (Montessori, 1917/2013b).

Scocchera (2002/2013), commented that this letter to Ferrari, reveals a particular time when Montessori showed a deep interest in psychological trauma in children, in particular, the trauma experienced by war-torn children (Scocchera, 2002/2013). He notes that Montessori had been involved in the past, in various ways, with orphans and child survivors of the 1908 Messina earthquake, but he adds that this was different, this was an attempt to establish a universal organization that would be active in virtually all continents and countries – the White Cross, which would complement the work of the Red Cross, but focusing on psychological as opposed to physical healing (Scocchera 2002/2013). He states that Montessori's aim was to ensure that this organization would be fronted by a team of specialist doctors, and teachers who would have the knowledge and expertise to investigate scientifically the psychological impacts of war on children so that a robust body of knowledge could be established (Scocchera, 2002/2013).

The Press in both Europe and America outlined Montessori's proposed plan to design and deliver *psychological trauma* courses for teachers and nurses. For example, on September 18, 1916, a London newspaper ran an article about Montessori's efforts to set up the White Cross to complement the work of the Red Cross. The article reported that Dr. Montessori's method had a remarkable calming effect on anxious children and that she was making plans to deliver a course comprising both theoretical and practical knowledge of the Montessori method as applied to children adversely affected by war conditions (*London Daily News*, September 18, 1916). It stated that medical specialists in mental health would assist in the delivery of the course. It further stated that Dr. Montessori's overall plan was to dispatch working groups to France, Belgium, Serbia, Romania, Russia, and other European countries where refugee children were already gathered and had the assistance of the Red Cross for physical care but needed assistance in psychological care Similarly, on September 24, 1917, The *London Times* published an article which stated that Dr. Montessori was establishing an organization designed to remediate war-torn children and aimed to save these traumatized children by means of her special method of education (*London Times*, September 24, 1917). However, despite Montessori's strenuous efforts, Scocchera tells us that Montessori's proposal did not succeed (Scocchera, 2002/2013, p. 49).

Summary of Chapter 1

Dr. Montessori

1. Had a strong interest in mental health and psychiatry both before and after her graduation as a medical doctor.
2. Became involved with children who were both trauma-affected and had developmental difficulties immediately following her graduation as a doctor (1896). She worked with the children intensively having such a high level of success that her achievements were described in the media as "miraculous."
3. Became the educational director of the San Lorenzo "experiment" (1907), which was a social project designed to improve the lives of low-income families living in the poverty stricken and hitherto crime-ridden district of San Lorenzo in Rome. This work produced remarkable improvements in the children, seeing them flourish from being shy, fretful, frightened children into confident, happy, joyful, children excelling in all domains – social, emotional, and cognitive within a few months.
4. Became involved in the support of trauma-affected child survivors of the Messina earthquake (December 28, 1908). Her method also helped these children to flourish from being silent, numbed, and trauma-affected children into calm, happy, children, developing well in all domains, again within a few months.
5. Became involved in the support of many French and Belgian child refugees during WWI (1914–1918). Her method helped these children to recover from the traumas of war which had left most of them orphaned and homeless. Once again, the children showed remarkable improvements in their emotional, social, and cognitive functioning, and overall wellbeing, within a few months.
6. Campaigned for the establishment of an organization to be called the White Cross, which would incorporate a free training course on psychological trauma for teachers and nurses working with children who had been adversely affected by the traumas of war. Despite her considerable efforts to establish the White Cross, her campaign did not succeed.

> **Questions for group discussion**
>
> 1 In your opinion, does Montessori's interest and expertise in mental health strengthen the Montessori Method as an educational approach?
> 2 In your opinion, is it possible that some of the children that Montessori first worked with in 1897 were trauma-affected as well as mentally disabled?
> 3 In your opinion, do the accounts of the impoverished children of San Lorenzo, the traumatized child survivors of the Messina earthquake, and the psychologically distressed French and Belgian refugee children hold important lessons for today's Montessori teachers?
> 4 What are your thoughts around Montessori's efforts to set up the White Cross organization, which would incorporate a free, interdisciplinary "psychological trauma" training course for teachers and nurses?

References

Babini, V. (2000). Science, feminism and education: The early work of Maria Montessori. *History Workshop Journal, 49*(1), 44–67. https://doi.org/10.1093/hwj/2000.49.44

Bailey, C. S. (1915). *Montessori children*. Holt.

Cimino, G., & Foschi, R. (2012). Chapter 15: Italy. In David B. Baker (Ed.), *The Oxford handbook of the history of psychology* (pp. 308–346). https://doi.org/10.1093/oxfordhb/9780195366556.013.0015

Cromwell, M. (2006). The Montessori method adapted to the little French and Belgian refugees. *AMI Communications, 2*, 11–13. (Original work published 1916)

De Stefano, C. (2022). *The child is the teacher*. Other Press.

Felitti, V. J., Anda, R. F., Nordenberg, D., Williamson, D. F., Spitz, A. M., Edwards, V., Koss, M. P., & Marks, J. S. (1998). Relationship of childhood abuse and household dysfunction to many of the leading causes of death in adults. The adverse childhood experiences (ACE) study. *American Journal of Preventive Medicine, 14*(4), 245–258. https://doi.org/10.1016/s0749-3797(98)00017-8

Fisher, D. C. (1912). *A Montessori mother*. Henry Holt & Company.

Foschi, R. (2008). Science and culture around the Montessori's first "Children's houses" in Rome (1907–1915). *Journal of the History of the Behavioral Sciences, 44*(3), 238–257.

Gutek, G., & Gutek, P. (2016). *Bringing Montessori to America: S.S. McClure, Maria Montessori, and the campaign to publicize Montessori education*. University of Alabama Press.

Kramer, R. (1976). *Maria Montessori: A biography*. Addison-Wesley.

London Daily News (1916, September 18). The White Cross: Dr. Montessori's scheme for healing the wounded minds of Child war victims.

London Times (1917, September 24). The White Cross: Care of child victims of the war.

Maccheroni, M. (1947). *A true romance: Dr. Maria Montessori as I knew her*. Darien Press.

MacKinnon, L. (2012). The neurosequential model of therapeutics: An interview with Bruce Perry. *The Australian and New Zealand Journal of Family Therapy, 33*(3), 210–218. https://doi.org/10.1017/aft.2012.26

Mayfield, M. (2006). Maria Montessori: Advocate for children. *AMI Communications, 2*, 4–9.

Montessori, M. (1909). *Il metodo della pedagogia scientifica applicato all'educazione infantile nelle case dei bambini*. Scipione Lapi.

Montessori, M. (1936). *The secret of childhood* (B.B. Carter, Ed. and Trans.). Longmans.
Montessori, M. (1964). *The Montessori method* (A. E. George, Trans.). Schocken Books. (Original work published 1912)
Montessori, M. (1966). *The secret of childhood* (M. J. Costelloe, Trans). Ballantine.
Montessori, M. (2008). The California lectures of Maria Montessori, 1915: *Collected speeches and writings*. In R. Buckenmeyer (Ed.), *The Clio Montessori series*. Montessori-Pierson.
Montessori, M. (2013a). The white cross. *AMI Journal*, 1–2, 37–41. (Original work published 1917)
Montessori, M. (2013b). Letter on the white cross addressed to professor Ferrari, physician at the Italian Societa Umanitaria, of Milan. *AMI Journal*, 1–2, 47. (Originally published 1917)
Moretti, E. (2014). Beyond biological ties: Sibilla Aleramo, Maria Montessori, and the construction of social motherhood. *Italian Culture*, 32(1), 32–49. https://doi.org/10.1179/0161462213Z.00000000022
Moretti, E. (2021). *The best weapon for peace: Maria Montessori, education, and children's rights*. University of Wisconsin Press.
Pino, N. A., Piatanesi, A., Valensisi, G., & Boschi, E. (2008). *The 28 December 1908, Messina Straits earthquake (M_w 7.1): A great earthquake through a century of seismology*. Istituto Nazionale di Geofisica e Vulcanologia. https://pubs.geoscienceworld.org/ssa/srl/article-abstract/80/2/243/143519/The-28-December-1908-Messina-Straits-Earthquake-MW
Povell, P. (2010). *Montessori comes to America: The leadership of Maria Montessori and Nancy McCormick Rambusch*. University Press of America.
Quarfood, C. (2023). Maria Montessori: Life and historical context. Chapter 1. In A. K. Murray, E. T. M. K. Ahlquist, & M. C. Debs (Eds.), *The Bloomsbury handbook of Montessori education* (pp. 5–19). Bloomsbury.
Radice, S. (1920). *The new children: Talks with Dr. Maria Montessori*. Stokes.
Scocchera, A. (2013). Montessori, the white cross, and prof. Ferrari. *AMI Journal*, 1–2, 48–50. (Original work published 2002)
Standing, E. M. (1957). *Maria Montessori: Her life and work*. Plume.
Trabalzini, P. (2013). Nobody left behind: Montessori's work in defence of children as victims of war. *AMI Journal*, 1–2, 42–45.
Wright, T. (2019). Growing Hope: Developing supportive Montessori classrooms for traumatized children. *Montessori Collaborative World Review*, 1(1), 134–145.

2 Devising a "healing" approach

Chapter objectives

- To explore Dr. Montessori's "healing" approach with trauma-affected children.
- To outline the materials and activities Dr. Montessori utilized to help children to "heal."

Learning outcomes

At the end of this chapter, the learner will have a knowledge of how Dr. Montessori:

- Ensured that children felt "valued and loved."
- Observed children through (what we now refer to as) a trauma-informed lens.
- Took steps to make children "feel safe" and "be safe."
- Used specific activities to bring regulation to children dysregulated by trauma.
- Used specific materials to organize the disorganized minds of traumatized children.
- Utilized "muscle memory" to prevent "mental strain" on trauma-affected children.
- Used art, music, dance, and drama which help to re-wire the brain.
- Empowered children by identifying their strengths and building on them.

Ensuring children feel valued and loved

As early as 1904, when Montessori delivered lectures to student teachers as part of her work as Chair of Pedagogical Anthropology at the University of Rome (these lectures were later published in book form as *Pedagogical Anthropology*, 1913), she emphasized the importance of love and told her students that the critical factor that really makes a great teacher is genuine love for the child (Montessori, 1913). In a series of articles on the history of her early work (published in 1915 in the San Francisco Call and Post), Montessori showed that her first priority as a teacher was to make sure that the children in her care felt valued and loved (Montessori, 2008). In these articles, when referring to her work in 1897 with the children from the Roman psychiatric hospitals, she stated that when the street children (i.e., homeless children) and the children from the psychiatric hospitals (which Montessori referred to as the asylums) entered her school, they were greeted with cheerful signs of welcome and with genuine warmth and friendliness. She added this was the first time they had ever been made to feel that they were really cared about and were genuinely welcomed (Montessori, 2008).

> When these children from the streets and from the asylums entered my school, they were greeted with hearty manifestations of welcome and with genuine cordiality. For the first time they were made to feel that they were wanted and desired.
> (Montessori, 2008, p. 264).

She said that she was guided in her work by feelings of respect for these children and genuine feelings of love and compassion for them (Montessori, 1967). In her work with these children, Montessori's application of Seguin's method, augmented by her own substantial research and original insights led to the remarkable social, emotional, and academic progress in the children in the Orthophrenic school, described in Chapter 1.

Montessori took this principle of making children feel valued and loved as the overriding principle in her later work with typically developing children, and she emphasized its importance to the students in her training courses. Many eyewitnesses to the early Case dei Bambini described the children's relationships with their teachers as warm, affectionate, and respectful. One eyewitness describing her experience of observing at the St Angelo school in Pescheria (a poverty-stricken area of Rome), wrote that she witnessed a warm, affectionate, and respectful relationship between the teachers and the children (George, 1912). Carolyn Bailey, another eyewitness, described the warm, emotionally attuned, and relational approach of the directresses in the schools she visited. She vividly described a directress at the Via Guisti school, who when responding to a little boy's state of withdrawal (this child had lost both his parents in the Messina earthquake) would stop beside the boy's chair and hold his hand for a few moments, and whisper words of comfort to him (Bailey, 1915). As we shall show in later chapters, current trauma literature points toward the importance of emotionally attuned, responsive relationships in the healing process (Ludy-Dobson & Perry, 2010; Maté, 2019; Perry & Szalavitz, 2017; Treisman, 2017), which suggests that the emphasis on positive relational interactions as part of the overall Montessori approach played a key role in promoting the recovery of these children.

Observing children through a "trauma-informed lens"

Montessori instructed her teachers to always be mindful of a child's possible past exposure to traumatic events, and so view the child through (what we now refer to as) a trauma-informed lens. She told them to keep a biological chart detailing the physical and psychological characteristics of each child. She said that this could be a guide to the staff so that knowing what stressors had occurred earlier in the child's life, they could estimate the level of harm done and the potential for recovery from interventions (Montessori, 1967). She told them exactly what should be kept on this chart. She said it should include information about the health of the mother during the pregnancy, the health of the child at birth, and the ages (of the parents) when the child was born (Montessori, 1967). Then she advised teachers to take note of the parenting style and whether the parents had an authoritarian or more relaxed style of parenting (Montessori, 1967). She advised her teachers to take note of any traumatic events the child may have been exposed to, and to especially note if the child had experienced fear or shock (Montessori, 1967). She recommended that if children had any challenging behaviors, the teachers should look for possible causes of these in the children's life experiences (Montessori, 1967). Montessori was effectively instructing her teachers not to ask themselves *What's wrong with this child?* but rather to consider the question *What happened to this child?* In this respect, she anticipated by more than a century, current insights, and understandings around the issue of trauma (see Perry & Winfrey, 2021).

Helping children to "feel" safe and "be" safe

As we shall see in later chapters, supporting children to feel safe is an essential principle of trauma-informed practice (Fallot & Harris, 2009). From the outset, Montessori ensured the physical and psychological safety of the children through certain deliberate practices which included (a) the abolition of rewards and punishments; (b) the use of self-correcting materials; (c) the provision of spaces for individual activity; (d) the reduction of bullying, and (e) the emphasis on reality-based activities. We now examine each of these practices.

The abolition of rewards and punishments

In May 1911, the first of a series of articles published in the hugely influential "McClure's Magazine" on the subject of the Montessori Method of Education appeared on the educational scene with extraordinary force (Kramer, 1976). Josephine Tozier, an American travel writer, who had spent several months in Rome talking with Montessori while observing children at her schools, was subsequently commissioned by S. S. McClure (1914/2009), to write an article on the Montessori Method. In the article, she declared that Dr. Montessori had banned all forms of punishments from her schools and had eliminated the practice of giving rewards which encourages competition and replaced this with an emphasis on mutuality and collaboration among the children (Tozier, 1911). Montessori's decision to abolish rewards and punishments was remarkable at this time when the physical punishment of children was commonplace, and rewards were frequently used to encourage good behavior. Without doubt, this abolition would have been a major factor in the psychological healing of the children, removing some of the children's anxiety and helping them to feel physically and psychologically safe. An eyewitness who was a frequent visitor to the Montessori school on the Via Guisti, which accommodated a large number of child survivors of the Messina earthquake, vividly described how one trauma-experienced child sat in the Montessori classroom in silence with fear in his eyes, waiting to dodge the blows that he expected, but in this school, never received (Bailey, 1915). With regard to rewards, Montessori was equally convinced that rewards are harmful because they insult children who have done the right thing because of the awakening of their moral sense, not because they wanted to receive a reward. Recent research suggests that rewards may be harmful in that they may lead to feelings of being manipulated. Children who have been exposed to trauma have frequently been manipulated usually by the people who are entrusted with their care (Treisman, 2017). Therefore, Montessori's decision to abolish rewards and punishments is likely to have played a significant role in providing the children with a sense of safety and consequently would have contributed to their psychological healing.

The use of self-correcting materials

In her work with children with developmental difficulties and her later work with typically developing children, Montessori used many materials, originally developed by Seguin, which were self-correcting in that the materials indicate error, requiring the user to repeat the activity until the error is corrected. For example, if a child fills the cylinder blocks incorrectly, there will be cylinders left with no place to insert them, requiring the child to repeat the activity until the block is filled correctly and each cylinder has a "home." This self-correcting element of the materials provides a built-in safety element for children in that they do not have to go to the teacher for help to complete the activity, which for many could be a fearful exercise based on their past experiences of being ridiculed or punished for not knowing how to do something. Current research shows that children who have experienced abuse have found that asking for help can frequently lead to humiliating criticism or ridicule (Sorrels, 2015).

Additionally, it is arguable that self-correcting materials can help children to build resilience because of the requirement that children repeatedly correct their mistakes. This requirement to correct one's mistakes may involve the kind of mild adaptive stress, that the neuroscientist Bruce Perry calls controllable stress or, predictable stress, which in time can help to build resilience in a child (Perry & Winfrey, 2021). It is also arguable that the continuous building of resilience leads to the development of self-esteem and autonomy, as does the experience of successfully mastering challenging activities (such as the cylinder blocks, just mentioned) and both self-esteem and autonomy are vital in the process of recovering from trauma.

The provision of spaces for individual activity

From the outset of her work with children, Montessori observed that children, especially those under six years, often feel a need to engage in individual activity. In later years, after working with children for many decades she stated emphatically that children often feel a need to have some personal space and a desire to engage in an occupation on their own (Montessori, 1944/2013b). There are many reasons for this, some having to do with the child's need to process their emotions. Frequently the reason is a psychological one and has to do with the child's need to feel physically and psychologically safe. Many eyewitnesses to the early Montessori schools recorded that although group activities such as dancing, singing, laying tables, and washing and drying dishes, took place daily, individual activity was also frequently chosen by the children themselves, often for long periods of time (Fisher, 1912; White, 1914). The children learned to designate their own personal space by spreading a mat on the floor, placing their materials on the mat, and carrying out their activity within the confines of the mat, which other children were required not to step on it. This practice would clearly have contributed to a child's feeling of safety, as many of these trauma-affected children would have needed a personal safe space in which to process their emotions without the added stress of having to engage with others at the same time (Perry & Winfrey, 2021).

The reduction of bullying

Many eyewitnesses, including Montessori, observed the absence of aggressive behavior or bullying among the children (Fisher, 1912; George, 1912; Montessori, 1964; White, 1914). They also noted the children's genuine concern for and helpfulness toward each other, and this featured prominently in many reports (Bailey, 1915; Fisher, 1912; George, 1912; Montessori, 1964; Tozier, 1911; White, 1914). For example, Dr. Jessie White observed that there was a complete absence of roughness in the children's demeanor, and she added very little correcting was done, even though disputes often took place in the playground, but for the most part, no one interfered with the children, and they sorted the problems out themselves, so that the atmosphere was a positive one marked by love, trust, and calm (White, 1914). White, also wrote that, the competitive spirit was entirely absent and that in the entire period she spent in the schools (which was substantial) she never heard any children being aggressive toward one another (White, 1914). Similarly, White wrote that during her time observing the schools, she never saw any child in conflict with the directresses. She said that the relational interactions between the adults and the children were completely loving, kind and trusting, and there was a courteous atmosphere in the schools. Comparatively recent research also showed emphatically that Montessori schools have significantly less ambiguous rough play than non-Montessori schools (Lillard & Else-Quest, 2006). This may well be related to Montessori's use of mixed age groups in her classes. From the outset of her work with children, Montessori mixed the age groups in her classes and she and many eyewitnesses were quick to observe the benefits of this arrangement from a relational point of view. One eyewitness to the early schools in

Rome wrote that she was always impressed by the fact that the Montessori method facilitated children of mixed ages working together, with the older children helping the younger ones and the younger ones observing (with great admiration) the older ones (George, 1912). This mixture of ages is likely to have promoted a feeling of connectedness and kinship, and this has been shown to be healing for trauma-affected children because it helps to offset the feeling of being cut-off or separate from others, frequently felt by children who have been exposed to trauma (Craig, 2016). This significant reduction, and in some cases total elimination of bullying in the schools, is likely to have contributed greatly to the children's feeling of physical and psychological safety.

The emphasis on reality-based activities

Montessori was aware that the presence of a fear state (Montessori, 1936) lies at the root of so many trauma-affected children's behaviors. Consequently, she tried to reduce fear by the provision of activities that are grounded in reality. She wrote that everything that keeps children grounded in reality and permits them to comprehend and acquire lived experience of their environment can free them from this unnerving state of fear (Montessori, 1936). She added that one of the clearest results of the efficacy of the Montessori approach to promote mental health is the disappearance of subconscious fears in children or their failure to appear (Montessori, 1936). She told the story of a revered Spanish writer who was the father of four daughters, the youngest of whom (by many years) attended one of Montessori's schools. She said that this man wanted the public to know of an intriguing fact he noticed in relation to fears. He recorded that whenever there was a thunderstorm during the night, his youngest daughter (who attended the Montessori school) was the only one out of his four daughters who did not show any fear. It is arguable that the youngest child's daily engagement in reality-based activities helped to avoid any over-activation of her stress response systems and reduced the possibility that something like a thunderstorm could trigger a fear-based reaction.

Providing children with regulating tasks – practical life activities

From the outset of her work with children, and building on the work of Seguin, Montessori put great emphasis on what she came to call "practical life activities." These activities involved both gross and small motor movements and included activities that came to be categorized as (a) "care of the self" – washing hands, combing hair, cleaning nails, fastening clothing; (b) "care of the outdoor environment" – sweeping patios, digging soil, raking leaves, watering flowers, planting seeds, feeding and grooming small animals; and (c) "care of the indoor environment" – dusting shelves, scrubbing tables, putting materials in order, rolling up floor mats, sweeping up, polishing, shining mirrors, and so on. As there were large numbers of children in the early classes, these types of activities were necessary to maintain a clean and orderly environment, but Montessori soon found that they also had an unexpected effect, they proved to be regulatory activities that brought calm to the children, some of whom were very dysregulated because of their exposure to traumatic life events. Montessori, being a scientist with rigorous training in the examination and scrutiny of phenomena, looked closely at the activities the children were attracted to and the effects those activities had on them, and she discovered that the activities the children were attracted to and engaged in repeatedly all involved something she called synthetic movement, that is, movement that is not random but that requires that the mind guides the hand movements (1936), with the body and the mind working in unison so that mental and motor elements of the activities are inseparable (Standing, 1957). She soon wrote that movement without thought was chaotic, and thought without movement induced fatigue (Montessori, 1964). The practical life activities just described all require that the child uses synthetic movements, and it is these synthetic movements that appear to promote repetition of the activity, which in turn brings regulation, calm, and tranquility (Bailey, 1915; Cromwell, 1916/2006; Fisher, 1912; George, 1912; Montessori, 1936).

Contemporary research from the field of neuroscience has demonstrated how neural dysregulation can occur in the aftermath of trauma. For example, Perry explains that in children who have been exposed to serious trauma, there will be a high probability of poor organization and consequently poor functioning in lower parts of the brain, particularly in the brainstem and diencephalon (MacKinnon, 2012). This often leaves children feeling anxious, impulsive, and emotionally unstable (Perry, 2009). Perry's research also shows how dysregulation can be brought back into equilibrium by engaging in activities that are rhythmic and repetitive and have the effect of reducing anxiety and other symptoms related to trauma (2009). He explains that in order to bring re-organization to the badly organized neural networks involved in the stress response, we need to provide the child with repetitive rhythmic activities that are patterned and somatosensory (MacKinnon, 2012). This is exactly what Dr. Montessori did through the use of practical life activities (and sensorial activities which we will discuss in the next section) which involved repetitive, rhythmic movements (Phillips et al., 2022).

Re-organizing disorganized minds – sensorial activities

Once again, building on the work of Seguin, Montessori used a large variety of "sensorial materials" with the children, which appeared to have the effect of re-organizing their trauma-affected minds (or more specifically re-organizing the neural networks which are poorly organized as a result of exposure to trauma). These sensorial materials required the children to sort, compare contrast, and finally match various items which included color tablets (to promote visual discrimination), sound cylinders (to promote auditory discrimination), smell bottles (to promote olfactory discrimination), taste jars (to promote gustatory discrimination), and baric tablets (to promote tactile and weight discrimination). Montessori carefully observed the children as they worked with these materials, and she said the first thing she noticed was the children's tendency to repeat the exercises over and over again. One child of about four years filled a cylinder block 42 times! (Montessori,

1936) and was so engrossed in the activity that she was oblivious to everyone and everything around her. Then, all of a sudden, she stopped, looked as though she was coming out of a dream, and showed by her facial expressions and body language that she was feeling happy, calm, and peaceful. This was the moment when Montessori began to recognize the effectiveness of what Perry would later refer to as "patterned, repetitive, rhythmic activities" (Perry, 2009, p. 252) in moving a child from a high anxiety state to a calmer more cognitive state. Media reports also referred to the tranquil effect that engagement with the sensorial exercises had on the children. One eyewitness who observed children engaged in these sensorial exercises wrote that nervousness becomes dissipated, and tranquility takes its place (George, 1912). In addition, the American philanthropist and Montessori teacher, Mary Rebecca Cromwell, who worked with the French and Belgian war refugees during WW1, also conveyed to Montessori her opinion that engagement with the sensorial materials provided a true remedy for all the children's problems (Montessori, 1917/2013a). Some eyewitnesses suggested that the Montessori sensorial activities were beneficial to the children because they were meticulously designed to enable them to focus their attention on a single task and element such as color, sound, smell, texture, or weight, thereby eliminating unnecessary distractions and fostering a sense of clarity and calm (Fisher, 1912).

As stated above, contemporary research shows that neural dysregulation can occur after exposure to trauma, often leaving the young child subject to constant confusion because of the intrusion of sudden and unsolicited fragmentary memories that mix up past and present experiences (Sorrels, 2015). It seems likely that the Montessori sensorial activities helped to reorganize the disorganized brains of the children (caused by traumatic experiences) through their emphasis on the meticulous sorting, comparing, contrasting, and categorizing of objects (Phillips et al., 2022). This engagement in repetitive activity with materials that are scientifically designed, with gradations and sequencing built into their construction, probably played a vital role in the children's recovery. It is certainly arguable that all of these activities have a regulatory effect on children, and they appear to facilitate re-organization of the brain through what the neuroscientist Bruce Perry calls "patterned, repetitive, neural input to the brain stem" (Perry, 2009, p. 243).

Preventing mental strain by using "muscle memory" – language and math activities

From the beginning of her work in education, Montessori took pre-emptive steps to make sure that when helping children in their development, her teachers would not impose any type of mental strain on them. Tozier speaking of Montessori wrote that the good doctor personally attends the classes, in order to demonstrate to her teachers how to interact with the children in a way that avoids stressing them (1911). Eyewitnesses noted that Montessori, by her use of muscle memory (i.e., a type of memory that involves committing a specific motor task into memory through repetition), avoided exposing the children to mental strain (Tozier, 1911). Montessori, referring to her early work with children, wrote that in order to teach children the outlines of the alphabetical letters, she tried to fix the shape of each letter in the muscle memory of the child, just as a touch typist does (2008). Media reports (Tozier, 1911) commented on how the children learned to feel sounds and numerals as the directress guided their fingers over Sandpaper Letters and Sandpaper Numbers so that they could develop a muscle memory of their shapes. Similarly, using the same principle, materials such as "the long rods" were used to teach mathematics. The rods required the children to stretch out their arms to hold the longest rod, with the basic premise being that the child can embody mathematical concepts such as "length" through the use of muscle memory and this was thought to reduce mental strain on the children. One observer wrote that one of the most remarkable of Montessori's achievements was her success in teaching very young children how to read and write without putting any strain on their nervous systems (Tozier, 1911). Another eyewitness wrote that Montessori, being a combination of physician and teacher, demonstrates how we can protect children's nervous systems from stress (Stevens, 1912).

Contemporary research in trauma shows that trauma-affected children often live in a perpetual state of fear and are continuously hypervigilant scanning the environment for danger and making efforts to protect themselves and possibly others from harm (Treisman, 2017). This perpetual fear state can leave the brain stressed and overtaxed, and therefore unable to apply itself to learning which involves thinking clearly. Montessori therefore circumvented this problem by making it possible for children to absorb academic content via muscle memory which did not involve strain and did not tax the children's brains. Clearly, the children did not find the exercises that involved procedural memory stressful, this was made evident by the fact that they voluntarily kept repeating the exercises (Tozier, 1911).

Re-wiring the brain – cultural activities, music, movement, art, and drama

Comments from some of Montessori's contemporaries reveal that Montessori as a scientist, doctor, and educator was aware of the property of brain plasticity (the brain's ability to create new connections and pathways), and she consciously made efforts to utilize it in her work with children. In 1911, America's most highly respected Kindergarten expert, Ellen Yale Stevens, traveled to Italy and spent close to two months having talks with Montessori about her method. Having examined the schools and the children with her own eyes, she stated with confidence that Montessori recognizes the nervous system's plasticity and the importance of building into its tissues (Stevens, 1912). Similarly, in 1919, the assistant editor of the *London Times Educational Supplement*, following months of discussions with Montessori about her method, wrote that the Montessori approach is focused on re-organizing the human brain (Radice, 1920).

As stated earlier, neuroscientific research suggests that in children who have been exposed to serious trauma, there may well be disorganization and consequently poor functioning in lower parts of the brain, especially in the brainstem and diencephalon (MacKinnon, 2012). However, Perry states that "patterned, repetitive neural input to the brainstem and diencephalon monoamine neural networks" (2009, p. 243) would have the capacity to provide the kind of regulating and organizing input that the brain stem requires, and therefore could be instrumental in in reducing the anxiety, impulsivity and other symptoms arising from trauma that occur when these systems are dysregulated.

In her early schools, Montessori, with the help of her student and colleague, Anna Maccheroni, as stated earlier, a professor of music, developed music and dance activities for the children that were rhythmic and repetitive. They added to these activities, clay modeling, coloring, and drawing which also involved rhythmic and repetitive movements. Many eyewitnesses commented on the calming effect these activities had on the children. Several eyewitnesses wrote that the children kept time to rhythmic music often marching to a piano tune, sometimes quickly, sometimes slowly, again and again (Bailey, 1915). Other teachers stated that art activities such as modeling with clay, or coloring outlines of flowers or animals calmed the children apparently through the repetitive movements involved. Others described the children's calm when playing outdoor dramatic games that required repeated movements (Fisher, 1912). It is likely that these cultural activities provided the type of repetitive neural input to the brainstem that can help to re-wire the trauma-affected brain.

Empowering children by building on their strengths

Montessori trained her teachers to observe children carefully so that they could discover children's strengths and build on them (1964). Many eyewitnesses to the early schools recorded examples of how the directresses, by close observation, identified the strengths of trauma-affected children and built on them to help promote healing and resilience in these children. For example, in her book, *Montessori Children* (1915), Carolyn Bailey, a writer and graduate of Columbia University's Teachers College, who spent a considerable period of time in Rome in 1913, observing children in several Montessori schools, wrote very poignant descriptions of children who had experienced much trauma, abuse, and neglect in their young lives but slowly began to recover because the Montessori directresses looking after them (through their careful observations) discovered children's hidden strengths and took the trouble to nurture them. For example, in the case of Bruno (whose story is told in the Introduction), Baily describes how the directress in the Via Guisti school (which accommodated large numbers of child survivors of the Messina earthquake, which left many children orphaned and homeless) carefully observed children to identify their strengths. She described how the directress noticed that Bruno showed evidence of an almost crushed but just about surviving, kind, and helpful spirit. She immediately took steps to nurture this strength and especially his growing relationship with one of his peers, and she facilitated his timid but emerging desire to help others, especially younger children. Bailey described how this child slowly began to recover chiefly because the directress, through her careful observations, discovered

Bruno's hidden, almost extinguished strengths and nurtured them and built on them. The teacher's sensitive, emotional attunement to this child helped the boy to blossom from a terrified, cowering, psychologically wounded child to a joyful, confident, helpful boy full of love and kindness for his fellow companions (Bailey, 1915).

Summary of Chapter 2

Dr. Montessori

1 Ensured that the children felt valued and loved.
2 Trained her teachers to look at children through a trauma-informed lens, i.e., keeping in mind the possibility that the children may have been exposed to adversity or trauma.
3 Took steps to help children to feel physically and psychologically safe. These included:

- The abolition of rewards and punishments
- The use of self-correcting materials
- The provision of spaces for individual activity
- The reduction and virtual elimination of bullying
- The emphasis on reality-based exercises and activities

4 Provided children with Practical Life tasks that regulated and calmed them.
5 Provided children with Sensorial exercises that helped to re-organize their minds which were dis-organized by trauma.
6 Prevented mental strain in children by utilizing muscle memory in the Language and Math activities.
7 Helped to promote positive brain change and re-wiring by giving the children cultural activities that were rhythmic and repetitive such as music and movement, clay modeling, drawing, painting, and little dramatic pieces.
8 Helped to empower children by identifying their strengths and building on them.

Questions for group discussion

1 In your opinion, how important is it for a teacher to make the children feel valued and loved?
2 What are your thoughts on Montessori's admonitions to her teachers to always consider that a child may have had previous exposure to adversity or trauma and that it might affect his current behavior?

3 How important do you think it is to help children to feel physically and psychologically safe?
4 In your experience, do practical life exercises help to calm children?
5 In your opinion, does working with the sensorial exercises help to re-organize children's confused minds?
6 What are your thoughts on Montessori's use of muscle memory to prevent "mental strain" in the language and mathematical activities?
7 In your opinion, did the use of Cultural exercises, which were rhythmic and repetitive play a role in changing and possibly rewiring the children's brains in the very early schools, so that the children changed from being shy, silent, numb, disengaged children, to being happy, joyful, social, empathic, productive, busy children, as witnessed by many eyewitnesses?
8 What are your thoughts on identifying and building on a child's strengths?

References

Bailey, C. S. (1915). *Montessori children*. Holt
Craig, S. E. (2016). *Trauma sensitive schools: Learning communities transforming children's lives, K–5* (Illustrated ed.). Teachers College Press.
Cromwell, M. (2006). The Montessori method adapted to the little French and Belgian refugees. *AMI Communications, 2*, 11–13. (Original work published 1916)
Fallot, R. D., & Harris, M. (2009). Creating cultures of trauma-informed care: A self-assessment and planning protocol. *Community Connections*. https://doi.org/10.13140/2.1.4843.6002
Fisher, D. C. (1912). *A Montessori mother*. Henry Holt & Company.
George, A. E. (1912). Dr. Maria Montessori: The achievement and personality of an Italian woman whose discovery is revolutionizing educational methods. *Good Housekeeping, 55*(1), 24–29.
Kramer, R. (1976). *Maria Montessori: A biography*. Addison-Wesley.
Lillard, A., & Else-Quest, N. (2006). Evaluating Montessori education. *Science, 313*(5795), 1893–1894. https://doi.org/10.1126/science.1132362
Ludy-Dobson, C., & Perry, B. (2010). The role of healthy relational interactions in buffering the impact of childhood trauma. In E. Gil (Ed.) *Working with children to heal interpersonal trauma: The power of play*. The Guilford Press.
MacKinnon, L. (2012). The neurosequential model of therapeutics: An interview with Bruce Perry. *The Australian and New Zealand Journal of Family Therapy, 33*(3), 210–218. https://doi.org/10.1017/aft.2012.26
Maté, G. (2019). *When the body says no: The cost of hidden stress*. Vermilion.
McClure, S. S. (2009). *My autobiography*. Cornell University Library. (Original work published 1914)
Montessori, M. (1913). *Pedagogical anthropology*. Frederick A. Stokes Company.
Montessori, M. (1936). *The secret of childhood* (B. B. Carter, Ed. and Trans.). Longmans.
Montessori, M. (1964). *The Montessori method* (A. E. George, Trans.). Schocken Books. (Original work published 1912)
Montessori, M. (1966). *The secret of childhood* (M. J. Costelloe, Trans). Ballantine.
Montessori, M. (2008). The California lectures of Maria Montessori, 1915: Collected speeches and writings (R. Buckenmeyer, Ed.). *The Clio Montessori series*. Montessori-Pierson.

Montessori, M. (2013a). The white cross. *AMI Journal*, *1-2*, 37–41. (Original work published 1917)

Montessori, M. (2013b). The house of children, lecture, Kodaikanal, 1944. *NAMTA Journal*, *38*(1), 11–19.

Montessori, M. (1967). *The absorbent mind* (C. A. Claremont, Trans). Dell. (Original work published 1949)

Perry, B. D. (2009). Examining child maltreatment through a neurodevelopment lens: Clinical applications of the neurosequential model of therapeutics. *Journal of Loss and Trauma*, *14*(4), 240–245. https://doi.org/10.1080/15325020903004350

Perry, B. D., & Szalavitz, M. (2017). *The boy who was raised as a dog: And other stories from a child psychiatrist's notebook—What traumatized children can teach us about loss, love, and healing*. Basic Books.

Perry, B. D., & Winfrey, O. (2021). *What happened to you? Conversations on trauma, resilience, and healing*. Pan Macmillan.

Phillips, B., O'Toole, C., McGilloway, S., & Phillips, S. (2022). Montessori, the white cross, and trauma-informed practice: Lessons for contemporary education. *Journal of Montessori Research*. *8*(1). 13–28.

Radice, S. (1920). *The new children: Talks with Dr. Maria Montessori*. Frederick A. Stokes Company.

Sorrels, B. (2015). *Reaching and teaching children exposed to trauma*. Gryphon House.

Standing, E. M. (1957). *Maria Montessori: Her life and work*. Plume.

Stevens, E. Y. (1912). The Montessori method and the American kindergarten. *McClure's Magazine*, *40*, 77–82.

Tozier, J. (1911). An educational wonder-worker: The methods of Maria Montessori. *McClure's Magazine*, *37*(1), 3–19.

Treisman, K. (2017). *Working with relational and developmental trauma in children and adolescents*. Routledge.

White, J. (1914). *Montessori schools: As seen in the early summer of 1913*. H. Milford.

Part II
Trauma

3 What is trauma?

Chapter objectives

- To explore various definitions of trauma and outline the different "types" of trauma.
- To examine types of stress and explain the stress response system.
- To list common signs and symptoms of trauma in children and young people.
- To explain the meaning of – "hypo-arousal" and "hyper-arousal" and "state-dependent" functioning.
- To explain the concept of a "window of tolerance" and the "polyvagal theory."
- To explain the PACE model.

Learning outcomes

At the end of this chapter, the learner will be able to:

- Define trauma.
- Give examples of types of trauma.
- Understand the connection between trauma and stress.
- Distinguish between types of stress.
- Briefly outline the stress response system.
- Recognize common signs and symptoms of trauma in children and young people.
- Explain "adaptive responses" and what hyper-arousal and hypo-arousal look like.
- Understand how "state-dependent functioning" affects children in school.
- Explain what is meant by the term "window of tolerance" and the "polyvagal theory."
- Describe the PACE model.

Defining the term "trauma" and looking at types of trauma

The word "trauma" first appeared in the English language in the seventeenth century (circa 1685). It derives from the Greek word "τραύμα" which originally referred to a physical "wound" in the body. Later on (circa 1894), the English word "trauma" was used to denote an experience that caused abnormal mental stress. Essentially, a traumatized individual is someone who has been "wounded" psychologically and research shows that this "wound" can have a very negative impact on both the mind and the body (Alexander, 2019; Burke Harris, 2019; Herman, 1997; Jennings, 2019; Levine, 1997; Mate, 2021, 2019; Perry et al., 2001, 2009; Perry & Szalavitz, 2017; Perry & Winfrey, 2021; Treisman, 2017; Van Der Kolk, 2014) and can be linked to a variety of physical illnesses such as heart disease, cancer, diabetes, and other chronic illnesses (Felitti at al., 1998; Mate, 2019).

> **KEY TERM**
>
> **TRAUMA**
>
> is a
>
> **PSYCHOLOGICAL WOUND**

Over the past four decades, numerous definitions of "trauma" have emerged, all with different emphases and nuances. However, in 2014, the Substance Abuse and Mental Health Services Administration SAMHSA arrived at their definition. They acknowledged that decades of work in the field of trauma had generated many definitions, and having weighed up the multiplicity of nuances and differences in the wealth of definitions, they, in collaboration with their expert panel, which included trauma survivors, crafted the following definition which is often referred to as the "3 Es" of trauma:

> Individual trauma results from an **event**, series of events, or set of circumstances that is **experienced** by an individual as physically or emotionally harmful or life-threatening and that has lasting adverse **effects** on the individual's functioning and mental, physical, social, emotional, or spiritual well-being.
> (SAMHSA, 2014, p.7).

This definition is important because it takes into account (a) that trauma may be a single event or a series of events; (b) how trauma is experienced by an individual is a key factor – something that is traumatic for one person, may not be traumatic for another; and (c) trauma may have lasting adverse effects, meaning, – the harmful event may have long passed but the adverse effects of that harmful event may linger in the body, often impacting an individual's cognitive, social, and emotional functioning, as well as their physical and spiritual well-being (Perry & Szalavitz, 2017; Van Der Kolk, 2014).

However, there is also the view put forward by other experts that trauma is not so much what happens to us, but rather it is what happens inside of us, because of what happened to us (Mate, 2021).

We offer the following definition:

> Trauma may be caused by our unique response to something we experienced which harmed or wounded us, or to something we didn't experience, the lack of which equally harmed or wounded us. Both can leave us with **invisible** but **enduring** emotional, social, and spiritual scars that negatively affect our ability to live a fulfilling life.

Looking at types of trauma

While experts in trauma theory may vary a little in their definitions of trauma, they all agree that there are many different types of traumas and adversities (Treisman, 2017) and that some of these overlap. For the sake of clarity, we will divide them into three main categories, namely, acute trauma, chronic trauma, and complex trauma.

Acute trauma

This refers to a single highly stressful and/or dangerous event that is limited in time (Perry et al., 1995).

Examples include exposure to:

- A sudden natural disaster such as an earthquake, tornado, storm, tsunami, fire, or flood.
- A sudden man-made disaster such as witnessing or being the victim of a shooting, a violent assault, (physical, sexual, or emotional), a robbery, or a burglary.
- A sudden catastrophic event such as a car crash.
- The sudden loss of a loved one through death, or the sudden separation from a loved one through incarceration, or illness.

Chronic trauma

This refers to the experience of multiple traumatic events that may be happening continually (Perry et al., 1995).

Examples include exposure to:

- Continuous physical, sexual, or emotional abuse.
- Continuous domestic violence.
- Continuous community violence.
- War.

Complex trauma

This refers to exposure to chronic trauma that occurs within the child's primary caregiving system, and it includes the emotional dis-regulation and psychological damage of this exposure on the child (Treisman, 2017).

Complex trauma:

- Is usually interpersonal (occurs between people, often a child, and a caregiver).
- Often makes the individual feel trapped.
- Is usually planned by the perpetrator and happens repeatedly.
- Often causes feelings of shame, causes mistrust of others, and emotional dysregulation.
- Often involves coping strategies that include alcohol or drug use, self-harm, or eating disorders.
- Usually has a negative effect on emotional, social and cognitive functioning.

Examples of complex trauma include chronic exposure to abuse (physical, sexual, or emotional) and exposure to neglect (physical and/or emotional) at the hands of someone within the child's primary caregiving system who acts as a predator rather than as a protector of the child. Specific examples would include:

- Repeated physical abuse of a child by a caregiver making the child feel terrified, helpless, and in pain.
- Repeated sexual abuse of a child by a caregiver, making the child feel ashamed, guilt-ridden, victimized, and helpless.
- Repeated emotional abuse of a child by a caregiver, making the child feel worthless, ashamed, and belittled.

Examining types of stress and explaining the stress response system

Types of stress

The National Scientific Council on the Developing Child (NSCDC), at Harvard University, has classified stress into three categories (2005, p.1). These are:

- Positive stress
- Tolerable stress
- Toxic stress

Positive stress

This category of stress is moderate, short-lived, and a normal part of life. Learning to adjust to positive stress is a mark of normal healthy development. Positive stress produces mild alterations in our body's stress hormone levels and often brief increases in our heart rate. Examples of positive stress include everyday challenges such as changes in routines, meeting new people, dealing with everyday frustrations, starting a new school or creche, getting a medical check-up, and trying to overcome a fear of something such as water, animals, or flying. If a child is supported (e.g., through the help of loving caregivers) in trying to face these positive stressors so that he/she can actually master and overcome these everyday challenges, the result will be a positive developmental milestone and an essential part of the normal developmental process. The NSCDC states that this kind of stress is a normal part of life and that learning to adjust to positive stress is an essential part of normal, healthy human development (2005).

Dr. Bruce Perry, child psychiatrist, developmental neuroscientist, and founder of the Child Trauma Academy, explains that experiencing stress during development is not necessarily a bad thing. He states that the development of stress response neural systems relies on exposure to moderate and controllable stress levels (Perry, 2007). He states that when human beings are allowed to experience moderate, controlled exposure to stress while in childhood, with the buffering support of an emotionally attuned available adult nearby, it is as if these children are inoculated against future, harsher stressors and that this helps to build healthy children (Perry, 2007).

Tolerable stress

This category of stress is potentially more damaging than positive stress because it has to do with events and experiences that could alter the developing brain in a negative way. However, these events and experiences are ones that usually occur for shorter periods and so give the brain time to recover and therefore prevent potentially damaging effects (NSCDC, 2005/2014). Examples of tolerable stress include such major adverse experiences as experiencing the death of a loved one, a frightening accident, or a contentious parental separation or divorce. If a child has the support of loving caregivers, learning to cope with and eventually overcome the pain of tolerable stress can be a positive thing (National Scientific Council on the Developing Child, 2005). However, without the buffer of positive relationships, tolerable stress can become toxic stress.

Toxic stress

This category of stress can be extremely damaging to the developing brain because it involves frequent, prolonged activation of the body's stress response. It activates either the hyper-arousal or hypo-arousal of the sympathetic nervous system. It is caused by seriously stressful events that are: (a) chronic, (b) out of the child's control, and (c) are experienced without the child having access to support from at least one, understanding, competent, and caring adult. Studies show that if a child is repeatedly exposed to experiences that he/she finds fearful, the very structure/architecture of the developing brain can be harmed by the repeated activation of the stress response triggered by these experiences (National Scientific Council on the Developing Child, 2005; Perry et al., 1995; Schore, 2003, 2008; Van Der Kolk, 2014).

Explaining the stress response system

As we have explained, trauma may be caused both by "events" that happened to us as well as "events" that didn't happen to us (such as experiencing nurturing during infancy), but the effect of these negative experiences or lack of certain positive experiences triggers the stress response and it is the repeated activation of the stress response that ultimately causes trauma. We now provide a step-by-step description of the neurobiological, neuroendocrine, and neuropsychological responses to the activation of the stress response system.

Every human being is wired from birth to respond in a predictable fashion to experiences they sense to be threatening. The human body is programmed to respond with one or a combination of specific responses to these experiences. This is called the fight, flight, or freeze response. For example, if we see someone running toward us brandishing a weapon, we either (a) run toward the aggressor and fight them, this is called the fight response; (b) run away as fast as we can, this is called the flight response; or (c) dissociate/detach from reality, this is called the freeze response. Each of these three reactions is triggered by chemical and biological responses in the body that have been designed to equip human beings to respond to impending danger and protect themselves. The fight, flight, or freeze response, also known as the "acute stress response," is an automatic response that is hormonally based. It is not something one chooses; the hormones in the bloodstream choose for us. The higher reasoning part of the brain, the pre-frontal cortex, is excluded from the process; it is the lower, more primitive part of the brain that controls the response. Here is a summary of what happens when the stress response is triggered.

- When we sense danger (either through something we see, hear, smell, or taste), a signal goes from our senses straight to the amygdala, which has been referred to as the brain's "smoke detector" (Van Der Kolk, 2014, p. 60), a structure in the brain that is concerned primarily with the survival of the organism (in this case, the human being).
- The amygdala does not waste any valuable time trying to communicate with the thinking part of the brain (i.e., the cortex) in order to rationalize the situation. To do that would waste valuable time and therefore could risk the life of the organism.
- The job of the amygdala is to fast track everything.

- In a situation that is perceived to be threatening, the amygdala has three main functions.
- First, the amygdala's job is to aid the human being to manage his/her emotions in the midst of the (perceived to be) threatening event so that he/she can react appropriately by either fighting, taking flight, or freezing. Each of these responses has the potential to save the life of the organism.
- Second, the amygdala's job is to create an emotional memory of the threatening event, because if the human being does not do this, he/she may fall prey to the same danger again.
- Third, the amygdala's job is to get a warning message out quickly to other structures in the body stating that the organism senses immediate danger.
- The amygdala does these three jobs by sending a distress signal straight to the hypothalamus.
- The hypothalamus operates like a command center in the brain. It is a structure that gets information out quickly to other parts of the body. Once it is signaled by the amygdala that the organism is in danger, the hypothalamus flies into action.
- The job of the hypothalamus is to activate various mechanisms in the body that can provide the organism with the energy and physical strength needed to either fight the source of danger or take flight from the source of danger. The hypothalamus must also activate the mechanisms that will ensure that the organism becomes hyper-vigilant and in a state of high alert so that it can protect itself. Here is what it does.
- The hypothalamus sends a signal to the adrenal medulla and the adrenal medulla responds by releasing surges of the hormone epinephrine (also called adrenaline) into the bloodstream.
- As epinephrine surges through the body, it stimulates a number of physiological changes.
- The heart beats faster than normal, and in so doing it pumps blood into the muscles and other essential body parts. It does this so that the legs are empowered to run fast if necessary and the arms are empowered to wrestle and fight if necessary.
- The breathing becomes rapid. The small airways in the lungs open wide so that the lungs can take in more oxygen than they normally would with each breath. This happens for a number of reasons. One reason is so that the organism, (if a human) can shout for help, or (if an animal), can growl or bark and possibly frighten off the aggressor. Another reason for this rapid breathing is that extra oxygen is sent to the brain to increase alertness in the parts of the body, such as the senses, which play a vital role in informing the organism as to where the danger lies. The effect on the senses is immediate.
- Sight. The pupils dilate (i.e., open wide) so that we can see more clearly, especially in the dark and we have tunnel vision (i.e., our focus is straight ahead). Our peripheral vision (i.e., side vision) is temporarily suspended, so that we don't focus on anything that could distract us to the side, we focus on what is in front of us, which is usually where the danger is located).

- Touch: The hair stands on end, making our skin very sensitive to anything that touches it. In animals, this reaction sometimes makes the animal look larger and thereby more intimidating to its attacker.
- Smell: The sense of smell is heightened so that we can make a memory of the scent of our attacker.
- Hearing: The hearing is altered so that we block out background noise and only hear what is going on in our immediate vicinity where the danger is located.
- Taste: The mouth becomes dry, so that our instinct to eat is impeded therefore we are not distracted by food.
- Epinephrine: Epinephrine also triggers the release of glucose, i.e., blood sugar, and the release of fats from their temporary storage cells in the body. These nutrients surge through the bloodstream, supplying oxygen to all parts of the body.
- All of these changes happen in milliseconds as a result of the hypothalamus's activation of the SAM axis (sympathetic–adreno–medulla axis).
- This is stage one of the fight/flight response.
- Now, as the initial surge of epinephrine subsides, the hypothalamus activates stage two of the fight/flight response.
- The hypothalamus now activates the HPA axis (hypothalamus–pituitary–adrenal axis).
- The HPA axis is activated when the brain continues to perceive something as dangerous.
- The hypothalamus releases a hormone called CRH (corticotropin-releasing hormone) which travels to the pituitary gland and triggers the release of ACTH (adrenocorticotropic hormone). This hormone travels to the adrenal glands activating the release of cortisol, a powerful stress hormone.
- The effect of all this is to keep the body on high alert, vigilant, revved up in top gear, ready and able to fight or take flight.
- If, for some reason, fight/flight is not an option, as is usually the case if the organism is a young child, the organism is programmed to freeze.
- The freeze response is a legitimate adaptive response, which is designed by nature to help save the life of the organism.
- When the threat passes, the brain, via the hypothalamus, stimulates the parasympathetic nervous system PNS to switch off the fight/flight response and calm the body down reversing all the biochemical and physiological responses that were triggered. So, heart rate, respiration, and blood pressure all go back to pre-stress stress levels. The digestive system, which was effectively shut down during the stressful event, is re-stimulated, and homeostasis is achieved.

(adapted from Van Der Kolk, 2014).

All of this chemical and biological activity is a good thing if:

a It propels the organism into a fight/flight or freeze response because the organism's life really is in danger and this response helps to save it.

b   The response is short-lived. The body is only in this hyper-vigilant state for a very short time, giving the organism just enough time to get out of harm's way. Then the body is restored to a normal, non-aroused, non-hyper-vigilant state, and the brain and the body start to repair.
c   This hyper-aroused state does not occur very often. It is the exception rather than the rule.
d   Homoeostasis (balance) is achieved quickly, i.e., heart rate, respiration, and blood pressure all return to normal levels quickly.

In this scenario, the fight, flight, or freeze response is a very helpful adaptive response capable of saving the life of the organism. However, a problem occurs when, for various reasons, the fight, flight, or freeze response does not switch off but is involuntarily activated over and over again, causing this cascade of chemical responses to become habitual, so that the child is constantly thrown into "adaptive response" mode and consequently left in a continuous state of being either "hyper-aroused" or "hypo-aroused." These adaptive responses are now examined.

Explaining the terms "adaptive responses" and "survival strategies"

As we have outlined above, the human brain is wired to respond to threat with a series of predictable neurobiological, neuroendocrine, and neuropsychological responses. The term "adaptive response" refers to how we as humans respond to serious stressors by initiating defensive reactions which are designed to counteract and restore to normalcy the disruption in the state of homeostasis (balance) brought about by trauma. The fight or flight response we referred to above is an adaptive response, which can also be called "hyper-arousal." The freeze response we referred to above is also an adaptive response, which can be called "hypo-arousal'"

KEY TERMS

Adaptive Responses
Hyper-arousal
Hypo-arousal
Homeostasis

Adaptive responses are often referred to as "survival strategies" because when an individual experiences or re-experiences the activation of the stress response system as described above, they unconsciously turn to "survival strategies" originally designed by nature to save their life, that take the form of either "hyper-arousal" or "hypo-arousal." These "adaptive responses" or "survival strategies" often show themselves in classrooms, if a child's stress response becomes activated by some "trigger," i.e., a reminder of a traumatic experience. These triggers can take the form of a sight, smell, sound, or other sensory stimulus.

Understanding "hyper-arousal" and "hypo-arousal"

Hyper-arousal: what can it look like in a classroom?

- *(fight response).*
- screaming, kicking, shouting, biting
- hitting others, breaking things
- scattering things, throwing things
- upturning chairs/tables
- looking defiant
- *(flight response).*
- running out of class
- running away from the teacher
- refusal to join a group
- hiding under tables
- covering the face with the hands
- putting hands over eyes and ears
- shutting out the teacher

Hypo-arousal: what can it look like in a classroom?

- *(freeze response).*
- withdrawn/unresponsive
- being in a world of their own
- looking sleepy
- daydreaming
- zoning out
- looking like they cannot hear
- not comprehending anything.

The crucial problem for many traumatized children is that these "adaptive responses," fight, flight, or freeze, which were designed by nature to only be activated sporadically when the organism was faced with real danger, may become habitual and therefore maladaptive. They may become habitual for the following reasons:

a The dangerous event is recurrent, so the chemical and biological response is repeated over and over and over again, allowing no opportunity for "repair" or recovery from the traumatic event. In this situation, the child is left "stuck" in a perpetual low-level fear state because the dangerous event is ongoing, homeostasis (balance) does not happen for very long, and the child is left in a persistent stress response state (Perry, 2001).

b The dangerous event has, in fact, gone away but the child is so "stuck" in a fear state that stress hormones are continually triggered when the child either:

- Sees, hears, smells, tastes, or touches something that reminds him/her of the dangerous event.
- Gets sudden, unsolicited flashbacks, or confused images of the dangerous event in the form of patchy memories.

Therefore, the repeated activation of the stress response (the fight/flight/freeze response) can become a very unhelpful, maladaptive response because the repeated activation prevents the organism from achieving homeostasis (balance). If homeostasis is delayed, and the child is left in a semi-permanent state of hyper- or hypo-arousal, the slightest trigger can cause a cascade of primal responses resulting in the types of behavior described above, which are essentially fight/flight/freeze responses which present as behaviors.

Recognizing signs and symptoms (which may be indicative) of traumatic stress

Children 0–3 years

Children aged 0–3 years who have been exposed to traumatic stress may exhibit some of the following behaviors and conditions:

- Poor verbal skills
- Poor memory
- Poor sleep habits
- Restless sleep
- Nightmares
- Poor appetite
- Low weight
- Digestive problems
- Are withdrawn
- Are anxious
- Become abnormally sad (suddenly)
- Become abnormally irritable (suddenly)
- Cry, scream, or fret excessively
- Be easily startled
- Be easily frightened in non-threatening situations
- Constantly look for attention
- Have extreme temper tantrums
- Show fear of being separated from primary carer

Children 3–6 years

Children aged 3–6 years who have been exposed to traumatic stress may exhibit some of the following behaviors and conditions:

- Be verbally abusive
- Have poor skill development
- Have poor sleep habits
- Have nightmares
- Have an erratic appetite
- Have digestive problems
- Have stomachaches
- Have headaches
- Are withdrawn
- Are anxious
- Are fearful
- Are distrustful
- Are suspicious of people's motives
- Can become abnormally sad (suddenly)
- Can become abnormally irritable (suddenly)
- Become easily startled
- Become easily frightened in non-intimidating settings
- Constantly demand attention
- Display excessive temper tantrums
- Behave aggressively
- Exhibit regressive behaviors, e.g., bedwetting
- Show a lack of self-confidence
- Act-out in social situations
- Show inability to make friends
- Show inability to trust others
- Believe he/she is to blame for the traumatic experience
- Difficulty concentrating in school
- Difficulty doing what peers are doing in school
- Show fear of being separated from primary carer
- Fear adults who remind them of the traumatic experience

Children 6–12 years

- Show signs of anxiety e.g., biting nails/bed-wetting
- Become suddenly fearful e.g., want light on at night
- Feel guilt or shame
- Are fearful of others
- Show inability to trust others
- Lose confidence in themselves
- Become argumentative
- Don't want to go to school

- Don't want to be with friends
- Want to isolate
- Show fear when separated from primary carer
- Have difficulty concentrating
- Develop sleep problems
- Have nightmares

Young people 12–18 years

- Develop eating disorders
- Show signs of depression
- Begin self-harming
- Start abusing alcohol
- Begin to use drugs
- Become sexually active
- School refusal

Vignette

Brandon was a new entrant to the Montessori 6–9 classroom. He was eight years old and had just moved with his mom to the city. He had previously attended a Montessori 3–6 program in another state, and according to his mom, he was very happy there and was doing well. During the first three days, he was very quiet and anxious looking. The teacher noticed that his nails were chewed down to the tips of his fingers, though she was careful not to comment on this. The teacher offered him various activities, but he refused them saying firmly (and what appeared to be defiantly), "I don't want anything." He insisted on sitting near the open classroom door, with his jacket on and zipped up, for three full days, expressionless, just staring into space.

Day three was a particularly beautiful day. The sun was shining and there was the sound of birdsong everywhere. At one point the birdsong was slightly interrupted by the distant sound of an ambulance and a police siren. Most of the children and teachers didn't appear to notice it… but Brandon did. He leapt up from his seat by the door and raced across the classroom to the window, knocking over the chequerboard (a Montessori mathematical material) that Amy and Ruth had been working on so carefully for over half an hour. He pulled on the window latches, shaking, and appearing to have a great need to get outside. The teacher quietly approached him, but he ran from her back to the open classroom door where he had been sitting, and then raced to the main door of the building which was, of course locked. He looked terrified, agitated, and panic-stricken. His mom was called, and when she arrived, he threw his arms around her still silent and shaking.

> Later that week, Brandon's mom confided in the teacher that, for over a year, she had been in an emotionally and physically abusive relationship and Brandon had witnessed very frightening scenes including her being removed to hospital by ambulance, following an assault committed by her former partner. Brandon's response upon hearing the faint sound of the ambulance siren was a classic "flight" response caused by a trigger – the sound of the siren. He had become hyper-aroused, and the "flight" response had kicked in suddenly and forcefully.

Not all negative behaviors are trauma-based, but many of them are, and because they are not recognized as such children are often unjustly criticized for behavior that is orchestrated by the stress response system and not the child's will. Many behaviors that are seen as willful defiance, such as screaming, kicking, shouting, biting, hitting others (fight response), and running as far away from the teacher as the classroom allows (flight response) and being in a world of their own (freeze response), are unconscious behaviors and are not voluntarily chosen by the child, therefore they are unintentional and are not done to defy the parent or teacher. They are survival-based stress responses that are triggered and re-triggered because the child is still holding trauma in the body. The trauma is literally under the skin. The behaviors are not calculated, planned, or selected by the child, they are activated by the amygdala, the fear center of the brain, which, as we explained above spends all its time scanning for danger to the organism so that it can fast track a survival strategy. What is happening has a serious effect on a child's ability to function in school and can best be explained through the concept of "state-dependent functioning."

Understanding the concept of "state-dependent functioning"

Dr. Bruce Perry states that "a traumatized child in a persisting state of arousal can sit in a classroom and not learn" (1999, p. 10). This statement sums up succinctly the effect of "state-dependent functioning" which is a concept that explains why we absorb, and process information differently depending on what state of mind, or more specifically, what state of arousal we are in at the time the information is coming to us. All human beings have an internal state or more specifically, a state of arousal which is on a continuum moving from a state of calm to a state of vigilance, to a state of alarm, to a state of fear, and finally reaching a state of terror. If we live in a secure environment with dependable caregivers, our state of arousal will be resting at "calm" on the continuum. If something happens to trigger our stress response, we will move from this state of calm along the continuum to either a state of vigilance, a state of alarm, a state of fear, or a state of terror. Our position on the continuum depends on a number of factors such as (a) whether or not the stress response was triggered by something acute or chronic, (b) whether or not the stress response was able to switch off so that homeostasis (balance) was achieved,

(c) whether or not the individual was an adult or a child, whether or not the individual had the benefit of having a supportive adult available to buffer the effect of the traumatic event, and so on (Perry, 2003).

However, children who are, or have been exposed to chronic or complex trauma such as chronic exposure to neglect or abuse, frequently live in a constant state of alertness because the nature of these types of trauma is such that they cause the stress response system to "stay on." Homeostasis is delayed and so the body and the brain are stuck in a constant state of alertness leaving the child hyper-vigilant, watching out for signs of danger, and living with the expectation that something bad will happen imminently. In this state of arousal, even innocent words or actions will look threatening to children causing them to prepare their body to either fight, flight, or freeze in order to protect themselves from possible attack. If nothing happens to relieve the perceived threat of danger (such as the presence of a trusted, sympathetic, and emotionally attuned adult), the child will enter either (a) a state of hyper-arousal (attempting to escape pain and danger by either fighting off the enemy, or taking flight to escape the enemy) or (b) a state of hypo-arousal (attempting to escape pain and danger by dissociating, i.e., screening out the attack by escaping through the mind into a safe, sometimes fantasy world). Both of these states have a seriously negative effect on a child's ability to function in school. Both states have the same result, the child cannot take in information and therefore may do what Perry says: sit in a classroom yet still be unable to learn (1999).

Also, as Perry et al. point out, when a child lives constantly in hyper-or hypo-aroused states, these adaptive states which were so necessary for survival, become maladaptive habits (1995). What this means is that the child's adaptive responses (which were good and necessary responses) to the repeated activation of the stress response can lead to permanent characteristics in the child's behavior and demeanor, and the neural systems in the child's brain will be altered in ways that are not conducive to healthy development (Perry et al., 1995). In other words, the child will develop the habit of either dissociating/tuning out, or the habit of being defensive, aggressive, and flying away from anything that appears to be threatening. Simply put, when we observe children who are either aggressive, defensive, and convinced that they are being threatened, or the opposite, disinterested, in a world of their own, we may well be observing the habits formed by "state-dependent" functioning.

Exploring the concept of a "window of tolerance"

Another concept known as the "window of tolerance" was originally developed by Dr. Daniel Siegel, a Clinical Professor of Psychiatry, and expert on trauma. According to Siegel, every person has a "window of tolerance" (2020). What this means is that when a person is operating within their particular optimum zone (or window of tolerance), they can manage and cope with their emotions without getting dangerously stressed. It may also be explained as a neuroscientific model used to describe the zone of arousal in which an individual is able to function most effectively. When an individual is within the confines of this zone, they are typically able to function well, learn effectively, relax, play, and relate well with others and generally thrive in everyday life. Within this window of tolerance, an individual feels grounded, regulated, present, capable of being curious and interested in relating to others, and they are also able to cope when heightened emotions threaten to have a negative impact on them. However, if we are pushed out of our window of tolerance, we can become hyper or hypo-aroused. As we have seen, hyper-arousal is characterized by emotions related to the (fight/flight) response, high energy, aggression, anger, and need to escape, which can present in a classroom as angry outbursts, irritability, destructive behavior, constant anxiety, hyper-vigilance, poor concentration, and so on. Hypo-arousal, on the other hand, is characterized by emotions related to the (freeze) response, numbness, withdrawal, shut down, and shame, which can present in a classroom as zoned out, showing no interest in anything, listless, depressed, and so on.

When someone experiences severe or repeated trauma, their worldview may change, and they can begin to see everything as a threat. Consequently, their window of tolerance becomes narrower, and even innocent everyday challenges can cause them to explode. For example, for children who have been exposed to trauma, a simple and ostensibly reasonable request from a parent or teacher asking the child to carry out an everyday task (e.g., a parent's request that the child take a shower, or a teacher's request that the child change classrooms) can cause a volcanic-like eruption of emotion that is incomprehensible to the non-trauma affected onlooker. The sheer explosiveness of the response is, in itself, an indication that the child has been pushed out of his/her window of tolerance. The good news is that most people can widen their particular window of tolerance with simple strategies such as (if they are hyper-aroused), listening to calming music, taking gentle exercises such as yoga or walking, to calm them down; or (if they are hypo-aroused), listening to fast-paced music with a strongly scented candle in the room to awaken their senses, or doing brisk exercise such as jogging or running, to enervate themselves. These strategies have been shown to increase the ability to manage stress when an individual's window of tolerance has become narrowed.

Examining the polyvagal theory (PVT)

This theory was first proposed by Dr. Stephen Porges (2004), an American psychologist, neuroscientist, and professor of psychiatry in 1994. Despite criticisms that it is not good science (Grossman, 2023), and oversimplifies and over emphasizes the role of the vagus nerve and its role in threat and social engagement, it paved the way for PVT to be used in psychotherapy, with many psychotherapists embracing it, and others dismissing it as pseudoscience. PVT aims to provide an understanding of the connections between brain and body processes from an evolutionary perspective. Basically, PVT proposes that our nervous systems are genetically wired to continually scan the environment to check whether we are safe or in danger. Porges used the word "neuroception" to refer to the neural circuitry involved in the continuous, unconscious scanning of our environment, looking for the presence of safety or danger. If danger is sensed, we respond with a survival response (a fight/flight or freeze response). To put it simply, neuroception explains why infants get excited and smile when their parents or caregivers get close to them but become unsettled and cry when a stranger does the same (Porges, 2004). However, according to Porges, when neuroception tells us that we are safe and the people in our environment are not a threat to us, our defense mechanisms are disabled, and we can behave in ways that promote social engagement helping us to make positive attachments (2004). Porges emphasizes the role of tone of voice, (angry or gentle) and facial expressions (friendly or threatening) in neuroception in the effort to tell us whether we are safe or in danger. Nicholson et al. point out that a young child is more likely to sense danger when adults are using a harsh or angry tone of voice and when their facial expressions are communicating lack of empathy, anger, or fear. Similarly, they say that in order to calm a distressed child, a nurturing tone of voice coupled with facial expressions that communicate love and kindness will be successful (Nicholson et al., 2023.) However, Porges points out that following traumatic experiences, our neuroception can become faulty so that we misread prosody of voice and facial expressions and perceive danger when in fact our environment is safe.

Explaining the PACE model

This model was developed by Dr. Dan Hughes, an American psychologist (Hughes & Golding, 2012). PACE stands for Playfulness, Acceptance, Curiosity, and Empathy. It is a model used with trauma-affected children and it aims to promote the feeling of safety in children in their interactions with adults.

Playfulness involves having a lighthearted relationship with children in which they sense that the relationship is not conditional on their being perfect. It therefore reduces the shame children might load upon themselves when they feel that things have gone wrong in their lives.

Acceptance means letting the child know that you are responding to their feelings in a non-judgmental way, and you are not trying to "reassure away" the feelings they have, however negative they may be. Acceptance usually involves sitting with the child as they pour out strong emotions such as "no one likes me." It involves showing that you accept how they feel (even if you do not actually agree with their perceptions). You are showing that you are accepting that their feelings represent their perception of reality.

Curiosity involves showing the child that you are genuinely interested in how they feel. However, it is better to avoid asking "why?" and instead ask questions such as "I wonder what makes you feel this" or "Would it be ok if I tell you what I think is going on here? I may be completely wrong here, but this is what I think is happening." This approach shows your genuine desire to understand the child's feelings and perceptions. It does not imply that you agree with these perceptions, but it shows that you are curious enough and care enough to want to try to understand what's going on for the child.

Empathy involves showing the child that you are standing shoulder to shoulder with them in their difficulties and genuinely trying to feel and understand how it they feel while going through such difficult circumstances. It is often helpful to express your own feelings such as "I feel sad that you think nobody cares about you."

> **Summary of Chapter 3**
>
> 1. There are several definitions of trauma but all of them accept that trauma is a psychological wound that can adversely affect our ability to live a fulfilling life.
> 2. There are three main types of trauma – acute, chronic and complex. Acute means a once-off event. Chronic means repeated events. Complex means repeated traumatic events usually perpetrated by a caregiver (SAMHSA, 2014).
> 3. Trauma and stress are not the same things. Trauma is an experience that induces an abnormally intense and prolonged stress response (Perry, 2007).
> 4. There are three types of stress – positive, tolerable, and toxic stress (NSCDC, 2005).
> 5. The stress response is a normal adaptive response to a perceived threat. Its function is to save our lives. It involves the fight, flight, and freeze response (Burke Harris, 2019).
> 6. Repeated activation of the stress response is not normal and it can result in adaptive behaviors or survival strategies, such as hyper-arousal (hypervigilance, always being on alert for danger), or hypo-arousal (becoming withdrawn, being in one's own world) or a mixture of both.
> 7. "State dependent functioning" is a concept that explains why we absorb, and process information differently depending on what state of mind, or more specifically, what state of arousal we are in at the time the information is coming to us. If a child is in a perpetual fear state he can sit in a classroom and still not be able to learn (Perry, 1999).
> 8. A "window of tolerance" (Daniel Siegel) is a neuroscientific model used to describe the zone of arousal in which an individual is able to function most effectively. When an individual is within the confines this zone, they are typically able to function well, learn effectively, relax, play, and relate well with others and generally thrive in everyday life, but if we are pushed out of our "window of tolerance" we can become hyper or hypo-aroused.
> 9. The "polyvagal theory" (Stephen Porges) proposes that our nervous systems continually scan our environment (using neuroception – neural circuitry) to check if we are safe or in danger.
> 10. The PACE model (Dan Hughes) stands for Playfulness, Acceptance, Curiosity, and Empathy. It is a model used with trauma-affected children and it aims to promote the feeling of safety in children in their interactions with adults.

Questions for group discussion

1. Describe your thoughts about "trauma." Do you think of "trauma" as something only caused by big events, or do you believe that trauma can be caused by more commonplace events?
2. Do you find the classification of "types of trauma" helpful in understanding what trauma is?
3. Does a knowledge of the fight/flight/freeze response help you to understand how trauma can impact children's behaviors in the classroom.
4. Do you find the distinction between "types of stress" helpful?
5. Do you find that an understanding of the "adaptive responses" or "survival strategies" known as "hyper-arousal" and "hypo-arousal" is helpful to you in responding to the diverse behaviors and demeanors of children who have been impacted by trauma?
6. Do you find the concept of "state-dependent functioning" helpful to you in your attempts to understand and respond to the behaviors of trauma-affected children?
7. Try to explain the concept of a "window of tolerance." Is it helpful to your understanding of trauma?
8. Discuss the polyvagal theory. Do you find it helpful to your understanding of trauma?
9. Do you find the PACE model helpful when responding to trauma-affected children?

References

Alexander, J. (2019). *Building trauma-sensitive schools: Your guide to creating safe, supportive learning environments for all students*. Brookes.

Burke Harris, N. (2019). *The deepest well: Healing the long-term effects of childhood adversity*. Mariner.

Felitti, V. J., Anda, R. F., Nordenberg, D., Williamson, D. F., Spitz, A. M., Edwards, V., Koss, M. P., & Marks, J. S. (1998). Relationship of childhood abuse and household dysfunction to many of the leading causes of death in adults: The adverse childhood experiences (ACE) study. *American Journal of Preventive Medicine, 14*(4), 245–258. https://doi.org/10.1016/s0749-3797(98)00017-8

Grossman, P. (2023). Fundamental challenges and likely refutations of the five basic premises of the polyvagal theory. *Biological Psychology, 180*(2023), 108589. https://doi.org/10.1016/j.biopsycho.2023.108589

Herman, J. (1997), *Trauma and recovery: The aftermath of violence, from domestic abuse to political terror*. Basic Books.

Hughes, D., & Golding, K. (2012). *Creating loving attachments: Parenting with PACE to nurture confidence and security in the troubled child*. Jessica Kingsley.

Jennings, P. (2019). *The trauma-sensitive classroom. Building resilience with compassionate teaching*. W.W. Norton & Company.

Levine, P. (1997). *Waking the tiger*. North Atlantic Books.

Mate, G. (2019). *When the body says no: The cost of hidden stress*. Vermillion.

Mate, G. (2021). Trauma is not what happens to you: It's what happens inside you. youtube.com

National Scientific Council on the Developing Child (NSCDC), (2005). *Excessive stress disrupts the architecture of the developing brain: Working Paper No 3*. Retrieved from www.developingchild.harvard.edu.

Nicholson, J., Perez, L., Kurtz, J., Bryant, S., & Giles, D. (2023). *Trauma-informed practices for early childhood educators: Relationship-based approaches that reduce stress, build resilience and support healing in young children*. Taylor & Francis.

Perry, B. D., Pollard, R. A., Blakley, Y. L., Baker, W. L., & Vigilante, D. (1995). Childhood trauma, the neurobiology of adaptation, and "Use-dependent" development of the brain: How "States" become traits". *Infant Mental Health Journal*, *16*(4), 271–291. https://doi.org/10.1002/1097-0355(199524)16:4<271::AID-IMHJ2280160404>3.0.CO;2-B

Perry, B. D. (1999). Memories of fear: How the brain stores and retrieves physiological States, feelings, behaviors and thoughts from traumatic events. In J. Goodwin & R. Attias (Ed.) *Splintered reflections: Images of the body in trauma*. Basic Books.

Perry, B.D., (2001) The neurodevelopmental impact of violence in childhood. Chapter 18: In D. Schetky & E. P. Benedek (Eds.), *Textbook of child and adolescent forensics psychiatry* (pp. 221–238). American Psychiatric Press, Inc.

Perry, B. D. (2003). *Effects of traumatic events on children*. The Child Trauma Academy.

Perry, B. D. (2007). *Stress, trauma and post-traumatic stress disorders in children* (pp. 1–15). Child Trauma Academy.

Perry, B. D. (2009). Examining child maltreatment through a neurodevelopmental Lens: Clinical applications of the neurosequential model of therapeutics. *Journal of Loss and Trauma*, *14*, 240–255.

Perry, B. D., & Szalavitz, M. (2017). *The boy who was raised as a dog and other stories from a child Psychiatrist's notebook: What traumatized children can teach us about loss, love and healing*. Basic Books.

Perry, B. D., & Winfrey, O. (2021). *What happened to you? Conversations on trauma, resilience and healing*. Pan Macmillan.

Porges, S. (2004). Neuroception: A subconscious system for detecting threats and safety. *Zero to Three: Bulletin of the National Centre for Clinical Infant Programs (J)*, *24*(5), 19–24.

SAMHSA, (2014). Substance abuse and mental health services administration. (2014, July). *SAMHSA's concept of trauma and guidance for a trauma-informed approach*. Retrieved from https://store.samhsa.gov/shin/content/SMA14-4884/SMA-4884.pdf

Schore, A. (2003). Early relational trauma, disorganized attachment, and the development of a predisposition to violence. In M. F. Solomon & D. J. Siegel (Eds.), *Healing trauma: Attachment, mind, body and brain* (pp. 107–167). Norton.

Schore, A. (2008). Modern attachment theory: The Central role of affect regulation in development and treatment. *Clinical Social Work Journal*, *36*, 9–20.

Siegel, D. J. (2020*). The developing mind: How relationships and the brain interact to shape who we are*. Guilford Press.

Treisman, K. (2017). *Working with relational and developmental trauma in children and adolescents*. Routledge.

Van Der Kolk, B. (2014). *The body keeps the score: Mind, brain and body in the transformation of trauma*. Penguin.

4 The effects of trauma on emotional, social, and cognitive functioning

Chapter objectives

- To explore the potential impact of trauma on children's emotional functioning.
- To outline the potential impact of trauma on children's social functioning.
- To explain the potential impact of trauma on children's cognitive functioning.

Learning outcomes

At the end of this chapter, the learner will be able to:

- **Explain the effects of trauma on emotional functioning including:**
- How trauma affects children's ability to control emotions.
- How trauma affects children's ability to form later attachments.

- **Outline the effects of trauma on social functioning including:**
- Children's ability to make friends.
- Children's ability to feel at ease in social situations.
- Children's ability to do what peers are doing.

- **Explain the effects of trauma on cognitive functioning including:**
- The effect of hypervigilance and dissociation on children's concentration.
- The effect of trauma on children's receptive and expressive language skills.
- The effect of trauma on memory.

In her very helpful book, Patricia Jennings emphasizes that "We now know that trauma can impact the development of social, emotional, and cognitive skills in ways that result in difficulties adjusting to the demands of school" (2019, p. 1).

DOI: 10.4324/9781003438021-7

This chapter examines the effects of exposure to trauma on the emotional, social, and cognitive functioning of children and young people.

Looking at the impact of trauma on children's emotional functioning

Trauma expert, Bessel van der Kolk (2003) states that "Lack of capacity for emotional self-regulation is probably the most striking feature of chronically traumatized children" (2003, p. 298). The trauma-affected child's difficulties with emotional regulation arise from a number of sources which include:

- A view of the world as a dangerous place.
- An over-stimulated stress response system.
- Emotional triggers.
- Difficulty understanding and naming their own emotions.
- Attachment problems.

A view of the world as a dangerous place

If a child grows up in a nurturing environment and has been provided with an opportunity to build an attachment with a loving caregiver, that child will generally have a view of the world that is fundamentally positive. Even if finances are limited and the home is basic, living in a stable environment with a secure attachment figure who recognizes and appreciates the child's value and worth will generally enable a child to feel safe and have a positive self-image and internal sense of self-worth. In general, children in such circumstances will have positive expectations, and essentially an optimism that they can have a happy, worthwhile life. However, if children grow up with chronic poverty, food scarcity, homelessness, neglect, or abuse, or alternatively, if children's happy, nurturing environment has collapsed due to the effects of a sudden traumatic event, their worldview may no longer be a positive one. Judith Herman explains that exposure to trauma takes away a person's basic assumptions about the inherent safety of the world (1997).

Therefore, children may develop a worldview that is fundamentally negative. They often view the world as a very dangerous place where everything and everyone poses a potential threat to their very survival. To some trauma-affected children, danger lurks everywhere and there seems to be no escape from it. This is particularly the case when a child is the victim of complex trauma, such as physical, emotional, or sexual abuse, when the very people who should be the protectors of children are the very ones who perpetrate harm against them (Treisman, 2017). For other children, whose life and worldview has been changed suddenly, as in the vignette below, the world can become a dangerous and unpredictable place overnight.

> **Vignette**
>
> **(An anonymized composite of a true event)**
>
> Ivanovic was a happy three-year-old with a mischievous grin. He had loving parents and although they were newcomers to the country, Ivan was sociable and mixed easily especially with his peers at his Montessori school. One winter morning, his happy, carefree life came to a dramatic end, when he went into his baby sister's bedroom and found that she was cold, blue, and didn't smile when he tried to tickle her feet as he did every morning. Tragically, she had passed away owing to sudden infant death syndrome sometime during the night. Ivan stood terrified as his mother screamed hysterically beside the cot and eventually collapsed onto the floor as Ivan's dad searched for his phone to call the ambulance.
>
> Ivan was away from school for more than three weeks as his parents took him back to their homeland to bury the baby next to the grave of their own parents, and only returned because they had to resume work. Upon their return, the whole family was veiled in sadness. Ivan's first week back in school was difficult for everyone. He was an anxious, tearful, frightened boy. He was no longer the happy, carefree child he used to be. He appeared to be frightened of everything. He jumped nervously at any sudden noise. He was even frightened by the laughter of the other children and could be heard muttering to himself through tears – "are they crying? – are they crying?" Ivan's whole worldview had been changed overnight from a positive one filled with hopes and aspirations to a negative one where fear predominates.

An over-stimulated stress response system

As explained in Chapter 3, the stress response system is a very positive mechanism designed by nature to protect the life of the organism. However, it was designed only to be activated when needed, not to be switched on all the time, because human beings are not designed to be permanently on "high alert." That is where the problem of trauma lies. The trauma-affected child frequently develops an over-stimulated stress response and is often on high alert or in a low-level fear state most of the time (Perry, 1999). This in itself is exhausting and it causes intense irritability in some children and intense reactivity to even minor events which would typically not bother children who had not experienced trauma. For example, trauma-affected preschool children can suddenly fly into a state of emotional upheaval with tears and screams simply because their lunchtime biscuit came out of the packet a little broken. Similarly, trauma-affected preschool children can erupt like a volcano because someone appeared to be smiling when they tripped and fell down. It is not uncommon for trauma-affected children to lash out in a violent and aggressive manner against other children who they (wrongfully) believe are threatening them.

Emotional triggers

Children who have experienced trauma are extremely sensitive to emotional triggers. Just as fear enters the mind via the senses, so also fear can be re-triggered through the senses. A sight, a sound, a smell, a taste, a touch, however innocuous, can catapult a trauma-affected child from an apparent (but deceiving) state of calm, into an explosive state of emotional dysregulation. The National Child Traumatic Stress Network (NCTSN) explains that a child who has been exposed to traumatic events may demonstrate emotional responses that are explosive and unpredictable. They state that these children may react to a reminder of a traumatic event with feelings of sadness, anger, or just avoidance and that in the case of a child with a history of complex trauma, the environment may be filled with reminders of traumatic events. They further explain that trauma-affected children may frequently have powerful reactions to triggers in the environment and have great difficulty calming down when they become upset (NCTSN). They also point out that since typically, the traumatic events experienced by the child have happened in the context of relationships, it follows that even innocuous interactions with others that should only be mildly stressful (for example, choosing sides for a football match) can trigger emotional responses that are intense and sometimes explosive (NCTSN).

Difficulty understanding and naming their own emotions.

Children who have been affected by complex trauma often have problems identifying, expressing, and managing their emotions (Jennings, 2019). They often have an impoverished vocabulary with which to express their feelings (Treisman, 2017). These children frequently internalize (bottle-up) or externalize (act-out) stress reactions and, as a result of this they may experience anxiety, depression, or anger. Cole et al. state that children who have been affected by trauma frequently experience feelings that include fear, anger, irritability, anxiety, shame, helplessness, guilt, and depression, but they are unable to accurately identify or describe these feelings because they have neither the cognitive nor the verbal skills to express what they are feeling (2005). Therefore, these children may express emotions without restraint and so can appear to be, impulsive, out of control, aggressive, oversensitive, and unable to be reflective about their emotional outbursts. They frequently appear to overreact to what they perceive to be "provocation" in the classroom and in the playground and their outbursts are often referred to as *externalizing* behaviors.

Conversely, other trauma-affected children block out uncomfortable or painful emotions and so they can appear to adults, or their peers to be aloof or disconnected with others (Cole et al., 2005), and their withdrawal is often referred to as *internalizing* behavior. If the emotions are at the most extreme end of the scale, a trauma-affected child can move into a state of dissociation. When children lack an understanding relating to why they feel as they do, and also do not have words to describe how they feel, this puts them at risk for "somatic" (bodily) symptoms which include headaches, stomach pains, eating disorders, body-image concerns, fatigue, and a general feeling of being unwell (Van der Kolk, 1998). In 2014, Van der Kolk stated that trauma-affected children have fifty times the rate of asthma as non-trauma-affected children (2014).

Attachment problems

According to Van Der Kolk, it is extremely difficult to discuss childhood trauma without addressing the issue of the parental attachment bond (2014). The term attachment refers to the formation of a close emotional bond between an infant/child and the adult or adults who care for them (Bowlby, 1969/1982). An attachment may be secure, insecure, ambivalent, or avoidant (Ainsworth et al., 1978/2015). Trauma experts describe attachment as the *template* for future relationships. They explain that attachment is developed in infancy when a child interacts with parents or caregivers who are loving and responsive to the infant and attentive to the infant's needs. Therefore, attachment is the capacity to form and maintain healthy emotional bonds with others (Perry and Szalavitz, 2017; Schore, 2003, 2008; Treisman, 2017; Van der Kolk, 2003).

Alexander (2019) explains that having a healthy attachment does not mean that the parent is available to the child 24/7, never leaves the child's side, and never causes a "break" in their relationship. On the contrary, having a healthy attachment usually involves what psychologists call "break and repair" experiences. This author provides an excellent example of this "break and repair" experience when describing a mother who returns to her child following a work trip which involved the separation of mother and child for several days (this is the "break") and instinctively drops her bags on the floor while she allows her child to cuddle on her lap (this is the "repair") giving him time and space to snuggle and reconnect for as long as he needs (Alexander, 2019). She points out that, in this way, a healthy attachment is not made by never leaving the child or never having a break in the child/caregiver relationship but rather in supporting the child to manage and overcome the positive stress involved in the "break and repair" situation referred to above. "Break and repair" experiences are ongoing as the child moves from babyhood to toddlerhood to early childhood, with the caregiver often having to say "no" to the child's wants or desires especially if these are unhealthy or dangerous (for example having an entire packet of cookies for breakfast). In fact, it is these "break and repair" experiences that build a healthy attachment between the child and the caregiver and also build resilience in the child.

Research shows that a child who is securely attached will have a "template" for developing other healthy interpersonal relationships in the future. Moreover, a child who has had the benefit of a secure attachment in early life will have a *built-in* protective element against the negative effects of exposure to trauma, and the experience of having a secure attachment in early life will act as a buffer against the activation of the stress response (Treisman, 2017). However, it follows that a child who does not have the experience of a secure attachment in early life does not have a protective buffer against this type of extreme stress. Van der Kolk states that the security of the attachment bond appears to be the most significant mitigating factor against the brain disorganization that is caused by early exposure to trauma (2003).

In the case of complex trauma, where a secure relationship of sorts had been built between the child and the caregiver, but now the caregiver is the source of the child's trauma, the child's sense of betrayal and confusion is devastating. This situation leads to the child becoming wary of any further attachment no matter how sympathetic the new person (for example, a teacher or foster parent) might be. Alexander (2019) says that we need to understand the critical importance of healthy attachments between children and their caregivers and that this understanding is even more important when we take into account the fact that many children have experienced abuse and subsequent trauma at the hands of the very caregivers they trusted. Research shows that the majority of neglected and abused children have difficulty developing a strong healthy attachment to a caregiver (Treisman, 2017), and children who do not have healthy attachments have been shown to be more vulnerable to stress, have difficulty expressing and controlling emotions, and may react inappropriately, even violently in social situations (Treisman, 2017). Our capacity to develop supportive, healthy relationships with others is dependent on our having first developed those kinds of relationships in our family units (Treisman, 2017).

Children who have been exposed to abuse, neglect, or other traumatic experiences will not have developed (or will have developed but now have a rupture), in these kinds of relationships. These children need emotional healing and ironically that healing can only come through relationships and positive attachments. Barbara Sorrels, referring to the work of Neufield and Mate (2006), emphasizes the importance of the attachment relationship that a caregiver has with a child and relates this to the capacity of a caregiver to influence a child's behavior (Sorrels, 2015). She further points out that children who have been psychologically wounded in the context of a relationship can only be healed through a relationship (Sorrels, 2015). However, she points out that this needs to be a relationship of unconditional love and acceptance. Teachers may have the opportunity to be among the persons who can provide that love and unconditional acceptance to the child.

Examining the impact of trauma on children's social functioning

Perry (1999) stated that "The traumatized child frequently has significant impairment in social and emotional functioning" (p. 10). Children who have experienced traumatic events or who are experiencing ongoing exposure to traumatic events, often exhibit a number of specific problems in their social functioning (Cole et al., 2005). These problems include:

- Difficulty making friendships
- Unease in social situations
- Challenges doing what peers are doing

Difficulty making friendships

Children who have experienced or are still experiencing traumatic events in their lives frequently exhibit difficulty making friendships and often their peers see them as being unpredictable and oblivious to the unspoken social rules that underly friendships (Craig & Stevens, 2016). The specific reason for this difficulty often lies in the tendency of the trauma-affected child to mis-read the non-verbal cues, such as the facial expressions, the tone of voice, or the body language of their peers (Perry, 1999). Perry states that this is because, out of fear and a need to survive, these children had to focus on non-verbal cues (1999). Trauma-affected children have learned the hard way to be hyper-vigilant to non-verbal signals. They have experienced how a look, a tone of voice, or a bodily stance can very rapidly become a precursor to a frightening incident. As a result of having experienced such frightening events, these children subconsciously remain in a state of hyper-vigilance in relation to non-verbal cues. They notice looks, tones of voice, and bodily movements that other children, who have never experienced trauma would not even register. The National Scientific Council on the Developing Child (NSCDC) also states that trauma-experienced young children can have difficulty identifying and responding to other people's expressions of emotions and consequently have difficulties forming healthy relationships which leads to general problems with social interactions (NSCDC, 2010). This hyper-sensitivity to non-verbal cues, coupled with the fact that trauma-affected children are usually in a state of low-level fear, can lead these children to jump rapidly to the wrong conclusions about what they are sensing through non-verbal signals. Therefore, it is important for teachers to be aware that children who have experienced traumatic events often struggle because they:

- Mis-read the facial expressions of others and interpret a positive expression as a negative one. For example, trauma-affected children in school often interpret the teacher's serious expression as an angry expression and believe the teacher is cross with them.
- Mis-read the tone of voice of others and interpret a positive tone of voice as a negative one. For example, in the school yard, children who are trauma-affected will often interpret the shouts of other children as threatening voices, when, in fact, the children are just playing.
- Mis-read the body language of others and interpret a positive movement as a negative one. For example, children who are trauma-affected will often interpret an innocent pat on the arm by another as a threatening gesture, or a prelude to a sexual assault.
- Mis-read the intentions of others and interpret an innocent action as a malevolent one. For example, trauma-affected child may believe the teacher put him/her in a certain group or team because the teacher doesn't like him/her, whereas, in fact, the teacher's decision was purely arbitrary.

This situation naturally interferes with the child's ability to form and maintain friendships in school with their peer group as well as form good relationships with their teachers. Van der Kolk writes that children with histories of physical abuse tend to have problems accurately reading social cues and consequently are out of tune with their peers so that they become either socially withdrawn or they bully other children. He says they often scare other children away because of their inability to control their emotions and therefore often lack playmates and friends (Van der Kolk, 2003).

This is a serious problem for trauma-affected children and can have serious consequences. In terms of the peer group, social success is vital for the child who has suffered traumatic events, because positive social interactions play a significant role in the healing process from past and even ongoing traumas (Cole et al., 2005). Social success in school usually comes from the child's ability to get along with others. However, the trauma-affected child, who constantly mis-reads facial expressions, tones of voice, and body stances, finds it extremely difficult to get along with others. Moreover, children affected by trauma may be so overwhelmed by the social demands of the classroom that they either freeze into a hypo-aroused dissociative state much of the time or become hyper-aroused and fight with anybody who looks or sounds like they might pose a threat to their safety. Neither of these behaviors are conducive to making or retaining friendships.

Unease in social situations

Children who have been impacted by trauma often feel a sense of intense unease in social situations, indeed, this unease has been described as a feeling of being in "*shark-infested waters*" (Treisman, 2017, p. 6). This is often caused, as we have explained above, by the trauma-affected child's tendency to mis-read non-verbal signals. However, it is also due to their tendency to be in a low-level state of fear, much of the time (Perry et al., 1995). This state can translate into behaviors that appear either **withdrawn** which occurs when a child is in a hypo-aroused "freeze" state, or **aggressive** which occurs when a child is in a hyper-aroused "fight/flight state." However, what is not generally known is that both of these presentations, the withdrawn state and the aggressive state, stem from the same source, which is "FEAR" (Perry et al., 1995).

The life of the trauma-impacted child is dominated by FEAR. The child is rarely relaxed, rarely at ease. At any moment, the child could explode into aggression or dissociate completely from reality. Cole and colleagues explain that children who have been exposed to trauma can present with very puzzling and perplexing behavior. This behavior, they explain, arises from internal states that are not fully understood by the children themselves (Cole et al., 2005) and are invisible to those looking on. They explain that children who are trauma-affected can be unpredictable, demanding, and ambivalent in their behavior, but the crucial thing to understand is that these perplexing behaviors usually stem from intense feelings of vulnerability. They explain that the feelings of vulnerability may lead to reluctance on the part of the child to engage in the life of the classroom, and some children affected by trauma will often disconnect themselves from the present by dissociating or going away in their minds. As it may be difficult for a teacher to recognize the dissociating child, a frustrated teacher can become exasperated by the child's behavior and respond to it with threats, which only serve to confirm the child's feeling of "unease in social situations" and reinforce the child's sense of fear. Another problematic aspect of the trauma-affected child's feeling of unease in social situations is the tendency of these children to present as though they are being defiant and stubborn. Cole and colleagues shed light on this. They explain that because children who have been affected by trauma are basically in a perpetual low-level state of fear, they often try to take control of their situation either by acting in a defiant way, or sometimes, as we have explained, by unconsciously freezing. Both of these stances leave the child unreceptive and unresponsive to both the teacher and the classroom. This poses real problems for teachers who usually try to make the defiant-looking child do what he is told, by threats, and similarly, they try to control the zoned-out child to fit in with everyone else by pleadings. None of these approaches will work because the underlying source of the problem is fear, and neither threats nor cajoling can eradicate that fear (Perry et al., 1995). Cole and colleagues state that because these behaviors can be based on fear, reactivity, misreading of social cues, and hyper-vigilance, it is now recognized that most children impacted by trauma cope best in classrooms that are calm and where bullying is not accepted and where negative behavior is kept under control (2005).

Challenges doing what peers are doing

Children who have been affected by trauma often present themselves in schools as children who have difficulty doing what their peers are doing. For example, in a pre-school setting, these children often refuse to join the other children in a circle if the teacher is trying to conduct "story-time," or "song-time." Similarly, when out in the garden, these children may appear to completely ignore teachers when they announce that it is time to line-up and come back into the classroom. Often, teachers are unsure if this behavior represents blatant defiance, a naturally "zoned-out" child, or something more elusive, but it presents a very real problem for them. They must decide what to do at that moment. Should they make the child join the circle? Should they make the child come in from the garden? These are questions that face teachers every day. However, these questions and the problems they cause might not arise at all if the teacher had some knowledge about why a child might be behaving in what looks like a defiant manner. The most common reasons why a child can appear to be unable or unwilling to do what their peers are doing may involve factors such as language and communication difficulties, memory problems, misreading of non-verbal cues, and dissociation, all possibly related to exposure to trauma.

It should not be surprising that a child with language and communication difficulties caused by exposure to trauma would have difficulty doing what his peers are doing. For example, if a trauma-affected child frequently has difficulty understanding the meanings of even common words, it is likely they will have difficulty following instructions (Coster & Cicchetti, 1993). Also, a child coming from a home that is relatively chaotic with very few routines may not have developed an adequate level of sequential memory to enable him to follow the necessary sequence of steps in a lesson or a game (Craig, 1992). The reality is, if the child cannot follow the necessary sequence of steps in a game, his peers may very well lose their patience with him and may even oust him from the game. Similarly, if he cannot follow a sequence of steps in a lesson, the teacher may get irritated with him, or he may fear that the teacher will get irritated with him, and so he may decide not to participate because he is expecting defeat and fears embarrassment or public reproof. Similarly, problems with memory may also make it impossible for the trauma-affected child to do what his peers are doing. In addition, the trauma-affected child's tendency to mis-read non-verbal cues is a major problem that often prevents this child from doing what his peers are doing. Frequently, a preschool or school child will genuinely believe that another child is sneering at him, making faces at him, giving him threatening looks, and so on. Often, these beliefs are unfounded, but the effect is that the child feels a strong reluctance to join in with his peers. Finally, the greatest challenge to the trauma-affected child's ability to do what his peers are doing may be his tendency to dissociate and remove himself mentally from his environment. The tendency to dissociate may have become an unconscious habit that the child falls into when he feels under threat, especially if trauma triggers are present in his school environment.

Understanding the impact of trauma on children's cognitive functioning

Craig and Stevens (2016) stated that "Early trauma affects every aspect of children's cognitive development: representational thought, language, memory, attention, and executive functioning" (p. 59). Children who have experienced traumatic events or who are suffering ongoing exposure to traumatic events, frequently exhibit problems in their cognitive functioning. The most frequent problems are:

- **Poor concentration**
- **Poor verbal skills**
- **Memory issues**

Poor concentration

As explained earlier, children who have experienced or are still experiencing trauma often live in a persistent state of either hyper-arousal (i.e., hyper-vigilance, perpetually scanning the environment for potential danger) or hypo-arousal (i.e., dissociation, perpetually zoning out, going into another world, to protect themselves from potential danger) (Perry et al., 1995). This is not something they choose to do, they have no control over this, it is a biological reality that has its roots in an initial traumatic experience (Perry et al., 1995). Living in survival mode becomes an everyday way of functioning for these children (Perry et al., 1995). Both of these states (hyper-vigilant/dissociative) have a deleterious effect on children leaving them unable to concentrate at school (Perry et al., 1995). Therefore, we need to examine the effects of both hyper-vigilance and dissociation on concentration.

The effect of hyper-vigilance on concentration

According to Van der Kolk (2003), "Traumatized children tend to become hyper-vigilant ... They become preoccupied with impending danger" (p. 299). As explained earlier, many children who have been affected by trauma become hyper-vigilant (i.e., constantly scanning their environment for danger). In a school environment, this perpetual state of hyper-vigilance creates very real barriers to the trauma-affected child's ability to concentrate and focus on the tasks at hand. When confronted with a hyper-vigilant child in the classroom, teachers often think they are dealing with a child who cannot concentrate on anything. Actually, the very opposite is true. This is a child who is concentrating on everything. Sorrels explains that children who have been maltreated are heightened to possible threats to both their emotional and physical well-being. These children notice everything, every sound, every gesture, every movement, and this makes it very difficult for them to concentrate (Sorrels, 2015).

> **Vignette**
>
> Piper is four and a half years old. She had attended a Montessori primary (i.e., 3–6 years) classroom from her third birthday until her fourth but has been out of school for six months. She had loved school, had settled in quickly, and her all-round development was excellent. She was kind, sociable, and generous, and she loved learning. She had amazing concentration and often seemed oblivious to everyone around her as she swept, polished, spooned, poured, counted, and made words with the moveable alphabet. The Montessori directress, who loved her dearly, was thrilled by her progress. For this reason, it was devastating, when six months ago, the school learned that Piper and her mom were captives in a store hold-up where the cashier was shot in front of them. Following the incident (which ended as suddenly as it began with the perpetrator turning the gun on himself), Piper lost all her speech, and so was unable to say what, if anything she remembered from the traumatic event. Her mom gave a statement to the Police in which she said that there was a lot of angry shouting from the perpetrator before he shot at the cashier, screaming "you're in trouble now – you're in trouble now." Just two weeks ago, Piper returned to school for the first time since the shooting incident. Now four and a half, she seems like a different child. She is nervous, hypervigilant, jumpy, and can't concentrate on anything even for a moment. She spends most of her day peeping nervously around her with her

head bowed down low. The directress, several times a day, gently whispers as she passes Piper's mat – "we love you Piper, you are safe here." Piper is still hypervigilant as a result of her relatively recent traumatic experience, and it is this hyper-vigilance that is at present preventing her from concentrating on any task.

Hyper-vigilant children hear everything, see everything, sense everything. They hear the sound of police sirens in the distance, the underlying tone in every voice, and appear to be constantly scanning their surroundings (Treisman, 2017). In the classroom, "sketchy" thoughts race into their heads flooding them with frightening and confusing images of disturbing events they have witnessed or experienced (Perry, 1999). All the while, the teacher and the other (non-trauma-impacted) children don't even notice these background noises. In addition, hyper-vigilant children are unconsciously concentrated on the teacher's mood. When the teacher is explaining something, or giving a direction, trauma-impacted children are unable to concentrate or take in the meaning of the words because their lower brain area will not stop sending them messages relating to possible dangers stemming even from the teacher. The amygdala alerts them to the teacher's tone of voice. "*Is she cross with someone?*" "*Is she going to shout?*" "*Am I in trouble?*" these are the panicky thoughts filling the heads of trauma-impacted children. Therefore, children who appear to be inattentive to the classroom task at hand (Cole, 2005) may actually be focused on *trying to* interpret the teacher's mood (Craig, 1992; McMahon, 2011). Patchy memories of angry voices flood their minds, filling them with anxiety and dread, while the other children are blissfully unaware of any problem (Cole et al., 2005). In circumstances such as this, concentration is next to impossible. This is the most serious impact of hyper-vigilance on concentration.

The effect of dissociation on concentration

When young children have been exposed to trauma, they often become dissociative (they unconsciously, disengage from the real world and go into an "internal" world of their own to protect themselves from potential danger). Streeck-Fisher and van der Kolk describe dissociation as a state where an individual detaches from the world by numbing, or going into a daydream (2000).

The problem is that dissociation prevents children from concentrating on the things that are happening in the real world around them. Dissociation, which originated as a survival response when danger was present, can become an unconscious habit even when the danger has passed. This means that young children who have been exposed to trauma frequently go (metaphorically) into a different location in their minds, sometimes having a sense of floating or looking at a film with them playing a part in it (Perry et al., 1995). To the on-looker, these children appear as though they are daydreaming, or just staring into space (Perry et al., 1995).

It follows then that when children have developed this habit of dissociating, they bring it into school with them. In a school environment, this perpetual slipping in and out of dissociative states creates very real barriers to the trauma-affected child's ability to concentrate on the tasks at hand. When confronted with a child who is dissociating in the classroom, teachers often think they are dealing with a child who is a daydreamer or a child who is just not interested in anything, or even worse, a child who is brazen enough to just ignore the teacher and stubbornly persist in staying in their own world. However, the reality is, the child is not making a conscious decision to dissociate. The child has become *used to* slipping into states of dissociation and now slips into these states unconsciously. Unfortunately, this tendency of the child to unconsciously slip into states of dissociation has a negative effect on the child's ability to concentrate in school or preschool. Simple activities, such as sitting in a circle in order to learn a nursery rhyme/song, listening to a story, following instructions for an art or craft activity, or repeating instructions for a fire drill, can be very difficult or even impossible for this child. This is the most serious impact of dissociation on the young child's ability to concentrate.

Poor verbal skills

Children who have been exposed to trauma, or who are experiencing on-going trauma in their lives, frequently demonstrate problems in both expressive and receptive language. Receptive language refers to how we understand the words that are spoken to us, and expressive language refers to how we use words to express ourselves. Therefore, it is necessary to examine the effect of childhood trauma on the development of both receptive and expressive language.

The effect of childhood trauma on the development of receptive language

When human babies are born, they do not have any pre-established language. However, with the exception of those born with medical or neurological problems, all babies are born with the potential to develop language. However, in order to develop language a child first of all needs to hear language and see the mouths of people as they speak language to them. Nature has taken care of this. Human babies are unable to feed themselves and rely on either a mother's breast milk or a bottle for sustenance. Since a newborn does not have the capacity to hold a bottle, the child must be fed by either the mother or another caregiver and as this happens, the infant stares into the face and especially the eyes of the mother or caregiver as he/she feeds either from the breast or from a bottle. Schore (2003, 2008) points out that if all goes well, this act of feeding the infant will promote a bond between the caregiver and the child and this bond will encourage the caregiver to speak to the child in a warm, loving tone using rhythmic, lilting phrases such as "aren't you a hungry little fellow?," or "there you go, nice warm milk for your little tummy" and so on. However, often there are obstacles preventing the development of this loving bond between an infant and the mother/caregiver, and these obstacles can play a role in preventing the development of optimum receptive language in the child. These obstacles include but are not limited to:

- Post-natal depression in the mother
- A history of adversity and trauma in the mother's own background
- Drug or alcohol problems in the mother or family unit
- Severe stress in the family unit caused by poverty, homelessness, separation, divorce, etc.
- Physical or mental illness in the mother or family unit
- Neglect and abuse endemic in the family unit
- Violence in the family unit

In circumstances such as these, it is clearly difficult for a relationship to develop between a mother/caregiver and the infant which would promote the development and progression of receptive language.

Another obstacle that can prevent the development of receptive language in infants and young children is the neurobiological impact on the brain of trauma triggers which remind the child of either the experience of a once-off sudden traumatic event or the experience of chronic traumatic events. Research shows that triggers evoking the recollection of traumatic events can impact various areas of the brain with the result that areas associated with language (especially Broca's area) become less active (Cole et al., 2005; Rauch et al., 1996). Treisman (2017) argues that if teachers are knowledgeable about trauma triggers, they may be able to take steps to resist the re-traumatization of children and so hopefully prevent the continuous "shutting down" of the language area in the brain in trauma-affected children. There is also the argument that traumatized children may have difficulty focusing on the content of language simply because they are always monitoring non-verbal messages (Craig, 1992).

The effect of childhood trauma on the development of expressive language

As stated above, expressive language refers to how we use words to express ourselves. It has to do with how we communicate our feelings and our thoughts through words and gestures. In the case of young children, it includes such gestures as stretching their arms out wide to indicate something abstract such as "I love my doggie ***this*** much." Expressive language develops through interactions with others. If these interactions are with loving caregivers, in most cases expressive language will develop normally (though in some cases it can be delayed, even though the child has loving and attentive caregivers). However, when a child does not have access to loving caregivers, things frequently go wrong with the development of expressive language. Studies show that the development of communication is influenced by the interactive styles and social context in which early language is established (Coster & Cicchetti, 1993). These authors explain that when a child lives in a home where the caregiver's primary verbal interactions with the child are concentrated on controlling the child, and especially the child's behaviors, and less time or in some cases, no time is given to using language to address the child's thoughts, opinions, or feelings, thoughts or even opinions (Coster & Cicchetti, 1993), the child may develop an understanding that language is a chiefly instrumental medium (Cole et al., 2005). For such children, language can become little more than a tool that works to get tasks done rather than a channel for social exchanges (Coster & Cicchetti, 1993). This leads to the child having difficulties in conveying abstract ideas and also having difficulties with the basic ability to engage in dialogue and narrative with peers and adults which is so necessary for normal social exchange. Therefore, when this pattern of language use persists during the child's early years (3–6 years), the ability of the child to use language for other purposes such as social and emotional communication, may become stifled and limited (Coster & Cicchetti, 1993). Ultimately, exposure to trauma has a negative effect on a child's language development and studies show that there is a correlation between deficits in both receptive and expressive language in children who have been exposed to neglect (Allen & Oliver, 1982). These authors hypothesize that the lack of stimulation suffered by neglected children probably accounts for this deficit, Sylvestre and colleagues state emphatically that exposure to neglect and abuse in childhood has a detrimental impact on children's language development and they add that the language skills of children who have been exposed to neglect or abuse are clearly delayed when compared to children who have not been exposed to these stressors (2016).

This impoverishment of verbal skills in the traumatized child poses very real problems for the child in terms of cognitive functioning. Teachers use language to teach, especially to teach abstract ideas. The child who lacks appropriate verbal skills is at a disadvantage academically. Linguistic competence is necessary to allow the child to explore ideas and philosophize about them. The child with an impoverished vocabulary who struggles with syntax and grammar will have a hard time trying to contribute to class discussions. This inability to converse holds a child back from higher levels of cognitive functioning.

Memory issues

Children who have experienced traumatic events frequently exhibit poor memory skills which may be related to damage to the hippocampus caused by surges of high levels of cortisol in the bloodstream during the acute stress response (Bremner, 2006). The hippocampus plays a crucial role in memory. It is part of the limbic system, and it is mostly responsible for storing and retrieving memories and differentiating between past and present experiences. It is especially vital for short-term memory. Short-term memory refers to the holding in the mind of a piece of information for a few moments, after which time it is either stored in a more long-term memory area, or it is just forgotten. Bremner (2006) states that the hippocampus is a part of the brain involved in memory and learning that is especially sensitive to stress. He says that child maltreatment and other serious stressors can have long-lasting negative effects on the areas of the brain that are involved in emotion and the organization of memory. Other research concurs with this view. Nelson and Carver previously wrote "It appears that parts of the brain that are critically involved in memory are uniquely impacted by stress" (1998, p. 805).

Research shows that exposure to trauma can impact explicit (conscious) memory which includes both semantic and episodic memory. For example, following a traumatic experience, children may have difficulty with memory concerned with general knowledge and facts (semantic memory), so that information such as words, sounds, and images are not processed effectively. They may also have difficulty with memory of events, including who was present at an event, and when and where the event took place (episodic memory). Trauma exposure can "shut down" episodic memory and fragment the sequence of events. Research shows that exposure to trauma can also impact implicit (unconscious) memory which includes both emotional memory and procedural memory. For example, following a traumatic experience, children may be triggered by their (emotional memory) consisting of a sight, sound, smell, touch, or taste, which brings back painful emotions, seemingly "out of the blue" and often without context. They may also find that following a traumatic experience procedural memory (i.e., the memory of how to perform a task without having to think about it, e.g., ride a bicycle) is impacted negatively. In schools, children who have been affected by trauma and have problems related to both explicit and implicit memory are likely to experience problems trying to absorb academic material.

Summary of Chapter 4

1 Exposure to trauma can affect a child's worldview, as well as cognitive, emotional, and social functioning (Cole et al., 2005).
2 A child's worldview may change from feeling that the world is a safe place to feeling that the world is a dangerous and fearful place (Herman, 1997).
3 In terms of emotional functioning, ability to regulate emotions can be compromised (a) by the fact that the child's worldview may become altered so that they may see the world as a dangerous place; (b) they may have an over-stimulated stress-response system; (c) they may be vulnerable to emotional triggers; and (d) they may have difficulty understanding and naming their own emotions (Alexander, 2019; Cole et al., 2005).
4 Attachment problems are common in trauma-affected children because there may have been a lack of, or damage to, an attachment bond in early childhood (Van der Kolk, 2003).
5 In terms of social functioning, the ability to relate to others, and make friends, can be adversely affected chiefly because trauma-affected children often misread non-verbal cues such as facial expressions, body language, and tone of voice, and may mistakenly believe that they are under threat, making friendships difficult if not impossible (Perry, 1999; Van der Kolk, 2003).

6 Unease in social situations is common in trauma-affected children because fear may make them either aggressive or withdrawn (Cole et al., 2005).
7 Challenges doing what peers are doing is common in trauma-affected children often because of problems with language, memory, hypervigilance, or dissociation (Perry, 1999).
8 In terms of cognitive functioning, poor concentration may arise in trauma-affected children because of hyper-vigilance or dissociation (Perry et al., 1995).
9 Poor verbal skills are common in trauma-affected children possibly because the language area of the brain (Broca's area) is sensitive to trauma and may "shut down" when traumatic events are re-triggered (Cole et al., 2005)
10 Poor memory is common in trauma-affected children possibly because of hippocampal damage (Bremner, 2006).

Questions for group discussion

1 How can exposure to trauma affect a child's worldview?
2 Discuss how trauma can affect children's emotional functioning.
3 What are the ways in which trauma can affect children's social functioning?
4 How does trauma affect children's cognitive functioning?

References

Ainsworth, M. D. S., Blehar, M. C., Waters, E., & Wall, S. N. (2015). *Patterns of attachment: A psychological study of the strange situation*. Psychology Press. (Original work published 1978)

Alexander, J. (2019). *Building trauma-sensitive schools: Your guide to creating safe, supportive learning environments for all students*. Brookes.

Allen, R. E., & Oliver, J. M. (1982). The effects of child maltreatment on language development. *Child Abuse and Neglect, 6*, 299–305.

Bowlby, J. (1982). *Attachment*. Basic Books. (Original work published 1969)

Bremner, J. D. (2006). Traumatic stress: Effects on the brain. *Dialogues in Clinical Neuroscience, 8*(4), 445–461. 10.31887/DCNS.2006.8.4/jbremner

Cole, S. F., O'Brien, J. G., Gadd, M. G., Ristuccia, J., Wallace, D. L., & Gregory, M. (2005). *Helping traumatized children learn: Supportive school environments for children traumatized by family violence* (1st ed.; Printing ed). Massachusetts Advocates for Children.

Coster, W., & Cicchetti, D. (1993). Research on the communicative development of maltreated children: Clinical implications. *Topics in Language Disorders, 13*(4), 25–38;31.

Craig, S. (1992). The educational needs of children living with violence. *Phi Delta Kappan, 74*, 67–71.

Craig, S. E., & Stevens, J. E. (2016). *Trauma sensitive schools: Learning communities transforming children's lives, K-5* (Illustrated ed.). Teachers College Press.

Herman, J. (1997). *Trauma and recovery: The aftermath of violence, from domestic abuse to political terror*. Perseus.

Jennings, P. (2019). *The trauma-sensitive classroom. Building resilience with compassionate teaching*. W.W. Norton & Company.

McMahon, A. (2011). Are you calm enough to be curious? http://annmcmahon.wordpress.com/2011/01/29/are-you-calm-enough-to-be-curious/

National Child Traumatic Stress Network (NCTSN). Effects emotional responses www.nctsn.org

National Scientific Council on the Developing Child (NSCDC), (2010). Persistent fear and anxiety can affect young children's learning and development: Working Paper No. 9. www.developingchild.net

Nelson, C. A., & Carver, L. J. (1998). The effects of stress and trauma on brain and memory: A view from developmental cognitive neuroscience. *Development and Psychopathology, 10*(4), 793–809. https://doi.org/10.1017/s0954579498001874

Neufield, G., & Mate, G. (2006). *Hold on to your kids: Why parents need to matter more than peers*. Random House.

Perry, B. D. (1999). Memories of fear: How the brain stores and retrieves physiological States, feelings, behaviours and thoughts from traumatic events. In J. Goodwin & R. Attias (Ed.), *Splintered reflections: Images of the body in trauma*. Basic Books.

Perry, B. D., Pollard, R. A., Blakley, Y. L., Baker, W. L., & Vigilante, D. (1995). Childhood trauma, the neurobiology of adaptation, and use-dependent development of the brain: How states become traits. *Infant Mental Health Journal, 16*(4), 271–291. https://doi.org/10.1002/1097-0355(199524)16:4<271::AID-IMHJ2280160404>3.0.CO;2-B

Perry, B. D., & Szalavitz, M. (2017). *The boy who was raised as a dog: And other stories from a child psychiatrist's notebook—What traumatized children can teach us about loss, love, and healing*. Basic Books.

Rauch, S. L., van der Kolk, B. A., Fisler, R. E., Alpert, N. M., Orr, S. P., Savage, C. R., Fischman, A. J., Jenike, M. A., & Pitman, R. K. (1996). A symptom provocation study of post-traumatic stress disorder using positron emission tomography and script-driven imagery. *Archives of General Psychiatry, 53*(5), 380–387.

Schore, A. (2003). Early relational trauma, disorganised attachment, and the development of a predisposition to violence. In M. F. Solomon & D. J. Siegel (Eds.), *Healing trauma: Attachment, mind, body and brain* (pp. 107–167). Norton.

Schore, A. (2008). Modern attachment theory: The Central role of affect regulation in development and treatment. *Clinical Social Work Journal, 36*, 9–20.

Sorrels, B. (2015). *Reaching and teaching children exposed to trauma*. Gryphon House.

Streeck-Fisher, A., & van der Kolk, B. A. (2000). Down will come baby, cradle and all: Diagnostic and therapeutic implications of chronic trauma on child development. *Australian and New Zealand Journal of Psychiatry, 34*, 903–918.

Sylvestre, A., Bussieres, E. L., & Bouchard, C. (2016). Language problems among abused and neglected children: A meta-analytic review. *Child Maltreatment, 21*(1), 47–58. https://doi.org/10.1177/1077559515616703

Treisman, K. (2017). *Working with relational and developmental trauma in children and adolescents*. Routledge.

Van der Kolk, B. A. (1998). Psychology and psychobiology of childhood trauma. *Praxis Der Kinderpsychologie Und Kinderpsychiatrie, 47*(1), 19.

Van der Kolk, B. A. (2003). The neurobiology of childhood trauma and abuse. *Child and Adolescent Psychiatric Clinics Nth America, 12*, 293–317.https://doi.org/10.1016/S1056-4993(03)00003-8

Van der Kolk, B. A. (2014). *The body keeps the score: Mind, brain and body in the transformation of trauma*. Penguin.

5 The prevalence and causes of trauma – the ACE study

Chapter objectives

- To introduce the adverse childhood experiences (ACE) study.
- To outline the main findings of the ACE study.
- To show the limitations of the ACE study.
- To discuss the on-going influence of the ACE study.
- To address some of the social determinants of physical and mental ill-health.

Learning outcomes

At the end of this chapter, the learner will be able to:

- Explain what the term "ACE study" refers to.
- Summarize the main findings of the ACE study.
- Discuss the limitations of the ACE study.
- Describe the on-going influence of the ACE study.
- Discuss some of the social determinants of physical and mental ill-health.

Revisiting the original ACE study

The adverse childhood experiences (ACE) study is an on-going collaborative research study conducted by the Centres for Disease Control (CDC), in Atlanta, Georgia, and the Kaiser Permanente Health Group in San Diego, California, USA (Felitti et al., 1998). It is the largest study ever conducted to examine, over the lifespan, the effects of ACEs on adult physical and mental health, as well as on later social and economic well-being. The initial phase of the ACE study took place from 1995 to 1997. The original participants have been in long-term follow up, to track their health outcomes. The co-principal investigators were

DOI: 10.4324/9781003438021-8

Dr. Robert Anda of the CDC and Dr. Vincent Felitti of the Kaiser Permanente Medical Group. The participants were mostly middle-income Americans. About half were female. Nearly three-quarters were white. The average age was 57. The participants consisted of more than 17,000 Kaiser Permanente patients who, having undergone a standard physical examination, volunteered for the study by completing a confidential survey that contained questions about their childhood experience or non-experience of abuse, neglect, or family dysfunction. This information was then combined and linked to their most recent physical examination, and this formed the base-line data for the study. The medical status of the participants is still being tracked from this base-line.

The purpose of the ACE study was to find out if stressful or traumatic experiences in childhood have a direct impact on adult health and well-being. Specifically, the aim of the study was to examine the link between stressful and traumatic events experiences in childhood and the development of behaviors that result in disease, disability, social problems, and even premature death in adulthood. Some of the concepts for the study had their origins years earlier when, Dr. Vincent Felitti, while working at the Kaiser Institute as a specialist in preventative medicine, discovered that people with obesity who were very successfully losing weight through his weight loss program were the very ones who were dropping out of the program. This didn't seem to make sense until, Dr. Felitti, on digging more deeply discovered that a significant number of these people had been sexually abused in childhood. Dr. Felitti made the connection that these people were subconsciously using obesity as a protective measure against further sexual abuse. These findings indicated that although these individuals were being treated for obesity, their obesity was in fact a mere manifestation of a deeper problem, and that problem was early childhood trauma caused by ACEs, in this case, childhood sexual abuse. It also became clear that some of these individuals had previously turned to smoking, drinking alcohol, or taking street drugs to alleviate the stress, anxiety, and despair they suffered. In many cases, it became clear that the obesity, although it was the most visibly obvious of the patient's problems, was actually a less serious and debilitating issue than the hidden problems that had led to the obesity. While Dr. Felitti was making these discoveries, Dr. Robert Anda was studying a multitude of medical and public health issues including obesity, alcohol abuse, smoking, and various chronic diseases, and he was curious about the possible psychological causes of these problems. Following an introduction, Dr. Felitti and Dr. Anda's interests merged into what became known as the ACE study.

For the purposes of the study, ACEs were categorized into three main areas with ten subdivisions as follows:

ABUSE

Emotional abuse
Physical abuse
Sexual abuse

NEGLECT

Emotional neglect
Physical neglect

HOUSEHOLD DYSFUNCTION

Mother treated violently
Household substance abuse
Household mental illness
Parental separation
Incarcerated household member

The ACE questionnaire

Participants were asked if they were exposed to any of the adverse effects in the ten subsections, before they were 18 years of age. Specifically, they were asked:

1 Did a parent or other adult in the household often or very often swear at you, insult you, put you down, or humiliate you? Or act in a way that made you feel afraid that you might be physically hurt? YES/NO. If yes, enter 1 (This answer revealed whether or not there was emotional abuse in childhood).
2 Did a parent or other adult in the household often or very often, push, grab, slap, or throw something at you? Or ever hit you so hard that you had marks or were injured? YES/NO. If yes, enter 1 (This answer revealed whether or not there was physical abuse in childhood).
3 Did an adult or person at least five years older than you ever touch or fondle you or have you touch their body in a sexual way? Or attempt to have oral, anal, or vaginal intercourse with you? YES/NO. If yes, enter 1 (This answer revealed whether or not there was sexual abuse in childhood).
4 Did you often or very often feel that no one in your family loved you or thought you were important or special? Or your family didn't look out for each other, feel close to each other, or support each other? YES/NO. If yes, enter 1 (This answer revealed whether or not there was emotional neglect in childhood).
5 Did you often or very often feel that you didn't have enough to eat, had to wear dirty clothes, and had no one to protect you? Or your parents were too drunk or high to take care of you or take you to the doctor if you needed it? YES/NO. If yes, enter 1 (This answer revealed whether or not there was physical neglect in childhood).
6 Was a biological parent ever lost to you through divorce, abandonment, or other reasons? YES/NO. If yes, enter 1 (This answer revealed whether or not there was parental separation in childhood).

7. Was your mother or stepmother often or very often pushed, grabbed, slapped, or had something thrown at her? Or sometimes, often, or very often kicked, bitten, hit with a fist, or hit with something hard? Or ever repeatedly hit over at least a few minutes or threatened with a gun or a knife? YES/NO. If yes, enter 1 (This answer revealed whether or not domestic violence was witnessed in childhood).
8. Did you live with anyone who was a problem drinker or alcoholic or who used street drugs? YES/NO. If yes, enter 1 (This answer revealed whether or not the person was exposed to substance abuse).
9. Was a household member depressed or mentally ill or did a household member attempt suicide? YES/NO. If yes, enter 1 (This answer revealed whether or not the person was exposed to mental illness).
10. Did a household member ever go to prison? YES/NO. If yes, enter 1 (This answer reveals whether or not there was an incarcerated household member).

The ACE study used a simple scoring method to determine the extent of each of the study participant's exposure to childhood trauma, i.e., trauma that occurred prior to their 18th birthday.

Exposure to each of the ten types of ACE counted as one point and the points were then totaled. Therefore, the ACE score had the potential to go from 0 to 10. In practice, what this means is that if a person has suffered physical abuse in childhood, and no other category of abuse, neglect, or household dysfunction the ACE score is 1. However, if a person was exposed to physical abuse, an alcoholic parent, and a mentally ill household member, that person's ACE score would be 3, one point for every category of ACE. An ACE score of 0 would mean that the person reported no exposure to any of the categories listed as ACEs. An ACE score of 10 would mean that the person reported exposure to all of the categories listed as ACEs.

Examining the findings of the ACE study

The major findings of the ACE study were summarized as follows:

Major findings

- Adverse childhood experiences (ACEs) are very *Common*.
- Adverse childhood experiences (ACEs) are *Interrelated*.
- Adverse childhood experiences (ACEs) are a *Common Pathway* toward negative behaviors that can lead to disease, disability, social problems, and sometimes, premature death.

The ACE study demonstrated clearly and persuasively that stressful or traumatic experiences in childhood such as abuse, neglect, witnessing domestic violence, or growing up with substance abuse, such as alcohol or drugs in the household, or growing up in a household where in there is mental illness or where there is parental conflict caused by divorce or separation, or where there is crime resulting in the incarceration of a parent, are a common pathway to social, emotional, and cognitive challenges that can lead to increased risk of unhealthy behaviors, risk of violence or re- traumatization, as well as disease, disability and premature death. These findings may be summarized in the simple statement:

> ACEs can lead to behaviors that lead to disease/disability, social problems, and early death.

Specific findings

Adverse childhood experiences are common

In this predominantly middle-class study, where the majority of the participants were middle-class and well-educated, the findings were surprisingly grave. For example:

- Only 1 in 3 of the participants reported no ACEs.
- As many as 2 out of 3 reported at least one ACE.
- More than 1 in 5 reported three or more ACEs.
- More than 1 in 10 had five or more ACEs.

Adverse childhood experiences are interrelated

The ACE study revealed that ACEs tend to occur in groups or clusters rather than single experiences. So, if a person had an ACE score of 1 for exposure to emotional abuse, it was likely that he/she would also have a score of 1 for exposure to an alcoholic or mentally ill parent. It was also highly likely that a person would have another ACE score of 1 for experiencing either physical or emotional neglect; therefore, making his/her total ACE score at least 3 points.

Adverse childhood experiences (ACEs) are a common pathway toward negative behaviors which may lead to disease, disability, social problems, and sometimes, premature death

The ACE study clearly showed that as the number of adverse experiences in childhood increases, so does the risk of future vulnerability to disease, disability, social problems, and premature death. An extremely concerning finding of the study was that persons with an ACE score of 4 or more were:

> 2 times more likely to be smokers.
> 2 times more likely to have cancer.
> 2 times more likely to have heart disease.
> 6 times more likely to have become sexually active before 15 years.
> 7 times more likely to abuse alcohol.
> 10 times more likely to take street drugs.
> 12 times more likely to have attempted suicide.

Looking at the limitations and on-going influence of the ACE study

The original ACE study has been criticized for a number of limitations which include:

1 The potential for ACEs to be seen as deterministic because of its failure to consider the resilience factors which can buffer the effects of exposure to adversities.
2 Its failure to include other adversities such as poverty, homelessness, reliance on the care system, discrimination, racism, community violence, or exposure to war/conflict, which are all social determinants of health.
3 Its failure to consider the timing of the adversity (i.e., the age of the child when exposed to the adversity, as well as the duration of the adversity).
4 The use of the ACE score as a measure of individual risk rather than population risk.
5 The overly simplistic nature of the study.
6 The make-up of the participant pool – predominantly white, middle-class individuals with private health insurance.
7 Its methodological flaws such as the self-reported and retrospective nature of the data.

These are all valid points and will now be addressed.

First, the ACE study has been criticized for appearing to be deterministic. However, it does not have to be read as deterministic, because research shows that positive childhood experiences (PCEs) can act as "protective factors" that can buffer the toxic stress caused by exposure to ACEs (Matjasko et al., 2022). The most important of these protective factors is the presence of a positive relationship with an emotionally attuned available adult (Ludy-Dobson & Perry, 2010). Studies claim that if trauma-affected children have even one adult who is emotionally available to them, who is empathic, kind, and understanding, this one positive relationship can be profoundly healing for them. This person may be a parent, a grandparent, a youth worker, a teacher, a coach, a guide, a caseworker, or anyone involved with the child who can offer a sense of nurture that increases the child's sense of stability and security. This person does not need to be a therapist, he/she simply needs to be emotionally available, and willing to share positive, relational moments with the child. For a teacher, these interactions may be brief, possibly just seconds long, they may be a high-five, a smile, or a hello in the school corridor, but they send a message to the child that he/she is seen, is appreciated, is worthy of being noticed, is cared about (Think TVPBS, 2020). This is very important because Craig (2016) states children with early exposure trauma often experience themselves as disconnected from others. These short but powerful opportunities to connect with others, through a high five or a smile, can mark the beginning of trauma recovery. A further important resilience factor relates to being accepted within one's family, or community and having a feeling of connectedness with others, by participating in community traditions, which give a child a feeling of belonging, and feeling safe and protected as part of a group (Matjasko et al., 2022). However, this sense of connectedness necessitates the absence of exclusion or discrimination based on race, ethnicity, gender, sexual orientation, disability, or other factors (Venet, 2021). Yet another resilience factor relates to helping children to manage their emotions and their behaviors. Jennings (2019) referred to the fact that trauma-affected children are often incapable of recognizing and naming emotions they are feeling. Helping children with their ability to read and label not only their emotional states but also the emotional states of others builds emotional intelligence, a type of intelligence that enables us to keep our composure, make good decisions, and helps us to develop and maintain positive and healthy relationships throughout the life course. Another resilience factor is having a sense of being able to regain the personal agency, or sense of control that exposure to trauma steals from an individual. Trauma frequently affects people who belong to vulnerable or marginalized groups, leaving them with the feeling (and sometimes the reality) that they have very little agency or control over their destiny. The input of an emotionally attuned, caring adult in a child's life can help to reverse this and aid a child to build their sense of agency or control by helping them to build self-esteem, self-confidence, a sense of self-worth, and self-belief. In summary, these resilience factors should always be presented alongside discussions of the original ACE study findings in order to dispel the notion that the ACE study is deterministic, and that people cannot thrive following exposure to adversities. McEwen and Gregerson (2019) emphasize that the original ACE study model should be supplemented by placing a focus on the factors that have a positive impact on the development of brain architecture, and buffer the negative impact of traumatic events, such as protective relationships. They also make suggestions for protective factors that promote resilience at the community level such as the provision of high-quality (and affordable) childcare, organized home visiting, increased safety in neighborhoods, better family leave policies in work places, and support through faith-based institutions or groups (McEwen & Gregerson, 2019). These initiatives have the capacity to counterbalance the negative effects of adversity.

Second, the original ACE study has been criticized for its failure to include other adversities above the original 10, such as racial segregation, poverty, low wages, unaffordable housing, and weak social supports for parents and caregivers (McEwen & Gregerson, 2019). These authors point out that these adversities all have their roots in social inequalities (McEwen & Gregerson, 2019). Similarly, Finkelhor et al. (2013) criticized the ACE study's failure to include such adversities as peer rejection, exposure to violence outside the family, low socioeconomic status (SES), and poor academic performance. In summary, the original ACE study has been criticized for ignoring the social determinants of health which include access to health care and basic resources, such as food, housing, employment, education, and transportation (McEwen & Gregerson, 2019). These authors also point out that low SES, for example, is correlated with difficulty in obtaining good quality housing which can lead to decreased physical health in children and adults (such as respiratory illnesses) caused by poor living conditions. McEwen and Gregerson write that although the ACE study showed that the ten ACE adversities are found in all socioeconomic groups, that view must be balanced by one that recognizes the reality that those ten adversities along with others not included in the original ACE study are not equally distributed. Simply put, children in poorer locations are more likely to be exposed to ACEs.

Third, the ACE study has also been criticized for the failure to consider the timing of the adversity, i.e., the age of the child when exposed to the adversity, as well as the duration of the adversity. This is a valid criticism because as Perry and others have shown, the timing of the adversity is crucial (Perry, 2001). Adverse experiences in very young children, especially infants under two months, are very impactful because this is the period when the brain is undergoing a very intense period of neural development (NSCDC, 2005/2014).

Fourth, the original ACE study has also been criticized for its use as a measure of individual health risk as opposed to population health risk. In an article co-authored by Dr. Robert Anda, one of the PIs of the original ACE study, he and colleagues discuss some of the limitations of the study and in particular the dangers of misuse of the ACE "score" as a measure of individual health risk as opposed to population health risk. He explains that despite the ACE study's usefulness in research and surveillance studies, it should not be used as a diagnostic tool to measure individual risk because the impact of ACEs can vary widely from person to person (Anda et al., 2020). He states that he and his co-authors are concerned about the use of ACE scores as a screening tool to infer individual risk (Anda et al., 2020). He acknowledges that the ACE score is increasingly being used and even promoted as a screening tool for individual use, rather than for public health surveillance, which is what it was designed for (Anda et al., 2020).

Fifth, the original ACE study has also been criticized for being overly simplistic. Lacey and Minnis (2020) see both advantages and limitations to the ACE score's simplicity. They state that the simplicity of the ACE measurement is an advantage but also a limitation. They argue that its simplicity facilitates public policy allowing wide-ranging applications, but risks sending out communications that may be stigmatizing for some groups of people and may imply a deterministic message, and an over simplified account of risk and causality (Lacey & Minnis, 2020).

Sixth, the original ACE study has also been criticized for the make-up of the participant pool which has been described as being unrepresentative of the population (McEwen & Gregerson, 2019). The participant pool in the original ACE study was predominantly white middle-class individuals with private health insurance because Felitti was working for Keiser Permanente and the participants were subscribers to that private health insurance company. However, since the original study, other studies have been carried out with different cohorts and the findings have been similar. Anda and colleagues state that ACE score use has expanded to most states in the USA through the work of the Centers for Disease Control and Prevention (CDC) and internationally through the efforts of the World Health Organization WHO (2020). They state that the findings from these studies are similar to those of the original ACE study and have raised awareness among legislators and policy makers of the childhood origins of many (serious and costly) public health problems (Anda et al., 2020).

Seventh, the ACE study has also been criticized for methodological flaws. Kelly-Irving and Delpierre (2019) argue that one serious methodological flaw present in many ACE studies is the fact that the data is self-reported and retrospective. They point out that since the adults are being asked questions about trauma and adversities they may have experienced during childhood, these questions are subject to recall bias, where adults now experiencing poor health may be more likely to report exposure to adverse experiences during childhood (Kelly-Irving & Delpierre, 2019). These authors point out that some more recent studies have developed ACE measures using prospective data collected during childhood; however, they say that this presents further problems in that prospectively collected information about ACEs presents other methodological challenges because the collection of this data is by proxy and frequently obtained from a teacher or parent who may not have full and reliable access to accurate information (Kelly-Irving & Delpierre, 2019). They state that in some cases it may be possible to interview the children themselves, however, this raises ethical difficulties, as it may be inappropriate to raise questions about experiences of physical or sexual abuse directly with children (Kelly-Irving & Delpierre, 2019). These authors state that this situation causes a methodological risk of misclassification bias, and may therefore risk under-reporting, owing to the sensitive nature of the content involved in these studies (Kelly-Irving and Delpierre, 2019).

On the positive side, the ACE study should be regarded as seminal research that laid the groundwork for further studies. McEwen and Gregerson state that positioning the original ACE research and the follow up studies it generated, in a wider context, especially in the context of studies on the neuroscience and neurobiology of childhood adversity, as well as studies on the social determinants of health, can enrich ACE research (2019). They add that this can extend the impact of the original ACE research so that it may shape primary prevention policies that examine the economic and social conditions that contribute to adversity (McEwen & Gregerson, 2019).

The on-going influence of the ACE study

Referring to the authors of the original ACE study (Dr. Robert Anda and Dr. Vincent Felitti), McEwen and Gregerson state that their work has led to a large (and growing) body of research that has stimulated an influential movement concerned with both resilience building in the face of adversity, and the establishment of trauma-informed practice approaches (2019). They point out that the work of Felitti and Anda in the original ACE study has been widely disseminated to the general public through hundreds of training courses, statewide ACE networks, and other means such as short films and short documentaries (McEwen and Gregerson, 2019). These authors also point out that parallel research in the area of neuroscience and into the serious adversities children face caused by factors such as poverty, racial segregation, low wages, unaffordable housing, and poor social supports for parents and caregivers, which is research that is mostly independent of the type of research presented by Felitti and Anda in the original ACE study, have now been imported and amalgamated into the ACE movement and ACEs training courses under the name "ACEs Science" (McEwen & Gregerson, 2019).

Addressing the social determinants of physical and mental ill-health

Recent research shows that people who are exposed to less favorable social circumstances are more likely to experience mental health issues over their lifecourse (Kirkbride et al., 2024). As stated above, the original ACE study has been criticized for its failure to include other adversities beyond the original 10, such as poverty, SES background, discrimination, oppression, racism, or refugee status. The National Scientific Council on the Developing Child at Harvard (NSCDC) states that there is a real necessity to confront social issues such as racism, violence, poverty, food insecurity, homelessness, and other sources of adversity that are serious stressors for families (2020).

They point out that simply putting a name to the problem or identifying children and families as being in a high-risk category has not resulted in any substantial or replicable impacts. They argue that to achieve greater *impact at scale* will require more efforts to confront structural inequalities – such as unequal access to healthcare, education, and wealth creation (NSCDC, 2020). They state that the implications of these facts for policy and practice are striking and that strategic financial investments in young children and their caregivers impact long-term physical and mental health just as much as they impact early learning (NSCDC, 2020). They further state that when access to supportive relationships and crucial resources is secure, the fundamental structure for resilience building (i.e., self-regulation and adaptive skills) and wellness (e.g., well-regulated stress response systems) is strengthened (NSCDC, 2020). However, they state that when deprivations and hardships are persistent, especially in the context of systemic racism, or intragenerational poverty, the knock-on effect is that, there can be major disruptions in an individual's biological systems and, down the line, the results of these disruptions can be manifested as poor achievements in education, low SES for individuals, increased healthcare costs for governments and higher rates of crime for societies (NSCDC, 2020).

A recent study by Bernard et al. (2021) proposes a reconceptualization of the original ACE model to highlight the adverse impact of racism on Black youth. The authors state that a considerable body of evidence has shown that there is a significant disproportion based on race, in relation to exposure to potentially traumatic events (PTEs) (Bernard et al., 2021). These authors state that this evidence indicates that Black youths in particular are harmfully and disproportionately exposed to these PTEs (Bernard et al., 2021). They add that "systemic racism" may well explain why Black youth are disproportionately exposed to PTEs. They also state that "systemic racism" may also explain why mental health disparities are more likely to be seen in Black youth following experiences of PTEs. They point out that despite the preponderance of evidence acknowledging racism as a significant life stressor for Black youth, our current theoretical models of early childhood adversity have to a large extent neglected the multifaceted influence of racism on mental health outcomes (Bernard et al., 2021). The authors argue that this evidence necessitates a reconceptualization of the original ACEs model. They propose an ACE model that is culturally informed, so that it takes into account the widespread and detrimental impact of racism on the mental health of Black youth (Bernard et al., 2021). These authors claim that their suggested model supports the progress of ACEs research by promoting a culturally informed approach to understanding the impact of racism on the mental health of Black youth, focusing on the multi-level and intergenerational impact racism can have (Bernard et al., 2021). Another recent study by Palma et al. (2023) suggests that Bernard and colleagues' study which focuses solely on Black youth may apply to other historically marginalized groups, including indigenous and other communities of color, especially those living in poverty.

Summary of Chapter 5

1 The term "ACE" study refers to the Adverse Childhood Experience study. This is a ground-breaking study begun in 1995 and still on-going, conducted by the Centers for Disease Control (CDC) and the Kaiser Permanente healthcare organization in San Diego, California.
2 The key investigators were Dr. Vincent Felitti and Dr. Robert Anda.
3 In that study, "ACEs" referred to three categories of adversity (with ten sub-divisions) experienced before the age of 18 years. The categories were abuse (physical, sexual, or emotional), neglect (physical or emotional), and household dysfunction which included living in a home where there was domestic abuse, household substance abuse, parental mental illness, parental separation, and incarcerated household member(s).

4 A person's ACE score was calculated by allocating a score of 1 to every category of adversity suffered. The maximum ACE score is ten. The minimum is zero.
5 The key findings of the original ACE study and more recent ACE studies are (1) ACEs are very common, even among middle-class populations: more than two-thirds of the population report experiencing one ACE, and nearly a quarter have experienced three or more ACEs.
6 There is a clear correlation between the more ACEs a person is exposed to in childhood and the greater possibility of poor outcomes later in life, including dramatically increased risk of heart disease, diabetes, obesity, depression, substance abuse, smoking, poor academic achievement, time out of work, and early death.
7 The original ACE study has been criticized for (a) failing to consider resilience factors that can buffer the effects of exposure to adversities; (b) failing to take into account other adversities above the original 10, such as poverty, SES background, discrimination, oppression, racism, or refugee status; (c) failing to note the timing of the adversity; (d) the capacity for ACE scores to be used as a measure of individual risk rather than population risk; (e) the overly simplistic nature of the study; (f) the make-up of the original participant pool; and (g) methodological flaws.
8 The influence of the original ACE study is on-going and new ACE models are being proposed.
9 The ACE study has indirectly inspired a move towards examining the social determinants of physical and mental ill-health.

Questions for group discussion

1 Discuss the original ACE study, when it was conducted, by whom, and for what purpose.
2 What were the major findings of the original ACE study?
3 Discuss the limitations of the original ACE study. What criticisms have been made about it?
4 Discuss the on-going influence of the original ACE study and the studies that followed it.

References

Anda, R. F., Porter, L. E., & Brown, D. W. (2020). Inside the adverse childhood experience score: Strengths, limitations, and misapplications. *American Journal of Preventive Medicine, 59*(2), 293–295. https://doi.org/10.1016/j.amepre.2020.01.009

Bernard, D. L., Calhoun, C. D., Banks, D. E., Halliday, C., Hughes-Halbert, A., & Danielson, C. (2021). Making the "C-ACE" for a culturally-informed adverse childhood experiences framework to understand the pervasive mental health impact of racism on black youth. *Journal of Child & Adolescent Trauma, 14*(2), 233–247.

Craig, S. E. (2016). *Trauma sensitive schools: Learning communities transforming children's lives, K–5* (Illustrated ed.). Teachers College Press.

Felitti, V. J., Anda, R. F., Nordenberg, D., Williamson, D. F., Spitz, A. M., Edwards, V., Koss, M. P., & Marks, J. S. (1998). Relationship of childhood abuse and household dysfunction to many of the leading causes of death in adults: The adverse childhood experiences (ACE) study. *American Journal of Preventive Medicine, 14*(4), 245–258. https://doi.org/10.1016/s0749-3797(98)00017-8

Finkelhor, D., Shattuck, A., Turner, H., & Hamby, S. (2013). Improving the adverse childhood experiences study scale. *JAMA Pediatrics, 167*(1), 70–75. https://doi.org/10.1001/jamapediatrics.2013.420

Jennings, P. A. (2019). *The trauma-sensitive classroom: Building resilience with compassionate teaching*. W. W. Norton & Company.

Kelly-Irving, M., & Delpierre, C. (2019). A critique of the adverse childhood experiences framework in epidemiology and public health: Uses and misuses. *Social Policy and Society, 18*(3), 445–456. https://doi.org/10.1017/S1474746419000101

Kirkbride, J. B., Anglin, D. M., Colman, I., Dykxhoorn, J., Jones, P. B., Patalay, P., Pitman, A., Soneson, E., Steare, T., Wright, T., & Griffiths, S. L. (2024). The social determinants of mental health and disorder: Evidence, prevention and recommendations. *World Psychiatry: Official Journal of the World Psychiatric Association (WPA, 23*(1), 58–90. https://doi.org/10.1002/wps.21160

Lacey, R. E., & Minnis, H. (2020). Practitioner review: Twenty years of research with adverse childhood experience scores - advantages, disadvantages and applications to practice. *Journal of Child Psychology and Psychiatry, and Allied Disciplines, 61*(2), 116–130. https://doi.org/10.1111/jcpp.13135

Ludy-Dobson, C., & Perry, B. (2010). The role of healthy relational interactions in buffering the impact of childhood trauma. In E. Gil (Ed.) *Working with children to heal interpersonal trauma: The power of play*. The Guilford Press.

Matjasko, J. L., Herbst, J. H., & Estefan, L. F. (2022). Preventing adverse childhood experiences: The role of etiological, evaluation, and implementation research. *American Journal of Preventive Medicine, 62*(6 Suppl 1), S6–S15. https://doi.org/10.1016/j.amepre.2021.10.024

McEwen, C. A., & Gregerson, S. F. (2019). A critical assessment of the adverse childhood experiences study at 20 years. *American Journal of Preventive Medicine, 56*(6), 790–794. https://doi.org/10.1016/j.amepre.2018.10.016

National Scientific Council on the Developing Child (NSCDC) ([2014]). *Excessive stress disrupts the architecture of the developing brain: working paper no. 3*. Updated 2014. https://www.developingchild.harvard.edu. (Original work published 2005)

National Scientific Council on the Developing Child (NSCDC) (2020). *Connecting the brain to the rest of the body: Early childhood development and lifelong health are deeply intertwined, Working Paper No. 15*. https://developingchild.harvard.edu/resources/connecting-the-brain-to-the-rest-of-the-body-early-childhood-development-and-lifelong-health-are-deeply-intertwined/

Palma, C., Abdou, A. S., Danforth, S., & Griffiths, A. J. (2023) Are deficit perspectives thriving in trauma-informed schools? A historical and anti-racist reflection, *Equity & Excellence in Education*, https://doi.org/10.1080/10665684.2023.2192983

Perry, B. D. (2001). The neuroarcheology of childhood maltreatment: The neurodevelopmental costs of adverse childhood events. In K. Franey, R. Geffner, & R. Falconer (Eds.), *The cost of maltreatment: Who pays? We all do family violence and sexual assault institute* (pp. 15–37). San Diego.

Think TVPBS. (2020, August 25). Stress, trauma, and the brain: Insights for educators-the power of connection [video]. You Tube. https://www.youtube.com/watch?v=3is3xHKKs&abchannel=ThinkTVPBS

Venet, A. S. (2021). *Equity-centered, trauma-informed education*. Norton & co. Inc.

Part III
Trauma-informed practice

6 What is trauma-informed practice?

Chapter objectives

- To provide a definition of the term "trauma-informed practice."
- To examine SAMHSA's four assumptions of trauma-informed practice.
- To explore SAMHSA's six key principles of trauma-informed practice.

Learning outcomes

At the end of this chapter, the learner will be able to:

- Define what is meant by the term trauma-informed practice (in general).
- Outline SAMHSA's "4 assumptions" of trauma-informed practice.
- List and explain SAMHSA's "6 key principles" of trauma-informed practice.

Defining the term "trauma-informed practice"

In 2001, Maxine Harris and Roger Fallot, two experts in mental health and trauma, published a groundbreaking paper that pioneered the concept of trauma-informed practice (TIP) in the USA. In this paper, they defined "trauma-informed" services as services whose mission is informed and consequently altered by an interdisciplinary knowledge and understanding of trauma and its potential impact on the lives of those using the service (Harris & Fallot, 2001). They wrote:

> ...to be trauma-informed means... to design service systems that accommodate the vulnerabilities of trauma survivors and ... facilitate consumer participation in treatment.
>
> (Harris & Fallot, 2001, p. 4).

DOI: 10.4324/9781003438021-10

Explaining the need for trauma-informed organizations, they state that given the fact that of those attending mental health and addiction services, a large number comprise survivors of physical and sexual abuse, there is a need for practitioners to become knowledgeable about the aftermath and impact of trauma (Harris & Fallot, 2001).

Harris and Fallot state that in a trauma-informed approach, the emphasis is on understanding the whole person (2001). According to them, the practitioner needs to focus on the question of how to understand the person in front of them, rather than focus on the symptoms that the person presents with. They explain that this approach shifts the focus toward the person in front of the practitioner, and away from some limited aspect of their functioning (such as problems with anxiety or depression). This approach gives the message that the person's life is understandable and that their behaviors make sense when they are seen as just one part of a whole picture. The authors emphasize that many trauma survivors see themselves as a confused and disordered collection of symptoms and that what these individuals need is to be shown that their behaviors make sense in the context of what they have been through, and that these behaviors are capable of being brought under the control of the trauma survivor. These authors argue that trauma survivors need to be given a structure for organizing and understanding their experiences that is holistic in nature, and trauma-informed by design.

In 2009, in a further report, Fallot and Harris stated that:

1. Trauma is widespread.
2. The impact of trauma is far-reaching.
3. The effects of trauma are frequently serious and life-altering.
4. Trauma involving violence can cause problems that perpetuate the problem.
5. Trauma preys on the most vulnerable people in society.
6. The experience of trauma influences the way individuals respond to potentially helpful relationships.
7. Trauma often occurs within services that are meant to be providing help.
8. Trauma can affect not just the service user but also the service staff members.

(Adapted from Fallot & Harris, 2009)

In this document, the authors outline a planning protocol for organizations wanting to create what they call "cultures of trauma-informed care" (Fallot & Harris, 2009, p. 3). They present what they perceive as the necessary core values of a trauma-informed organization – *safety, trustworthiness, choice, collaboration,* and *empowerment*. They emphasize what they call "organizational culture" (Fallot & Harris, 2009, p. 3) meaning that all aspects of an organization's functioning must be driven by this new trauma-informed approach (Fallot & Harris, 2009). They state that in order to accomplish this culture change in any given organization they recommend the following four steps:

> 1. **Preliminary stage:** where the staff of an organization must meet together to consider their level of commitment to becoming a trauma-informed organization.
> 2. **Commencement of basic training:** where staff attend presentations demonstrating (among other things) that TIP is a shift in both understanding as well as practice.
> 3. **Follow-up (short-term):** in which all staff attend training. The authors explain that this training is designed to discuss the impact of trauma, its prevalence, as well as some of the multiple paths to recovery, emphasizing the ways in which trauma may present in the lives of consumers and the work experience of staff. A second educational event focuses on staff support and care and emphasizes that a shift in an organization's culture toward a trauma-informed system of care rests on staff members' experiences of safety, trustworthiness, choice, collaboration, and empowerment. The authors state that these training events should be offered by experienced trainers whose aim is to train some of the staff to become trainers themselves so that they might become capable of passing along important information about trauma to newer staff members.
> 4. **Follow-up (longer term):** this happens after about six to nine months, and it is basically a meeting in which the progress to date is reviewed. The authors state that the most important goal at this stage is to maintain the momentum established after the initial training until the point where change in the organization's culture becomes established.
>
> (Paraphrased from Fallot & Harris, 2009).

The authors emphasize that the overarching goal of a trauma-informed service system should be to return a sense of control and autonomy to the trauma survivor. They emphasize that in a trauma-informed approach, services should be "strengths-based." Therefore, one of the roles of a trauma-informed organization is to help the person to take the skills they used as survival strategies in the past and put these skills to greater use to protect themselves in the future. For example, they explain that if a woman has had to be guarded and hypervigilant to protect herself in the past, she has learned to pay attention to details. This means she has learned to be a quick judge of people and to get a quick sense of who can be trusted and who cannot. The authors state that these capacities should now be seen as skills that will help this individual in the future, for example, these skills may help this individual to choose relationships wisely, and to use skills of vigilance and attention to detail, to help her in a career or profession. One of the chief roles then of a trauma-informed organization is to build on an individual's strengths rather than putting the focus on managing their symptoms.

Outlining the key principles and assumptions of trauma-informed practice

In 2014, the Substance Abuse and Mental Health Services Administration (SAMHSA) built on the work of Fallot and Harris (2009) by publishing a document entitled, *SAMHSA's Concept of Trauma and Guidance for a Trauma-Informed Approach*. This document has become a key resource for the definition of TIP. It states that a trauma-informed approach is grounded in a set of four assumptions and six key principles (SAMHSA, 2014, p. 9). The assumptions and key principles are elaborated on in the two sections below.

The four assumptions of TIP

According to SAMHSA (2014), a trauma-informed program, organization, or system adheres to four assumptions. These assumptions are that a trauma-informed system adheres to the following four Rs: realizes, recognizes, responds, and resists (SAMHSA, 2014, p. 9).

> - *Realizes* [the pervasiveness of trauma and comprehends the possible routes to recovery]
> - *Recognizes* [signs/symptoms of exposure to trauma in individuals and groups]
> - *Responds* [by incorporating into its policies & practices, knowledge about trauma]
> - *Resists* [the risk of re-traumatization of individuals and groups, in an active manner]
>
> (Paraphrased from SAMHSA, 2014).

SAMHSA elaborates on these four assumptions explaining that:

1. With regard to realization, SAMHSA states that, in a trauma-informed organization, all people at all levels of the organization need to have a basic understanding of trauma and how it can impact not just individuals but also families, groups, organizations, and communities. There also needs to be a realization that the behavior/attitudes of trauma-affected individuals or groups need to be understood in the context of coping strategies that they may have had to rely on when faced with overwhelmingly stressful events or circumstances (SAMHSA, 2014). These stressful events or circumstances may have occurred in the past (e.g., it may be a client dealing with past child abuse); may be current (e.g., it may be a staff member living with domestic abuse); or the stressful events may be the result of secondary or vicarious trauma experienced by a professional

working directly with a trauma-affected client. These authors emphasize that in a trauma-informed organization, there is also an understanding that exposure to adversity and subsequent trauma is linked to such issues as substance misuse and mental health problems, and should be addressed rather than overlooked in prevention, treatment, and recovery settings, where appropriate. Also, in a trauma-informed organization, there should be a realization that trauma is found in many systems including the criminal justice system, the educational system, and the child welfare system and is often a barrier to optimal or effective outcomes in these systems.

2 With regard to recognition, SAMHSA states that a trauma-informed organization should be able to *recognize* the signs and symptoms of trauma which are often specific to a particular age-group, gender, or other factor. This ability to *recognize* the signs and symptoms of trauma should be promoted through workforce training (SAMHSA, 2014).

3 With regard to response, SAMHSA states that a trauma-informed organization *responds* by integrating the principles of a trauma-informed approach throughout the organization. This response should be reflected in the organization's specific mission statements. Their staff handbooks and manuals need to promote a culture based on beliefs about resilience, recovery, and healing from trauma (SAMHSA, 2014. The organization also needs to *respond* by providing service users with an environment that is physically and psychologically safe (SAMHSA, 2014).

4 With regard to re-traumatization, SAMHSA states that a trauma-informed organization actively seeks to *resist re-traumatization* of its clients and staff. This is achieved by teaching staff to recognize how practices within an organization may trigger painful memories and therefore be instrumental in re-traumatizing clients with a history of trauma. For example, they explain that actions such as placing a child who has been neglected and abandoned in a seclusion room may be re-traumatizing and may have an adverse effect on that child's healing and recovery" (SAMHSA, 2014).

The six key principles of TIP

According to SAMHSA, a trauma-informed organization adheres to six key principles: (these include the five core principles listed by Fallot and Harris (2009). The principles are:

- Safety
- Trust and transparency
- Peer support
- Collaboration and mutuality
- Empowerment, voice, and choice
- Cultural, historical, and gender issues

SAMHSA elaborates on these six key principles as follows:

Safety

In a trauma-informed organization, all staff and the people they serve should feel physically and psychologically safe (SAMHSA, 2014). In practice, what this means is having an understanding that people who have experienced trauma tend to feel unsafe, especially in unfamiliar environments such as offices (a welfare office, a doctor's office, a social worker's office) and most likely have experienced powerlessness and boundary violations in the past that make them feel vulnerable. They therefore have a vital need to feel physically safe from harm, and psychologically safe from humiliation, or embarrassment. In practice, for example, this may mean not publicly asking people to either read or fill out a form, when in fact they might be illiterate and therefore feel humiliated by this (seemingly) reasonable request.

Trust and transparency

SAMHSA states that in a trauma-informed organization, all decisions affecting the organization should be conducted with transparency and have the goal of establishing and maintaining trust with clients and their family members and with anyone involved in the organization (2014). In practice, what this means is understanding that many people who have experienced trauma tend to feel distrustful of others because they have experienced a breach of their trust, often by the very people they most trusted. Therefore, they have a vital need to discover, slowly but surely, that they can trust again, and that not everyone will breach their trust. In practice, this means that a trauma-informed organization should not make promises they cannot keep and should not break the promises they make.

Peer support

According to SAMHSA, a trauma-informed organization should recognize that peer support is a key factor in helping to promote recovery and healing (SAMHSA, 2014). "Peers" refers to people with lived experiences of trauma, or "trauma-survivors" (SAMHSA, 2014).

Collaboration and mutuality

SAMHSA emphasizes that a trauma-informed organization recognizes that healing happens in collaborative relationships and the sharing of power and decision-making (2014). Therefore, the organization recognizes that everyone at every level of the organization has a role to play and there is a genuine leveling of power differences. For example, in educational settings, this could mean involving the parents or caregivers, and the children in decision-making as much as is practically possible. In practice, this may mean sending regular newsletters to families asking for their opinions, ideas, or suggestions about matters pertaining to the school such as up-coming events or changes to the school building, and giving serious consideration to these opinions, and acting on them where appropriate. Actions such as these help to reduce the power imbalance often felt by those using the services of an organization.

Empowerment, voice, and choice

According to SAMHSA, a trauma-informed organization fosters empowerment for staff and clients alike. It promotes the voices and choices of both staff and clients. The experiences and strengths of individuals or groups are recognized and built on. The organization believes in the people it serves and strives to promote their resilience. It believes in the capacity of individuals and groups to overcome trauma. It seeks to foster empowerment in staff and service users alike. It recognizes that historically both voice and choice in organizations have often been diminished and were frequently replaced by coercive treatments. It recognizes that the role of staff is to facilitate recovery rather than control recovery in service users (SAMHSA, 2014).

Cultural, historical, and gender issues

SAMHSA states that a trauma-informed organization moves beyond past cultural stereotypes and prejudices (based on gender identity, race, age, ethnicity, sexual orientation, religion, geography, etc.) and offers culturally responsive services, recognizing and addressing historical trauma (2014).

Vignette

Trigger warning
This vignette contains content of a sensitive nature.
Maureen is a 70-year-old woman, attending an adult mental health clinic. She has been attending this clinic for over three years having attended similar clinics in different towns and cities for most of her adult life. She is being treated for anxiety and depression, and the treatment consists almost entirely of medication. Maureen first attended a mental health clinic in London, UK when she was just 20 years old, a month after she had tried to end her life (by taking an overdose of paracetamol and alcohol). Thankfully, her young flatmate came home from work early that day and found Maureen unconscious on the kitchen floor. Maureen does not recall much about the week she spent in hospital, having her stomach pumped, and her wrist put into plaster, which presumably fractured when she hit the floor. However, she remembers her first mental health session. She was asked a lot of questions about her current job, her relationships, her marital status, and her education. However, the vital question (which Maureen secretly hoped she would never be asked)

> related to her childhood. Maureen went on to have countless mental health sessions over the years, some of them follow-up sessions after Maureen tried again to end her life. These sometimes resulted in her being sectioned and placed in locked psychiatric units where she was sometimes restrained, constantly monitored (frequently by male staff) and mostly given no choices about anything relating to her care. All of this made her constantly fearful, and each time Maureen was discharged from one of these facilities, she often had nightmares for weeks, and even in the daytime she had no sense of safety. Maureen could never really comprehend why she felt so much worse after treatment.

What Maureen's mental health professionals did not know, because they did not ask, was that Maureen had a long history of child sexual abuse. Between the ages of six and nine years, Maureen was seriously sexually abused by her second foster father, whom she had believed loved her. Maureen had been placed in foster care when she was just ten months old. Her teenage mother was a lone parent and unable to care for a baby. Maureen was initially placed with two very loving foster parents and was with them for five years but was forced to go to another placement when her foster mother died of cancer and her foster father, in despair, became dependent on alcoholic, to sooth his grief. The second placement was difficult for Maureen. She desperately missed the only mother and father she had ever known. Her new foster parents seemed very kind, but after eight or nine months, her new foster father started to abuse her sexually, when her foster mother went out to work for a few hours each evening. It was a full three years before the abuse, almost accidentally, came to light when Maureen was taken into hospital for treatment for recurrent urinary tract infections. Maureen didn't understand why she was not allowed to go back to her foster parents, nor why she had to go to more than six different placements over the next eight years. Nor did Maureen understand why or even when she started to have what were later called "serious behavior issues." She didn't understand why she couldn't learn in school, or why she couldn't make friends, or be civil with her teachers. Her life became what she calls a "mess," a chaotic and unpredictable collection of symptoms that she could neither understand nor explain. Her treatment, over the decades, which consisted mostly of medications, gave her some short-term relief from her misery, but taking so much medication contributed to her belief that she had a host of mental illnesses including anxiety and depression, that she would live and die with. She was given no explanation from her treatment sessions that her "serious behavior issues" in her teens and 20s had actually been coping adaptations to her past traumas, and her deep depression and anxiety in later life was a direct result of what happened to her, and not what is currently being seen as what is "wrong" with her.

Now, in her 70s, Maureen still attends a mental health clinic, once a month. Mental health sessions have changed over the years, and now Maureen is asked about her childhood and given an opportunity to tell her story, which she often finds to be more damaging to her than helpful. What makes the situation worse is that each time she attends the mental health clinic, there is a new mental health professional in place, and Maureen is usually asked to tell her story again, and again, and again. This is re-traumatizing for her, and when she leaves the clinic, she often feels very low for days on end.

Maureen's story might have been different if the psychiatric units she was placed in and the mental health clinics she attended had been trauma-informed and committed to providing trauma-informed care. First, there would have been a realization that because of the pervasiveness of trauma, it was more likely than not that Maureen had been a victim of a traumatic event. Second, there would have been a recognition of the signs and symptoms of trauma (Bloom, 2004). Third, the psychiatric unit would have responded to the reality of the pervasiveness of trauma (Felitti et al., 1998) and reflected this knowledge in their policies, practices, and procedures. Therefore, making Maureen feel safe would have been a priority, and they would have given consideration to whether the presence of male nurses in Maureen's room would impede her capacity to feel safe. Fourth, there would have been an understanding that the use of restraints on a person who may have suffered abuse, could be re-traumatizing, and there would have been an awareness that re-traumatization is to be avoided at all costs.

Also, at the mental health clinic, there would have been a real paradigm shift. Maureen would have been looked upon as a whole person, rather than a person with a collection of symptoms such as anxiety or depression. The mental health professionals would have focused on the question "what happened to you?" rather than "what's wrong with you?" They would have held a genuine belief that Maureen could heal from trauma (not just be medicated), and they would have understood that their role was to support Maureen, in identifying and building on her strengths and participating in a very real way in her own recovery. They would have made sure that Maureen's voice was heard and that she had choices and was not coerced in any way. The power differential between Maureen and the mental health professionals would have been leveled, and efforts would have been made to help Maureen to become empowered and therefore have the capacity to play a major role in her own recovery. A trauma-informed approach such as this is indeed a change in perspective. It views the service user as the expert in their own life. It recognizes that the service user has had to develop skills to survive their traumatic experiences, and it attempts to help them utilize these skills in their own recovery. For example, a person who endured abuse as a child, frequently develops a heightened sensitivity to non-verbal cues. This sensitivity to non-verbal cues may be used by a trauma survivor to aid them in future personal relationships, helping them to be discerning. Overall, a trauma-informed approach will encourage trauma survivors to engage with services that may be able to help them. Without a trauma-informed approach, many trauma-affected people may cease to use mental health services. Since these services play a vital role in the protection of people with mental health challenges, a disinclination among some people to attend these services may lead to negative and even tragic results.

> **Summary of Chapter 6**
>
> 1 The concept of trauma-informed practice takes its origins from a seminal document published by Harris and Fallot (2001).
> 2 This document defined trauma-informed services as services whose mission is informed and consequently altered by an interdisciplinary knowledge and understanding of trauma and its potential impact on the lives of those using the service.
> 3 Harris and Fallot (2001) emphasized that in a trauma-informed approach, the emphasis is on understanding the whole person, rather than focusing on a collection of symptoms.
> 4 Harris and Fallot (2001) emphasized that a trauma-informed approach sends a message to the trauma survivor that their life is understandable, and that their behaviors do make sense, when they are understood as part of a whole picture.
> 5 Harris and Fallot (2001) emphasized that trauma survivors need to be shown that their collection of symptoms make sense in the light of their experiences, and they can (with compassionate support) bring them under control.
> 6 Harris and Fallot (2001) emphasized that a trauma focused understanding can provide trauma survivors with a structure for organizing an understanding their own experiences.
> 7 In a follow-up publication, Fallot and Harris (2009) outlined a planning protocol for organizations that wish to create a culture of trauma-informed care in their settings.
> 8 In this document, they presented their five core values for a trauma-informed organization.
> 9 These values are – *safety, trustworthiness, choice, collaboration, and empowerment*.
> 10 Fallot and Harris (2009) outlined four steps for institutions wanting to move toward a trauma-informed approach – Initial planning; A kick-off training event; Short-term follow-up; and Longer-term follow-up.
> 11 Fallot and Harris (2009) emphasize that the overarching goal of a trauma-informed organization is to return a sense of autonomy and control to the trauma survivor.
> 12 Therefore, one of the chief roles of a trauma-informed organization is to build on the trauma survivor's strengths, so that they can become empowered and so can help themselves to recover from the effects of trauma.
> 13 In 2014, SAMHSA built on the work of these pioneers in their document – *SAMHSA's Concept of Trauma and Guidance for a Trauma-Informed*

Approach. This document states that a trauma-informed approach is grounded in four assumptions and six key principles.

14 SAMHSA's four assumptions are – that a trauma-informed system *realizes* the widespread impact of trauma; *recognizes* its signs and symptoms; *responds* by integrating knowledge about trauma into its policies, procedures, and practices; and *resists* re-traumatization of clients in an active fashion.

15 SAMHSA's six principles are *safety; trustworthiness and transparency; peer support; collaboration and mutuality; empowerment, voice, and choice;* and *cultural, historical, and gender issues.*

Questions for group discussion

1 How would you define trauma-informed practice?
2 What did Fallot and Harris emphasize as crucial in a trauma-informed approach?
3 Discuss the four stages of the planning protocol outlined by Fallot and Harris (2009) for the establishment of a trauma-informed approach in an organization.
4 What are the five core principles outlined by Fallot and Harris for the establishment of a trauma-informed organization?
5 Discuss the four assumptions listed by SAMHSA (2014) (i.e., the 4Rs).
6 Discuss the six key principles of trauma-informed practice as listed by SAMHSA (2014).

References

Bloom, S. L. (1995). Creating sanctuary in the school. *Journal for a Just and Caring Education, 1,* 403–433.

Bloom, S. L. (2004). Neither liberty nor safety: The impact of trauma on individuals, institutions, and societies. Part 1. *Psychotherapy and Politics International, 2*(2), 78–98.

Fallot, R. D., & Harris, M. (2009). Creating cultures of trauma-informed care: A self-assessment and planning protocol. *Community Connections.* https://doi.org/10.13140/2.1.4843.6002

Felitti, V. J., Anda, R. F., Nordenberg, D., Williamson, D. F., Spitz, A. M., Edwards, V., Koss, M. P., & Marks, J. S. (1998). Relationship of childhood abuse and household dysfunction to many of the leading causes of death in adults: The adverse childhood experiences (ACE) study. *American Journal of Preventive Medicine, 14*(4), 245–258. https://doi.org/10.1016/s0749-3797(98)00017-8

Harris, M., & Fallot, R. D. (2001). Envisioning a trauma-informed service system: A vital paradigm shift. *New Directions for Mental Health Services,* (89), 3–22. https://doi.org/10.1002/yd.23320018903

Substance Abuse and Mental Health Services Administration (2014). *SAMHSA's concept of trauma and guidance for a trauma-informed approach.* SAMHSA's Trauma and Justice Strategic Initiative. https://ncsacw.acf.hhs.gov/userfiles/files/SAMHSA_Trauma.pdf

7 Trauma-informed practice in education

> **Chapter objectives**
>
> - To discuss the current movement toward TIP in education.
> - To explain how a TIP in education approach changes our perspective from a deficit lens to a trauma-informed lens.
> - To discuss the vital importance of positive, attuned relationships in the process of healing from traumatic experiences.
> - To examine the importance of searching for a child's strengths and building on them.
> - To show how TIP in education promotes a culture of safety, collaboration, and empowerment.
> - To explain why TIP in education needs to be a "whole school" approach.
> - To discuss the benefits of TIP in education for children, teachers, and families.
> - To outline the importance of self-care for educators.
> - To discuss the steps necessary to infuse "trauma-informed practice" into a school.

> **Learning outcomes**
>
> At the end of this chapter, the learner will be able to:
>
> - Explain the reasons for the current movement toward TIP in education.
> - Explain how a TIP approach shifts the perspective of educators away from the question – "What's wrong with this child?" toward the question – "What happened to this child?."
> - Explain why trauma-informed practice needs to be a relationship-based approach.
> - Recognize why trauma-informed practice needs to be a strengths-based approach.
> - Describe how TIP promotes a culture of safety, collaboration, and empowerment.

DOI: 10.4324/9781003438021-11

- Justify why TIP needs to be a "whole school" approach.
- List the benefits of trauma-informed practice for children, teachers, and other staff.
- Explain why a TIP approach promotes self-care for educators.
- Outline the steps necessary to infuse "trauma-informed practice" into a school.

Looking at trauma-informed practice in education

According to Wolpow et al. (2009) "Focusing on academics while struggling with trauma is like trying to play chess in a hurricane" (p. 3). It is not surprising then that over the last two decades, there has been a veritable explosion of publications, relating to the prevalence of childhood trauma and the extent of the social, emotional, and cognitive harm it causes to children (Thomas et al., 2019). It is not surprising, therefore, that there is a clear sense of urgency among educators to promote trauma-informed practice (TIP) in education (Alexander, 2019; Blodgett & Dorado, 2016; Bomber, 2020; Brooks, 2020; Brummer, 2021; Brunzell & Norrish, 2021; Cole et al., 2005, 2013; Craig, 2016; Jennings, 2019; Nicholson et al., 2023; Venet, 2021, Wolpow et al., 2009; Wright, 2023). In 2019, Thomas et al. correctly pointed out that, currently, there is no single agreed upon framework for TIPs (2019), and they stated that much of the widely promoted content designed specifically for educators use the trauma-informed approach developed in 2014 by SAMHSA Substance Abuse and Mental Health Services Administration (SAMHSA, 2014; Thomas et al., 2019). Despite this lack of a formally agreed upon framework for TIPs, there is a general consensus among educators on what makes a school trauma informed. This consensus accepts that there are a number of essential elements working together to make a school trauma-informed and trauma-responsive. These essential elements include seeing TIP as:

- An approach that changes our perspective.
- A relationship-based approach.
- A strengths-based approach.
- An approach that promotes safety, collaboration, and empowerment
- A "whole-school" approach.
- An approach that benefits children, teachers, and other staff.
- An approach that promotes self-care for educators.
- An approach that moves in stages from becoming trauma-aware, to trauma-sensitive, to trauma-informed, making it possible to finally become trauma-responsive.

These essential elements are now examined.

Shifting the perspective from a deficit lens to a trauma-informed lens

Alexander (2019) states that "Considering 'What happened to you?' instead of 'What's wrong with you?' is a mindset change for educators" (2019, p. 82). She emphasizes that changing the question shifts our perspective from a deficit lens to a trauma-informed lens. As educators, we don't need to know all the details of what the child has been through (unless we suspect an ongoing safeguarding issue). All we need to know is that the child has been affected by trauma and therefore is more likely than not to demonstrate behaviors in school (often quite suddenly, and often because of some trigger that we are unaware of) that have to do with the *fight flight or freeze* response. Alexander (2019) gives the example of a student who, by all appearances, looked like he was being defiant and disruptive every day in the school cafeteria. A knowledge of "what happened to him" revealed that he lived with domestic violence, and he did not feel safe when he had to sit in the cafeteria with his back to other students as this made him feel too vulnerable and consequently, he quickly became dysregulated, and problems with behavior followed (Alexander, 2019). Alexander points out that if the staff had known earlier what was triggering this student, they could have allowed him to sit with his back to a wall or window which would most likely have helped to make him feel less vulnerable.

Vignette

Fourteen-year-old Juanita attends a public Montessori school about 5 miles from her home where she lives with her dad and younger sister. She has been attending the school for two years now and loves it, and she is recognized as a nice child and a good student. However, over the last month, she has become different. She seems sleepy in school and unfocused. She appears to be losing interest in things that she was formally quite excited about, such as dance, music, and drama. She also seems dazed on some occasions and looks as if she is daydreaming or zoning out. The Montessori class teacher, who has had some training in trauma-informed practice, is keeping an eye on this change in Juanita's behavior, and he is considering the possibility that something traumatic may be happening to Juanita. The teacher is aware that Juanita is a private person and doesn't talk much about her family life or her feelings. He has a good relationship with all the students, and although Juanita is reserved, he looks for an opportunity to talk with her. One afternoon, when the class goes out for a shopping trip to buy the ingredients for some meals, they are going to cook that week, Juanita asks if she can stay back at school because she is not feeling well. This gave the class teacher an opportunity to talk with her in the presence of a trusted assistant teacher. The talk revealed that Juanita's dad who is a widower, has begun to date a divorced woman who has a 15-year-old son, named Carlos. When Juanita's father goes out to dinner with this lady, he pays Carlos to be the sitter for Juanita and her younger sibling. Unknowns to Juanita's dad, Carlos is addicted to pornography and watches it on his tablet while sitting. He keeps inviting Juanita to watch it with him and keeps pushing his tablet in front of her face telling her what she's missing. She feels scared, shocked, and disturbed when her dad is out for the evening and she and her little sister are left at home with Carlos. She can't sleep at night thinking about it. She did not tell her dad about this, because he seems so happy with his new lady friend, and she knows how sad he's been for the last two years after her mom died. She cried when she told the class teacher about this, but she also said she felt a great relief to have told someone about it. The class teacher asked Juanita if it would be okay if he spoke with her dad, and Juanita agreed. The class teacher was so glad that he had focused not on what's wrong with you, but on what happened to you.

Explaining TIP as a relationship-based approach

According to Perry and Szalavitz (2006), "The more healthy relationships a child has, the more likely he will be to recover from trauma and thrive" and they also claim that "Relationships are the agents of change, and the most powerful therapy is human love" (2006, p. 230). A TIP approach in education acknowledges that healthy relationships are key in the healing of trauma (Alexander, 2019; Jennings, 2019; Ludy-Dobson & Perry, 2010; Nicholson et al., 2023; Sorrels, 2015; Treisman, 2017; van der Kolk, 2014; Wright, 2023). Dr. Barbara Sorrels points out the seeming contradiction that children who have been exposed to trauma in the context of a relationship can only find healing within a relationship (Sorrels, 2015). However, she also points out that this relationship needs to be one marked by trust and unconditional acceptance. Teachers who are trauma-informed therefore, have the potential to change trauma-affected children's lives for the better (Treisman, 2017). However, it is not just the teachers who can help here, all school staff (who have a TIP understanding) can be agents of change in a trauma-affected child's life. Jen Alexander writes that bus drivers, school secretaries, cafeteria workers, and anyone who interacts with students and parents needs to be knowledgeable about meeting the needs of traumatized children and young people through a relationship-based school culture (Alexander, 2019, p. 100).

This does not require the teacher or other staff to spend hours and hours in a one-on-one relationship with the child, as this would not be practical nor helpful and it could lead to dependency. Instead, teachers and other staff can learn how to be the providers of droplets of positive relational interactions all through the school day. As explained above, teachers and other staff can relate by giving a smile in the child's direction, by giving a high five as they pass a child in the corridor, or by saying something like – *Hi there Sam – how are you doing to-day?* as the child enters the school building. All of these two-second interactions send a message to the child's brain and that message is "I'm noticed and not for a negative reason," "someone is glad to see me," "someone genuinely recognizes something in me that is worthwhile," "someone has taken the time to nod to me, smile at me, say a kind word to me, remember my name." These brief, positive, relational interactions, given several times a day, send the child a key message and that message is "you're safe," "there's no danger here, this is a safe space." Without relational safety, a child cannot learn in school (Perry, 1999). In a school situation, when children experience a lack of relational safety in their interactions with their teachers and/or their peers, their brains are forced to focus on protecting themselves from such things as criticism, derision, punishment, and so on. While the brain is involved with the issue of safety, the cortex is not open for learning (Perry & Graner, 2018). In this situation, children's ability to concentrate and learn is seriously compromised. Therefore, relational safety is fundamental to the learning process (Perry & Graner, 2018).

> **Vignette**
>
> Germaine is an 11-year-old Black boy who recently moved with his mom and little sister to a new city and got a place in the local Montessori public school just opened a few years ago. Neither Germaine nor his mum know much about Montessori, they are both just hoping that the school will be a good one. Germaine is hoping he will settle in quickly and make some new friends. At Germain's previous school, in another city, he was constantly faced with the trauma of systemic racism, whereby it was clear that black children (both girls and boys) were treated more harshly than white children by the predominantly white female teachers. The injustice of this was ingrained in Germaine, you could say it was "under his skin." On Germain's first day at his new school, he was greeted, like all the other kids, with a high-five by the bus driver who was a very friendly Latino man probably in his 60s. All the kids seemed to love him and not one failed to high-five him when getting on and off the bus. This greeting was like a friendly ritual that settled everyone down before they took their seats on the bus. When the bus pulled up at the school, Thomas, a young teaching assistant was standing at the front door of the school to greet everyone. With a huge welcoming smile, he greeted each child one by one with a variety of handshakes, high-fives, and other more creative greetings including a few dance steps from one of the girl students which Thomas mirrored with some moves of his own. The combination of smiles, high-fives, and short dances, contributed to a very positive mood as the children entered the school and created a sense of belonging and community that Germaine had never encountered in his previous school.

As he followed the queue into his new classroom, he heard the teacher's friendly voice also uttering greetings such as "how are you doing Jay?" or "great see you Sofia" or "how's that sore knee Bobby?." These comments created a friendly and welcoming atmosphere, and when Germaine came through the door and was greeted with "hi Germaine, how's it going, hope you and your mom are settling into your new home, let me know if you need help getting school materials," Germain felt an immediate sense of being in an atmosphere of care, where the teacher actually liked the students and cared both for them, and about them. As the days and weeks went on, Germaine could see that the teacher took a real interest in the students' lives. She knew things such as the names of their parents/caregivers, and siblings, even sometimes, the names of their pets! This atmosphere of care was present in the cafeteria staff, the administration staff, the coaches, and guides. It was a culture of care that contributed to helping Germaine to feel a sense of belonging, a sense of being welcomed, a sense of being in a community, that was healing for him. He began to apply himself to school life and soon began to show evidence that he was flourishing emotionally, socially, and cognitively.

In time, Germaine's mom, who had never attended a parent meeting before (first because she had no transportation, and second because she always felt uncomfortable and inferior going into a school building, probably because she did not have a high level of education herself), decided to attend her first parent–teacher meeting. Attendance was made possible because the teacher, discretely had a habit of finding out which families had transport and could get to school events or parent–teacher meetings, and which families did not, and so could not. She would then quietly and discretely arrange lifts to events for those families who had no transport or gas cards to help with the cost of travel. She managed to do all this without falling into the trap of developing a deficit or savior mentality which is when teachers see themselves as the rescuers and fixers of children from what they regard as dysfunctional homes. This teacher did not have that mindset, instead, she had a mindset that focused on supporting children and families to develop their inherent skills and capacities and to direct their own lives, with a little support (if wanted, or asked for) to help them work toward their own particular goals. This is what a relationship-based approach means.

Explaining TIP as a strengths-based approach

Brunzell and Norrish (2021) state that "Trauma-informed approaches can be greatly enhanced by deliberately focusing on identifying and cultivating students' strengths" (p. 37). To find and celebrate a child's strengths, we must use our observational skills to determine:

- What does this child do well?
- What are the child's talents?
- What makes this child happy?

A TIP approach recognizes that it is crucial to find the child's strengths (Brunzell & Norrish, 2021). All of us have something we are good at. Cole et al. (2005) write that every child or young person has a strength. Sometimes, this strength is in academics, though often it is in sport, music, or art. Cole et al. say when teachers identify and build on a child's strength, they help that child to experience success, and they derive all the self-esteem and self-belief from their accomplishments (2005). Historically, schools have given priority to academic strengths over a child's physical, social, emotional, and spiritual strengths. Every human being is made up of more than just intellect. As educators, we need to train ourselves to look for both the academic and the non-academic strengths which children possess. Cole et al. point out that one of the most effective ways for a teacher to support a trauma-affected child is by building a (healthy) relationship with them that does not focus on their academic standing. They state that when children feel cared for and appreciated by a teacher, regardless of their academic abilities or academic standing, a feeling of safety develops, and this results in children becoming more open to learning (Cole et al., 2005).

Sometimes, a trauma-affected child's particular strength will be the one that is least expected. For example, children who have experienced adversity and/or trauma are often (when they are not in a state of hyper- or hypo-arousal), very sensitive to other children's pain or distress. They notice the teacher's tone of voice toward other children, and they often stand up to defend them. This sometimes gets them into trouble because they frequently do not have the social or verbal skills to handle things appropriately and therefore may come across to teachers as if they are being cheeky or impudent, when in fact, they are just being protective of other children. They are actually being heroes, not troublemakers.

Similarly, children, who are overly controlled in their homes and often coerced, can appear to be very bossy in a school setting, always wanting to control things or perhaps dictate the rules of the games. However, if we look at their behaviors using a trauma-informed lens, we will understand that these children are often placed in roles in their homes that are essentially adult roles, for example, it is often these children who have to feed and dress their siblings because their parent or caregiver is either unable or unwilling to do so. Therefore, these children have developed leadership skills, and this is why they can appear to be bossy or controlling.

As teachers we need to recognize the strengths in these children and promote them rather than suppress them. We need to find ways to help these children to take on a leadership role but give them the supervision they need so that they do not become coercive like the negative adults in their family. Other strengths that may be hidden in a trauma-affected child could be the ability to sing, dance, or perform in a dramatic production. Opportunities to do these things have the potential to build back, trauma-affected children's self-esteem and give, or return to them the self-belief that they so much need, and that the experience of trauma has taken from them. As educators, if we pay attention to these (often hidden) strengths in trauma-affected children, we may be able to offer them opportunities to build on these strengths and in so doing help them to heal from the negative effects of exposure to trauma.

> **Vignette**
>
> Five-year-old Heather really tested the directress's patience during her first week at Montessori school. She was a total newcomer to the Children's House Nursery, and the other children complained that she was bossy and rude to them. She snatched materials out of their hands saying, "you're not doing that right" and she pushed the two little lunch servers of the day, Charlotte and Harry, out of the way grabbing their serving spoons from them, and saying crossly, "this is how it's done." Heather had been brought to school that first week by her auntie Kate who was quite evasive when asked about Heather's mum and would only divulge that Heather's mum was in a clinic and was feeling a bit down, and that she (Kate) would be minding Heather and her six-month-old baby brother Timothy, for a bit. Fast forward six months. Heather is still attending school, and she is now perceived by her peers to be friendly and helpful. She learned (especially through the Montessori Grace and Courtesy Exercises) how to relate in a helpful manner toward others.

It turns out that Heather's mum had a long history of depression that she could usually control with medication. However, because she came off the medication during pregnancy and for months after the birth, she developed what was most likely to be post-natal depression and for months, lay in bed most of the day. Heather, who was only four years old, would climb into the cot and change little Timothy's nappy and then feed him using the ready-prepared bottles that her mum (who was a lone parent) kept in a low cupboard. Then she would make jam butties (an English sandwich) for herself and her mum. No one knew how bad the situation was until auntie Kate arrived one morning and found Heather sitting in the cot changing the baby's nappy. It was at that point that Heather's mum went into hospital for a few weeks and Heather started attending the Montessori school.

In this case, there was no intentional neglect of Heather, but there was neglect. In the midst of this, Heather developed certain strengths. She learned to make basic sandwiches (jam butties) that were probably her only food on many occasions. She kept the baby from being dehydrated by feeding him bottles when her mum was half asleep, and she saved him from many a nappy rash by changing him. She coped by using natural leadership and practical strengths that were probably part of her make-up. By doing this she became a little heavy handed, but this characteristic is related to what she had to do to survive. Now, that the directress understands what happened to Heather, she can better understand her former behavior, and is creating activities that allow Heather to use her natural born strengths. For example, almost every day, Heather organizes little groups to go around the classroom with her, dusting shelves, cleaning tables, and sweeping the floor. Heather is an excellent leader and organizer, and these skills developed when she was in a situation that must have been very stressful for her at the time.

Explaining TIP as a "whole-school" approach

A TIP approach recognizes the need for a whole-school approach in which the aim is to infuse a trauma-informed culture into every element of the school (Cole et al., 2013). A trauma-informed approach will be less effective if the whole-school is not on the same page (Cole et al., 2013). Each and every member of the school staff, whether the bus driver, the principal, or the teachers, must be on the same page, that is they must understand what trauma is, and how it affects the social, emotional, and cognitive functioning of children (Alexander, 2019). They must also understand what this looks like in a school setting, specifically, what are the likely "triggers" for a child who has been exposed to trauma, what are the likely behaviors of a child who has been exposed to trauma, and what are the likely reactions of a child who has been exposed to trauma to non-verbal signals such as tone of voice, facial expressions, physical stance (van der Kolk, 2003). All staff need to understand the power of relationships to bring healing. They need to understand that even two-second-long doses of positive relational interactions can be healing for a child (Bomber, 2020). Everyone needs to know how important and how valuable they are in the healing of a child who has been exposed to trauma. All staff need to understand that every human being has strengths and that we must promote those strengths in our efforts to bring healing to children who have been exposed to trauma. They need to understand the importance of physical and psychological safety for a trauma-experienced child. Everyone needs to understand the importance of collaboration for all children but especially those who have been affected by trauma and they should be encouraged to look for ways to help children to collaborate with adults and with their peers. Similarly, all staff need to understand the importance of empowering children who have been disempowered by their experience of trauma, in order to help them to overcome the negative effects of this on their young lives.

Discussing how TIP promotes a culture of safety, collaboration, and empowerment

According to Venet (2021) "A ... trauma-informed approach requires that we are intentional in creating safety and trust. ... we need to prioritize the empowerment and agency of each person in our school community ... We need to collaborate with students, families, and communities regularly and proactively in ways that promote agency and ownership" (p. 69). A TIP approach actively creates and promotes a culture of safety, collaboration, and empowerment (Fallot & Harris, 2009; Harris & Fallot, 2001). It is not sufficient to simply recognize and empathize with trauma-affected individuals, a trauma-informed organization recognizes that it has a duty to actively promote safety and provide opportunities for collaboration with the aim of helping trauma-affected individuals to become empowered. Herman (2015) pointed out that "Traumatic events destroy the victim's fundamental assumptions about the safety of the world" (p. 51). Therefore, the first priority of a trauma-informed school is to actively promote safety. A TIP approach recognizes the child's need for both physical and psychological safety (SAMHSA, 2014). If a child does not have the assurance of physical safety (for example from being bullied by peers), or the assurance of psychological safety (for example from being publicly embarrassed or humiliated by a teacher or by peers), the child will be forced to operate at the level of the survival brain (Nicholson et al., 2023). As the survival brain is focused on safety, it operates from either a state of hyper-vigilance or disengagement. As we have shown, when a child is in either of these states, he is unable to access the cortex, and therefore will be unable to absorb academic information (Bomber, 2020). With regard to collaboration, a TIP approach recognizes that healing happens in the sharing of decision-making and power (SAMHSA, 2014). A TIP approach also recognizes that these collaborations must be free from power-differentials. For collaborations to be healing there must be no element of threat and so there must be a leveling of power differences (SAMHSA, 2014). All parties in the collaboration must be given equal respect, even if they are mixed age groups. As teachers, we must protect children who are trying to collaborate and keep a watchful eye on any power differentials that could prove to be harmful or re-traumatizing for the trauma-affected child. With regard to empowerment, a TIP approach recognizes that children who have been exposed to trauma have been disempowered. Traumatic experiences strip children of their agency, power, and sense of control. For example, it is common for many children who have experienced over controlling and coercive caregivers, to be left feeling completely disempowered (Treisman, 2017). They often feel a strong sense that they have no say over their own lives and are often resigned to living a life of subservience to others. Educators can provide children with a sense of empowerment in their classrooms by actively listening to their opinions and giving them the power to make practical decisions such as what activity they wish to do and for how long, and if they wish to do the activity alone or with another child. Also, empowerment comes through developing skills and becoming aware of one's abilities. Therefore, teachers can empower children by helping them to gain skills, which others can see and perhaps praise, giving the child a sense of self-worth, and self-esteem all of which build a sense of empowerment in a child (Brunzell & Norrish, 2021).

Outlining the benefits of TIP for children, teachers, and families

Summary of the benefits of TIP for children:

Children:

- Feel safer
- Feel happier
- Can start making friends
- Can engage in learning
- Can develop self-understanding
- Can develop empathy and compassion

- Start to feel empowered
- Can begin to recover
- Can avoid being re-traumatized

Summary of the benefits of trauma-informed practice for teachers:

Teachers:

- Gain increased understanding of children/young people
- Develop empathy and compassion for their students
- Become infused with "Hope" and a vision for the great potential of their students
- Experience a reduction in work-related stress
- Begin to understand the dangers of "vicarious trauma"
- Learn that "self-care" is not a luxury but a necessity
- Develop "self-care" routines
- Learn how to balance work and home life
- Achieve more job satisfaction

Summary of the benefits of trauma-informed practice for families:

Families:

- Children may become calmer at home
- Children may become happier and more content at home
- Parents may become less stressed by their children's behaviors

Promoting the health of educators by highlighting self-care in TIP

Craig (2016) highlights the fact that "Teachers get little training in recognizing symptoms of primary trauma in their students and virtually no training in the self-care needed to prevent secondary traumatic stress" and she says that this "has serious implications for their effectiveness and rates of attrition" (p. 90). A TIP approach promotes self-care for educators because it recognizes that educators are vulnerable to secondary trauma and that a dysregulated adult cannot help a dysregulated child (Jennings, 2019).

Educators are vulnerable to secondary trauma

According to Perry (2014) "Secondary traumatic stress is a risk we incur when we engage empathically with an adult or child who has been traumatized" (p. 10).

This type of trauma happens when adults who are working with trauma-affected children start to exhibit signs and symptoms similar to those who experienced the trauma directly (Perry, 2014). Perry points out that this is sometimes confused with burnout, but he makes it clear that it should not be (2014). However, Perry also points out that the term secondary trauma may be used interchangeably with the term vicarious trauma (Perry, 2014). He explains that the term "vicarious" trauma is used to refer to the traumatic impact on those who feel the intensity of the traumatic event through another person (Perry, 2014). The impact of this on a teacher's *personal* life can present as changes in sleep habits, fatigue, reduced energy, irritability, feelings of sadness, inability to concentrate, desire to withdraw from others, physical aches and pains such as stomach upsets (Alexander, 2019). The impact of this on a teacher's *professional* life can present as lack of motivation, decreased confidence, isolation from other colleagues, overworking, and absenteeism (Alexander, 2019). Secondary trauma is more common when teachers have had their own personal experience of trauma, and when the teacher feels that he/she has very little resources or capacity to help these children (Craig, 2016).

A dysregulated adult cannot help a dysregulated child

Perry and Ablon, explain that a dysregulated adult cannot help a dysregulated child (2019). Human beings are relational creatures, and we are contagious to the mood, the feelings, and the behaviors of other people (Perry & Szalavitz, 2006). We are particularly impacted by the moods and feelings of people who are, at a particular point in time, dominant in our lives. Therefore, the emotions of teachers in the classroom will significantly influence the emotions of the children in the classroom. It follows then, if educators wish to get to a child's cortex, they need to remember that they must be regulated themselves (Perry & Graner, 2018). Teachers need to remember to take care of themselves and to always keep in the forefront of their minds that if they are not regulated, they are not going to be effective in bringing regulation to children.

Suggestions for self-care:

Jennings (2019) emphasizes that "It helps to create a self-care plan that is balanced across the domains of our physical, emotional, intellectual, and spiritual well-being and growth" (p. 114).

Suggestions for physical self-care:

- Try to develop a regular sleep routine
- Try to have a healthy diet
- Try to have a regular lunch break
- Try to have a brief walk at lunchtime
- Try to use your allocated sick leave
- Try to get some exercise before starting work

Suggestions for emotional self-care:

- Do things you enjoy
- Do things that make you laugh
- Play a sport you enjoy
- Watch a movie you enjoy
- Play a musical instrument
- Sing, dance, and move
- Develop supportive friendships
- Talk to a trusted friend

Suggestions for psychological self-care:

- Try to take up a non-work-related hobby
- Try to avoid "working" outside of work hours
- Try to make time for relaxation
- Try to spend time with friends and family

Suggestions for spiritual self-care:

- Try to engage in practices such as meditation
- Try to spend time in nature
- Join a faith-based community

Suggestions for relational self-care:

- Avoid negative colleagues
- Avoid complainers
- Avoid areas where negative talk is commonplace
- Prioritize close relationships with family/friends
- Attend special events with family and friends

Professional Supervision for educators:

According to Venet (2021), "Leaders must make teacher wellness a school-wide priority rather than leaving it up to individual teachers to self-care their way out of it" (p. 132). Many professions that involve the care and protection of children provide professional supervision for staff, e.g., social workers and medical professionals. Sadly, this is not universally the case in the field of education. A survey carried out by Barnardos in Scotland found that nearly all staff working in education said that they would welcome Supervision in Education programs (2020). The report states that educators discussed their increasing levels of stress, and the emotional load of teaching as a caring profession. One participant quoted in the report stated that "Having worked with children with adverse childhood experiences, ... there have been times when I've had to close my classroom door and cry for the full of break time due to what's being disclosed" (p. 7). Another participant quoted in the report stated that educators hold in themselves a lot of emotions from children who are trauma-experienced, and educators need to learn how to reflect, but also move on and let go. Overall, there was consensus on the need for Professional Supervision.

Explaining the steps in the journey to becoming a trauma-informed school

Several steps need to be taken to begin the process of becoming a trauma-aware, trauma-sensitive, trauma-responsive, and ultimately a trauma-informed school. These may differ from school to school. However, it is safe to say that most schools will have to take the following steps:

1 Have at least one "whole-school" meeting informing all staff on the nature, prevalence, and impact of trauma on children so that all staff share an understanding of this and recognize the need for a school-wide approach to helping children to recover from trauma and avoid re-traumatization.
2 Provide teachers and other staff with specific strategies to use when a child shows the signs or symptoms of exposure to trauma.
3 Provide parents with information on TIP.
4 Managers must make sure that all school policies reflect a commitment to TIP.
5 Regular "whole-school" reflection on the experience of implementing a trauma-informed approach is recommended.

Summary of Chapter 7

1 TIP in education is an approach that changes our perspective from – *What's wrong with you?* to *What happened to you?*
2 TIP in education is a relationship-based approach.
3 TIP in education is a strengths-based approach.
4 TIP in education is an approach that promotes safety, collaboration, and empowerment.

5 TIP in education is a whole-school approach.
6 TIP in education is an approach that benefits children, teachers, and other school staff.
7 TIP in education is an approach that promotes self-care for educators.
8 TIP in education is an approach that moves in stages from becoming trauma-aware to trauma-sensitive, to trauma-responsive, making it possible to become trauma-informed.

Questions for group discussion

1 Discuss the current trend toward TIP in education. What fueled it, and is it warranted?
2 How does a TIP approach change an educator's perspective?
3 How important are relationships in the healing of trauma?
4 What is a strengths-based approach? How does it operate in Montessori classrooms?
5 How does a TIP approach promote a culture of safety, collaboration, and empowerment?
6 Does TIP need to be a whole school approach? Discuss.
7 What are the benefits of TIP to children, teachers, and families?
8 Explain why a TIP approach promotes self-care for educators. Give examples of self-care.
9 Discuss the basic steps necessary to infuse trauma-informed practice into a school.

References

Alexander, J. (2019). *Building trauma-sensitive schools: Your guide to creating safe, supportive learning environments for all students*. Brookes.

Barnardos. (2020). Supervision in education – healthier schools for all: Barnardos Scotland report on the use of professional or reflective supervision in education. Trauma-informed schools – paper No. 2. https://www.barnardos.org.uk/files/uploads

Blodgett, C., & Dorado, J. (2016). *A selected review of trauma-informed school practice and alignment with educational practice*. California and Endowment.

Bomber, L. (2020). *Know me to teach me: Differentiated discipline for those recovering from adverse childhood experiences*. Worth Publishing.com.

Brooks, R. (2020). *The trauma and attachment aware classroom: A practical guide to supporting children who have encountered trauma and adverse childhood experiences*. Jessica Kingsley Publishers.

Brummer, J. (2021). *Building a trauma-informed restorative school: Skills and approaches for improving culture and behaviour*. Jessica Kingsley Publishers.

Brunzell, T., & Norrish, J. (2021). *Creating trauma informed, strengths-based classrooms: Teacher strategies for nurturing student's healing, growth, and learning.* Jessica Kingsley Publishers.

Cole, S. F., Eisner, A., Gregory, M., & Ristuccia, J. (2013). *Helping traumatized children learn: Creating and advocating for trauma sensitive schools.* Massachusetts Advocates for Children, Trauma and Learning Policy Initiative. https://traumasensitiveschools.org/wp-content/uploads/2013/06/Helping-Traumatized-Children-Learn.pdf

Cole, S. F., Greenwald O'Brien, J., Gadd, M. G., Ristuccia, J., Wallace, D. L., & Gregory, M. (2005). *Helping traumatized children learn: Supportive school environments for children traumatized by family violence.* Massachusetts Advocates for Children, Trauma and Learning Policy Initiative. https://traumasensitiveschools.org/wp-content/uploads/2013/06/Helping-Traumatized-Children-Learn.pdf

Craig, S. E. (2016). *Trauma sensitive schools: Learning communities transforming children's lives, K–5* (Illustrated ed.). Teachers College Press

Fallot, R. D., & Harris, M. (2009). Creating cultures of trauma-informed care: A self-assessment and planning protocol. *Community Connections.* https://doi.org/10.13140/2.1.4843.6002

Harris, M., & Fallot, R. D. (2001). Envisioning A trauma-informed service system: A vital paradigm shift. *New Directions for Mental Health Services,* Spring (89), 3–22. https://doi.org/10.1002/yd.23320018903

Herman, J. L. (2015). *Trauma and recovery: The aftermath of violence—From domestic abuse to political terror.* Basic Books.

Jennings, P. A. (2019). *The trauma-sensitive classroom: Building resilience with compassionate teaching.* W. W. Norton & Company.

Ludy-Dobson, C., & Perry, B., D. (2010). The role of healthy relational interactions in buffering the impact of childhood trauma. In E. Gil (Ed.) *Working with children to heal interpersonal trauma: The power of play.* The Guilford Press.

Nicholson, J., Perez, L., Kurtz, J., Bryant, S., & Giles, D. (2023). *Trauma-informed practices for early childhood educators: Relationship-based approached that reduce stress, build resilience and support healing in young children.* Routledge.

Perry, B. D. (1999). Memories of fear: How the brain stores and retrieves traumatic experience. In J. M. Goodwin & R. Attias (Eds.), *Splintered reflections: Images of the body in trauma.* Basic Books.

Perry, B. D. (2014). The cost of caring: Understanding and preventing secondary traumatic stress when working with traumatized and maltreated children. *CTA Parent and caregiver education series.* Vol. 2: Issue 7. https://www.childtrauma.org/trauma-ptsd

Perry, B. D., & Ablon, J. S. (2019). CPS as a neurodevelopmentally sensitive and trauma-informed approach. In Pollastri, A., Ablon, J., & Hone, M. (Eds.), *Collaborative problem solving. Current clinical psychiatry.* Springer. https://doi.org/10.1007/978-3-030-12630-8_2

Perry, B. D., & Graner, S. (2018). *The neurosequential model in education: Introduction to the NME series: Trainer's guide (NME training guide).* Child Trauma Academy.

Perry, B. D., & Szalavitz, M. (2006). *The boy who was raised as a dog: And other stories from a child psychiatrist's notebook—What traumatized children can teach us about loss, love, and healing.* Basic Books.

Substance Abuse and Mental Health Services Administration (SAMHSA) (2014). Substance abuse and mental health services administration. In *SAMHSA's concept of trauma and guidance for a trauma-informed approach.* https://store.samhsa.gov/shin/content/SMA14-4884/SMA-4884.pdf

Sorrels, B. (2015). *Reaching and teaching children exposed to trauma.* Gryphon House.

Thomas, M. S., Crosby, S., & Vanderhaar, J. (2019). Trauma-informed practices in schools across two decades: An interdisciplinary review of research. *Review of Research in Education, 43*(1), 422–452. https://doi.org/10.3102/0091732X18821123

Treisman, K. (2017). *Working with relational and developmental trauma in children and adolescents.* Routledge.

van der Kolk, B. (2014). *The body keeps the score: Mind, brain and body in the transformation of trauma*. Penguin.

van der Kolk, B. A. (2003). The neurobiology of childhood trauma and abuse. *Child and Adolescent Psychiatric Clinics of North America, 12*(2), 293. https://doi.org/10.1016/s1056-4993(03)00003-8

Venet, A. S. (2021). *Equity-centered, trauma-informed education*. Norton & co. Inc.

Wolpow, R., Johnson, M. M., Hertel, R., & Kincaid, S. O. (2009). *The heart of learning and teaching: Compassion, resiliency, and academic success*. https://www.k12.wa.us/sites/default/files/public/compassionateschools/pubdocs/theheartoflearningandteaching.pdf

Wright, T. (2023). *Emotionally responsive teaching: Expanding trauma informed practice with young children*. Teachers College Press.

Part IV
Contemporary Montessori schools and trauma-informed practice

8 How the six TIP principles are incorporated into Montessori schools

Chapter objectives

- To provide examples of how *safety* can be promoted in Montessori schools.
- To show how *trustworthiness and transparency* are integrated into Montessori schools.
- To show how *peer support* can be promoted in Montessori schools.
- To examine how *collaboration and mutuality* are supported in Montessori schools.
- To examine how *empowerment, voice, and choice* are promoted in Montessori schools.
- To see how *cultural, historical, and gender issues* are responded to in Montessori schools.
- To examine how *diversity, equity and inclusion (DEI) and anti-bias, anti-racism (ABAR)* principles are responded to in Montessori schools.

Learning outcomes

At the end of this chapter, the learner will have a knowledge of:

- How physical and psychological **safety** can be supported in Montessori schools.
- How to promote **trustworthiness and transparency** in Montessori schools.
- How **peer support** can be promoted in Montessori schools.
- How **collaboration and mutuality** are supported in Montessori schools.

DOI: 10.4324/9781003438021-13

- How **empowerment, voice, and choice** are promoted in Montessori schools.
- How **cultural, historical, and gender issues** are responded to in Montessori schools.
- How **DEI and ABAR** principles are responded to in contemporary Montessori schools.

Looking at factors that promote *safety* in Montessori schools

As we saw in Chapter 3 in the section on the stress response system, certain parts of the human brain, particularly the amygdala, are specifically concerned with the protection of the organism. This means that certain parts of our brains are constantly scanning our environment for signs of danger, in order to give us the opportunity to escape that danger, if possible, and remain safe. This scanning for safety is related to the concept of neuroception (Porges, 2004). In practice, this means that when a trauma-experienced child or young person enters a new environment, such as a new school or classroom, they unconsciously scan the environment for danger so as to protect themselves from physical or psychological harm.

Montessori made physical and psychological *safety* a priority in her schools. She did this by focusing on what she called *the spiritual preparation of the teacher* (Montessori, 1936, 1967). She prepared her teachers to provide *safety cues* to children through their tone of voice, facial expressions, and overall body language. In her practice, she provided physical and psychological safety to children by the abolition of rewards and punishments, the use of self-correcting materials, and the promotion of positive relational interactions between the teachers (called directresses) and the children, for example, the morning handshake, which started the day. These all represent *safety cues* and *safety measures* that children, especially trauma-affected children, will notice and be affected by. We now examine these elements and comment on how they relate to the promotion of *felt safety* and *real safety* (both psychological and physical) in contemporary Montessori schools.

Psychological safety cues – our facial expressions with children and our greetings

As stated in Chapter 2, in a series of articles published in 1915, in the San Francisco Call and Post, wherein Montessori reflected on her early work with children who were deemed to have intellectual disabilities, but who were also trauma-affected, it is significant that the first thing she tells us is how she prioritized the morning greeting to help the children to feel safe and warmly welcomed. She wrote that when the children from the psychiatric hospitals and some homeless children from the streets entered her school, they were met with genuine signs of welcome and real friendliness and were made to feel that they were welcomed and wanted (Montessori, 2008). Montessori was very aware of how our facial expressions can convey either a sense of safety or a sense of fear in children. She doesn't specifically say that she met the children with smiles or handshakes, but this is implied in her words. Essentially, what she was doing here was taking a pre-emptive step from the moment the children entered her schools that sent out a psychological *safety cue* to them. As stated in Chapter 4, in the section on the impact of trauma on social functioning, children who have been affected by trauma, often misinterpret non-verbal cues (Perry, 1999; van der Kolk, 2003) and wrongly interpret non-verbal cues such as innocuous facial expressions as being threatening. The safety cue that Montessori provided in the form of a genuinely warm welcome would have been instrumental in promoting a state of calm in these children that prevented the sending of a signal to the amygdala that could have caused an activation of the stress response. This pre-emptive step arguably had a positive impact on these children and likely contributed to their healing from the effects of traumatic experiences.

As stated, over 100 years ago, Montessori established this practice of greeting the children individually on arrival, and many Montessori schools have followed this practice and teachers typically welcome children each day by stooping down to their level and shaking hands with them if they are in the 3–6 age group or high fiving them if they are in the 6–9 or 9–12 age group or older. Currently, because of the spread of TIP information about the importance of giving children *safety cues* on arrival, some non-Montessori schools are starting to adopt this long-established Montessori practice. The importance of this practice cannot be over emphasized because it has huge psychological significance for children and young people in terms of giving them a felt sense of safety. In 1911, Anne George, one of Montessori's first students, reported on how she witnessed the importance of the morning greeting to students. She saw how this simple act appeared to put the children in a positive frame of mind and helped them to settle into the day. The children she was describing were from the St. Angelo school in Pescheria, an extremely impoverished area of Rome. George wrote that as she was in conversation with the teacher, she turned around only to find a group of little girls behind her, who had come in quietly, and were queuing up to wish her good morning. Following the greeting, each child (all over six years in this particular school) went immediately to the cupboard to get some materials to work on (Tozier, 1911).

The impact on children, especially those living with poverty or some other adversity, of a personal morning greeting is significant. This personal greeting tells them *I'm seen, I'm cared about, I'm safe in this environment* (Bomber, 2020). For many children, this is a vital start to their day. Contemporary Montessori schools should make sure to continue this century-old Montessori practice whereby each child is personally greeted each morning keeping in mind, not just its social and emotional function, but its important role as a *safety cue* to a child. In addition, teachers need to be very careful in relation to their facial expressions with all children but in particular with children they suspect may be trauma-affected. This means being aware at all times that trauma-affected children may be extra sensitive to every raised eyebrow, frown, grin, or grimace, on our faces, and may react strongly to them. We need to pre-empt negative reactions by being very aware of the sensitivity of trauma-affected children.

Psychological safety cues – our language and tone of voice with children

Again, as we saw in Chapter 4, in the section on the impact of trauma on social functioning, children who have been affected by trauma have a tendency to have difficulty interpreting social cues (Perry, 1999; van der Kolk, 2003) and often wrongly interpret social cues such as tone of voice as being threatening. For this reason, teachers need to be very careful in relation to their language and tone of voice with all children but in particular with children they suspect may be trauma-affected. Montessori, in describing her efforts to give grammar lessons to the children with intellectual disabilities that she first worked with, who were also survivors of traumatic experiences, gives us some beautiful examples of how she addressed these children. Referring to the children, she said that one of her most original pedagogical approaches was used when she set out to give them some basic grammar lessons (Montessori, 2008). She describes the dramatic and playful game she invented whereby she would stand in the center of a group of these children and using dramatic emphasis and a loud expressive voice would beckon the children to come to her, but she would deliberately omit the name of the person she wished to call. She said the children would look perplexed and the little ones, in puzzlement, would ask her who was she calling. She said, on another occasion, she would ask the children to bring her certain items from the shelves, but she would deliberately omit the name of the item she wanted, i.e., the noun. She describes how the children would bring her all sorts of objects, to which she would reply (using the sweetest and most loving words) that these were not the items she was requesting (Montessori, 2008). These descriptions (which we are so fortunate to still have) tell us so much about the language and the tone of voice that Montessori used with children. It is extraordinary that although she was telling the children that the items they were offering her were all the wrong ones, she managed to do this using gentle and affectionate words such as "my child," "dear," "little one" and she clearly used a playful tone of voice at all times during this interaction with the children. She states that the children would eventually respond with laughter asking her animatedly to state what exactly she wanted. She would then use a noun, and the children would grasp the grammar lesson!

Using this affectionate, kind, and respectful language, along with playfulness, she anticipated to an extent, the work of Dr. Dan Hughes, and his PACE (Playfulness, Acceptance, Curiosity, Empathy) model which was designed to promote a secure attachment and experience of safety in children and young people when interacting with adults such as parents or other caregivers (Hughes & Golding, 2012). Since Montessori was working with these children for long hours each day, she was arguably acting in loco parentis and took on some of the responsibility of a caregiver. Contemporary Montessori schools should follow Montessori's use of playfulness with trauma-affected children in order to promote a sense of safety between the child and the teacher. With regard to the use of kind language and a gentle tone of voice (which Montessori regarded as a vital part of the teacher's training, known as the "spiritual preparation" of the teacher), Montessori teachers who have heeded these admonitions, have been leaders in this area (1936, 1967).

Psychological safety cues – our body language with children

Montessori was very aware of the impact of the teacher's body language on the children in the class. She wrote that the teacher should examine her own movements, to make sure they were as graceful (and therefore as non-threatening) as possible (Montessori, 1967). Louise Bomber, a contemporary author on childhood adversity and childhood trauma, states that teachers who use warm body language will give a message of safety to students, but those who use the opposite type of body language, for example, cross their arms and stand in a manner that emphasizes that they are bigger and stronger than the children or young people around them, will run the risk of increasing the students' perception of threat, and increase their fears and feelings of distress (2020). From the outset, Montessori told her students that as part of their "spiritual preparation" to become teachers, they needed to rid themselves of pride and become humble (1936). This humility would automatically affect body language, for example, if teachers are humble, they will not fold their arms and puff themselves up to appear bigger and stronger and therefore threatening to children. By stating emphatically that the teacher should examine her own movements, Montessori was building *safety cues* into the teachers' body language. The *safety cues* were literally embodied in the teacher. This attention to such minute details as the teacher's body language was for a long time unique to Montessori education and should be recognized as a major strength of the Montessori method. It is especially important in view of the fact that because of the pervasiveness of adversity and trauma, most schools are almost guaranteed to have some children in them who have been impacted by traumatic experiences. Therefore, quality contemporary Montessori schools have the built in-infrastructure, *embodied in the very teachers*, among other factors, to help trauma-affected children to feel safe.

One advantage of these trauma-sensitive and safety-promoting practices is that they cost NOTHING. All teachers can use their eyes to give a child a kind glance, their voice to provide a comforting comment, and their body language to convey positive messages such as "you are wanted here," "you are valued here," "you belong here," and "you are part of this community." These practices are all inseparable from what Perry calls the power of belonging and connectedness which has been shown to be a powerful factor in bringing healing from trauma (Perry & Winfrey, 2021). Perry explains that the brain is constantly scanning our environment looking for signals that indicate whether we belong or do not belong and when the brain gets a message (via tone of voice, facial expression, or body language) that we belong, our stress systems become calm and settle down, because the brain gets the message that we are safe (2021). Historically, Montessori teacher training courses have been unique among teacher training courses in giving prominence to what Montessori called the spiritual preparation of the teacher, but it is that spiritual preparation that helps to make Montessori schools trauma-sensitive. Without adequate "spiritual preparation," a Montessori teacher cannot embody the *safety cues* that the trauma-affected child needs to sense. Contemporary teachers need to really understand this so that they can carry on Montessori's legacy of providing healing environments for trauma-affected children.

Physical safety – protection from bullying

For many children in contemporary schools, a key safety challenge relates to the risk of physical (or psychological) bullying, which for some children may be constant, especially during recess. Montessori had personal experience of the threat of bullying in her own second-level school days at The Royal Technical Institute of Rome where she and one other girl were the only female students. During recess, she and the other girl would be locked inside the classroom to protect them from the taunts of the male students (De Stefano, 2022). In 2006, in a very significant publication, Lillard and Else-Quest produced findings that have very real bearing on the issue of bullying in contemporary schools, both Montessori and non-Montessori, especially during recess. Their study compared both social and academic scores of children in a Montessori school with those of children in other elementary school education programs. The authors' findings were very significant. They recorded that "Observations at the playground during recess indicated Montessori children were significantly more likely to be involved in positive shared peer play and significantly less likely to be involved in rough play that was ambiguous in intent (such as wrestling without smiling)" (Lillard & Else-Quest, 2006, p. 1894). In the same study, as part of *Social/Behavioral Measures*, the authors state that the children were told five stories about social issues, such as a child not sharing a swing, and were asked how they would approach and try to solve each problem. The results were compelling. The authors state that the figures showed (43% versus 18% of responses) that the Montessori children were significantly more likely to opt for a social justice/fairness reasoning approach to convince the other child to share the swing. These findings confirm those of eyewitnesses to many of Montessori's early schools. As stated in chapter two Dr. Jessie White (1914), observing playground behavior in a number of early Montessori schools wrote that the atmosphere was positive and there was virtually no aggressive behavior. Other eyewitnesses (Bailey, 1915; Fisher, 1912; George, 1912) remarked on the children's genuine concern for each other, and helpfulness toward each other both in the classroom and in the playground.

A recent systematic review, while not dealing specifically with the topic of bullying, found that "Montessori education has a meaningful and positive impact on child outcomes, both academic and non-academic, relative to outcomes seen when using traditional educational methods" (Randolph et al., 2023, p. 2). It defined non-academic outcomes as those pertaining to such factors as social and emotional outcomes, creativity, and executive functions. The authors state that "this Montessori result is highly significant" (p. 46) because as they point out executive function is an important predictor of future outcomes. This research is indirectly relevant to the issue of bullying because it is arguable that any educational model that enhances executive function, which involves exercising inhibitory control (i.e., the ability to control our automatic urges by pausing and then using our attention and reasoning faculties to respond appropriately), could have a knock-on positive impact on children's behaviors and ultimately reduce or eliminate bullying as seems to have happened in Montessori's early schools.

Physical safety – protection from dangers in the outdoor and indoor school environment

In a lecture given in Kodaikanal in 1944, Montessori, speaking on the design of environments for young children emphasized the importance of physical safety. Clearly, she knew that it was not enough for children to have "felt safety," there must also be "real safety." She said "children will never be free unless the environment is safe, such that there is no danger to the child. If there is any possibility of danger, the children cannot be left alone" (Montessori, 1944/2013, p. 17). In this context, she was speaking of safety in the outdoor environment, specifically the garden. She recommended that the garden be protected from dangers by erecting an enclosure wall. She stated that physical safety is a very important issue because if the children have to be closely monitored because the environment is dangerous, this will result in a lack of freedom and the need for adult supervision, which ultimately curbs the children's feeling of freedom and spontaneity.

In contemporary schools the risks to safety for children either traveling to schools or within schools have increased. The threat of experiencing or witnessing gun violence or knife crime is very real and could potentially occur in any city or town (Holloway et al., 2023). Jennings (2019) states that traumatic events such as school shootings can have a very strong negative impact on children and teens especially those who have been exposed to trauma. She cautions that these kinds of traumatic events can be re-triggering for trauma-affected children (Jennings, 2019). No school can offer children or young people total protection from either experiencing or witnessing violent events, but schools can and must take all possible steps to provide physical safety to children and young people both inside and outside of the school.

Paula Lillard Preschlack recounts a story from a program volunteer at a Montessori public school in a location where children were exposed to very real threats to their safety on a regular basis. It was also the case that some of the children were being exposed to trauma in their homes and as a result showed challenging behaviors in the classroom (Preschlack, 2023). The volunteer said how sometimes street rules would invade the classroom and aggression would break out whenever someone (either accidently or deliberately) bumped someone else (Preschlack, 2023). The volunteer said that it became clear to the adults that what lay behind this behavior was really a survival issue (Preschlack, 2023). The solution they found was to tell the children that they were all safe in the school so they did not need to be defensive (Preschlack, 2023). The volunteer stated that the children were then able to understand and accept that they had alternative choices about what to do if someone pushed them in school (Preschlack, 2023). Explaining to children that there were alternative choices available actively promoted the safety of everyone.

Wright (2019) says that rather than viewing trauma-affected children's actions as behavioral challenges, we need to recognize that these actions may be necessary to keep children safe in other areas of their lives where risks to personal safety are a constant reality. However, he cautions us not to simply accept challenging behaviors without question, because these behaviors may place the child at risk of social, emotional, and academic struggles even in Montessori classrooms where safety and respect are valued and promoted experiences, and are the very experiences that a trauma-affected child most needs. He states that he approaches this problem by using the terms *in here* and *out there*. So, for example, when a child's behavior in the classroom is inappropriate (but he is aware that in the child's local neighborhood this behavior might well be a survival strategy that protects them from something such as an assault), he might express to children his understanding that out there, in the children's neighborhood, they might have no option but to behave in a certain way, but in here, in the classroom, they are in a safe zone and the teacher is there to protect them. He says that he explains to children that behaving inappropriately will not help them to make friends or to learn, but he offers them positive ways to act and re-act in the classroom. Wright reminds us that deep respect for children, and their real-life experiences is central to the Montessori approach (2019).

Considering how *trustworthiness* and *transparency* are promoted in Montessori schools

One of the core principles of trauma-informed practice is the concept of *trustworthiness* and *transparency* (SAMHSA, 2014). In their 2014 document, the Substance Abuse and Mental Health Administration (SAMHSA) recommends that in a trauma-informed organization, decisions should be conducted with transparency with the aim of building trust with all those involved in the service. From the outset of her work with children, Montessori made trustworthiness and transparency paramount. She established a practice that was very unusual for the time, i.e., an "open door" policy, whereby parents, at that time mostly mothers, were given the opportunity to come into the school any time they wanted to (Montessori, 1912/1964). In addition, she approved an arrangement whereby a parent could talk regularly with the teacher of her child(ren) (Montessori, 1912/1964). This invitation was included in the Rules and Regulations which were posted on the door of the first Montessori school in San Lorenzo in 1907.

In addition, Montessori allowed visitors from numerous professions and walks of life to come and observe the children at work, though she stipulated that they were merely to observe and not interrupt the children's work. In some schools, such as the one on the Via Giusti in the Franciscan nuns' convent, very large numbers of visitors could observe the children at work from an upper gallery (Fisher, 1912). The numbers of interested people wishing to observe the children were often so large that attendance passes had to be issued (White, 1914). Later, Montessori made provision for people to view the children at their work by creating a Glass Classroom at the San Francisco Panama-Pacific International Exposition in 1915. Sobe (2004) describing the Glass Classroom writes that Montessori's pedagogical methods were demonstrated to the world for four months there, with very large numbers of observers watching the classroom from the bleachers.

In these examples, transparency was Montessori's goal as she wanted observers to see with their own eyes how Montessori schools work. In particular, she wanted people to see how the children respond to the ordered environment and the concrete materials. Specifically, she wanted to demonstrate how the materials and exercises promote concentration on a task and how out of this concentration comes an integration of the personality. This phenomenon of integration (which she called by the technical term "normalization"), she argued, helps the child to become calm, tranquil, and subsequently kind and sociable toward others (Montessori, 1967). Contemporary Montessori schools can replicate this transparency by providing parents with photos and often video clips of their children at work and play. Many schools also attach to these photos a few sentences or paragraphs explaining what material the child is using and what the purpose of the activity is. This type of transparency is important for any parent because all parents appreciate feedback on their child's activities, but for parents of trauma-affected children, it is vital and often very comforting for them to see how the teachers daily help their child to regulate themselves by working with certain materials.

As for the children, the principles of trustworthiness and transparency are conveyed by simple acts such as (1) teachers and other staff speaking positively and respectfully to them so that they know they can trust that these members of staff care for them and want what is best for them; (2) behavioral expectations are made simple and clear, but kindness and empathy prevails when a child does not meet up to these expectations, in addition practical help is offered and suggestions are made to help the child to comply with these behavioral expectations; (3) activities, especially potentially trauma triggering activities such as fire alarm drills, are sensitively and gently flagged up well in advance of occurrence, so that children, especially trauma-affected children, are not re-traumatized; (4) changes of any kind including staff changes are gently flagged up in advance so that children, especially trauma-affected children are not taken by surprise, or re-traumatized; and (5) transitions from one place to another are gently flagged up because transitions, especially for trauma-affected children can be difficult and upsetting. All of these measures help children, especially those who have been affected by trauma, to sense that their teachers are trustworthy and that their actions are transparent. They also help to prevent re-traumatization as recommended by the trauma specialists (SAMHSA, 2014). Once again, most children need to sense that they can trust their teachers and that school practices are transparent, but for children who have been affected by trauma, the need to sense trustworthiness and transparency in their school is vital.

Showing how *peer support* can be promoted in Montessori schools

Another of the core principles of trauma-informed practice is the concept of peer support (SAMHSA, 2014). In their 2014 document, SAMHSA states that peer support is a key factor in establishing safety and hope for trauma survivors. By "peers" they mean persons who have lived experiences of trauma, or family members of children who have been affected by trauma and are directly involved in their recovery. In contemporary Montessori schools, peer support can be promoted by helping trauma-affected children to develop positive relationships with their teachers and peers. As explained in Chapter 4, children who have been exposed to trauma can have difficulty with social functioning and are prone to mis-read non-verbal signals leading to difficulties both forming and maintaining positive relationships.

Wright (2023) states that a vital task to be accomplished in early childhood is learning how to form and maintain positive relationships with peers. He notes that because of their focus on self-preservation, trauma-affected children tend to be less skilled socially (Wright, 2023). He states that often trauma-affected children reveal that they are challenged in social situations and often believe (wrongly) that other children are trying to cause problems for them and this can lead them to behave aggressively toward their peers. Wright suggests that teachers can support trauma-affected children's peer relationships in a number of ways which include providing opportunities for both individual and group play, providing spaces where children can take a break, role-playing conflict resolution, teaching children to recognize and name positive relational interactions (2023). Wright says that these "strategies" can support children who may be fearful of trusting others (2023).

An important aspect of the Montessori approach that promotes peer support is the fact that Montessori education does not encourage children to compete against each other, but rather to help each other so that one child's mastery of an activity or task is celebrated by their peers. Preschlack records the comments of a Public school teacher implementing Montessori, who said that she observed that Montessori students at all ages are inclusive and help each other. She believed this was due to the lack of competitiveness in Montessori classrooms (Preschlack, 2023). The lack of competition in Montessori classrooms at all ages and levels does much to promote peer support. Many decades ago, Montessori wrote about how the mixture of ages in her schools promoted peer support. She wrote that in her schools five year old children saw themselves as protectors of younger children (Montessori, 1967) and this led to real bonding among the classmates. She said that the children in her classes were almost glued together by affection Montessori (1967).

Looking at how *collaboration* and *mutuality* are promoted in Montessori schools

Another of the core principles of trauma-informed practice is the concept of collaboration (Fallot & Harris, 2009). In their 2014 document, SAMHSA explained the term "collaboration" by stating that a trauma-informed organization recognizes that healing happens in the context of collaborative relationships with others, and through the sharing of decision-making and the sharing of power. Therefore, a trauma-informed organization recognizes that all staff members have a role to play and there is a leveling of power differences. When Montessori agreed to direct the educational aspects of the first school in San Lorenzo, she agreed with Eduardo Talamo and their mutual friend Olga Lodi that the school should be called the Casa dei Bambini or Children's House (Kramer, 1976). Montessori meant this literally. She envisioned the school as an institution run as a true collaboration between the parents and the children. She envisioned it literally as the children's own home. From the outset, the children began treating it as *their* home and engaged in a very meaningful sharing of power and decision-making with the adults involved. E. M.

Standing, who was Montessori's first biographer, 1957, gives a very interesting account of how on one occasion, when the school was in its infancy an important visitor (the Argentine ambassador to Rome) came to see the school with his own eyes, being skeptical of the glowing reports he had heard (Standing, 1957). He deliberately visited the school unannounced in order to make sure that no artificial preparations were made to impress him. However, when he arrived, he found that the school was closed that day. Standing explains that:

> "Whilst this was being explained to him by the hall porter, a little child in passing overheard the conversation, and at once said, 'Oh that's alright. You've got the key (addressing the hall porter) and all the children live here (in the tenement house)'. So the porter opened the door, and the little child went around and collected his comrades. Then they all went into the classroom and did the honours to the ambassador by carrying on with 'business as usual'".
>
> (1957, p. 56).

In terms of any previous educational model, this understanding by the children that the school was a collaboration between the owners of the building and the "customer" served (that is, the children) was remarkable. This is a clear example of the type of collaboration being recommended by Fallot and Harris (2009).

The impact of this collaborative approach on the "customer" (i.e. the children) was extraordinary. Within a few months of attending the Casa dei Bambini, the crying, frightened children who had entered 58 Via di Marsi, on January 7, 1907, for the inaugural celebration of the opening of the school, had changed almost beyond recognition. Physically they looked healthier, though there had been no change to their diet, socially they had changed from being shy and fretful to being confident and sociable, emotionally, they were stronger and more resilient, psychologically, they appeared to be on the road to healing from their experiences of adversity (Montessori, 1936). Many factors account for this but one factor in particular had a decisive influence for good on their mental health and that was the collaborative environment that Montessori had created for them, in which there was a very real sharing of power (and responsibility) in the day to day running of the school. This collaboration was also extended to the parents of the children (most of whom were nonliterate) whom Montessori invited to talk at least weekly with the teacher so that they could share any information relevant to the welfare of the child. For these unschooled, nonliterate parents, this was a leveling of power differences and a sharing of power that was unheard of before and it had a very positive influence on them, making them want to become involved in the children's education. This Montessori institution, therefore, right from the outset, promoted collaboration between the teacher and the parents, collaboration among the teacher and the children, and ultimately this promoted collaboration between the children and their peers. From the point of view of childhood trauma, research shows that collaborative activity either with trusted adults or with trusted peers can be healing for children who have experienced trauma because it removes the feeling of being separate from others often felt by children who have experienced adversity or trauma (Craig, 2016).

Relational neurobiology (Ludy-Dobson & Perry, 2010) shows that although trauma often arises from relationships, healing from trauma often happens in relationships with trusted adults or peers. Historically, Montessori schools have always promoted collaboration and mutuality between children, both in the outdoor and indoor environments. Montessori was very clear about the human biological tendency to reach out to others and collaborate with them. Archival photographs of Montessori's early schools show the numerous ways the children naturally and spontaneously collaborated with each other and offered mutual support to each other, in carrying out the necessary tasks and activities during the school day. For example, there are photographs of the very impoverished children (some of whom were homeless) in the St Angelo school in Pescheria, collaborating to carry heavy classroom materials such as the geometric cabinet down the long flight of steps to the courtyard so that they could do their activities together outdoors.

Other photographs, some taken in the large gardens of the Via Guisti school, situated in the Franciscan nuns' convent, show two or three children serving ladles of soup to their classmates while the other little servers walked around the long beautifully laid out tables carrying large jugs of water with which they filled each child's glass, managing, for the most part, not to spill a drop. Eyewitnesses noted that if a drop of water did happen to spill, some of the smaller children would rush over with cloths to clean it up, thrilled to be collaborating with, and offering mutual support to, the servers of the day, and longing for their turn to come later in the week (Fisher, 1912). Other photographs depict children in the outdoors happily collaborating in kitchen work, such as washing, drying, and stacking plates following the communal midday meal in an orderly and systematic fashion. Still more photographs show small groups of children happily sweeping courtyards together with brooms, digging and weeding gardens together, and transferring soil from one place to another in wheelbarrows together. Everywhere, in these archival photographs, there is evidence of calm and joyful collaboration and mutuality. Montessori spoke clearly of the vital importance of collaboration for the human child and the necessity for children to be allowed to follow their biological instinct to collaborate with others.

In the lecture she gave in Kodaikanal, on the design of schools both indoors and outdoors, Montessori recommended that even when working in the garden, weeding, harvesting, and so on, the children should collaborate. She said that she rejected the idea of a garden where individual children work alone on their own strips of land. Standing also emphasized the importance of mutual aid rather than competition in Montessori environments. He states:

> Far from trying to outdo each other, or displaying any jealousy, these children are always helping one another. The older and more advanced show a keen interest in the progress of the younger and more backward; and it is often quite touching to observe the way in which the former regard the triumphs of the latter with as much joy as if they had been their own achievements
>
> (Standing, 1957, p. 177).

Standing attributes much of this mutual aid to the fact that Montessori classrooms do not have horizontal grading according to age, but rather have mixed age groups, which promotes mutuality and collaboration (1957). From the start, Montessori employed the two practices, mixed age groups and peer teaching, to promote collaboration and mutuality between children. These two practices need to be present as much as possible in contemporary Montessori schools to promote collaboration between children.

How mixed age groups and peer teaching promote collaboration between children

Contemporary Montessori schools promote collaboration by adhering to the principle of having mixed age groups in the classes, because when age groups are mixed (i.e., children from 3 to 6, 6 to 9, or 9 to12 years, in the same class), children will naturally show a tendency to collaborate and help each other and peer teaching spontaneously becomes the norm. Many eyewitnesses to the early Montessori schools were hugely impressed by the way that the mixture of age groups naturally and spontaneously led to peer teaching which promoted collaboration among the children. George (1912) wrote that she never ceased to be impressed by the fact that the Montessori approach made it possible for children of different ages to work together. She referred to the admirable way the older children helped the younger ones, and the younger ones looked up to the older ones (George, 1912).

In a 3–6 classroom, many of the activities that promote collaboration are spontaneous activities that arise in the course of daily life. For example, when children arrive at school, a six-year-old child may notice that his three-year-old classmate is having trouble opening the buttons on his coat, or the laces on his boots, and the older child may feel a compulsion to offer help. This offer may be politely refused if the younger child feels a desire to conquer the challenge of buttons and laces himself that day, but if not, a happy collaboration may arise and there will be benefits for both sides. The younger child will feel loved and cared for by his older classmate and the older child will feel that he is a useful and important member of the community. Similarly, necessary daily tasks, such as washing, drying, and stacking dishes, provide perfect opportunities for collaboration, as do sweeping, dusting, scrubbing tables, washing dish cloths, hanging out clothes to dry, and generally keeping the classroom tidy inside and out.

From 6 to 12 years, children move into what Montessori called the Second Plane of Development, a period in which "The children's focus shifts from individual formation to development as social beings" (Lillard, 1996, p. 44). During this period of development, the child feels a strong urge to join with others and form social groups or gangs. In Montessori communities for children from 6 to 12 (which are usually subdivided into 6–9 and 9–12 communities), children naturally and spontaneously collaborate with each other. However, for children who have been affected by trauma, collaborative activities, which ultimately will be so beneficial to them, may initially pose difficulties that teachers need to be aware of. First, trauma-affected children's tendency to mis-read facial expressions and misunderstand tones of voice may cause problems for them, so if teachers are aware of this tendency, they can take steps to pre-empt the kinds of misunderstandings that could be triggering for a trauma-affected child. For example, the teacher might need to initially pair the trauma-affected child with a small group of one or possibly two other children who have quiet personalities and would be less likely to trigger a trauma reaction in the trauma-affected child than if he/she were in a group with children with more exuberant personalities.

In terms of activities that promote collaboration, the teacher trying to help a trauma-affected child would be wise to focus initially on activities that involve patterned, repetitive, rhythmic movements because they calm the amygdala and can prevent any activation of the stress response. For example, a trauma-affected child who is new to a 6–9 or 9–12 community might collaborate very well with another child on an outdoor activity such as painting a fence, raking leaves, shoveling snow, washing and polishing a car, or indoor activities such as kneading bread dough, icing a cake, and cutting up vegetables or fruits. Because peer-teaching is such a spontaneous occurrence when children are in a mixed-age setting, it is inevitable that trauma-affected new children will soon find themselves either being taught something by a child who is older than them, or they will find themselves being asked by a child who is younger than them for help with an activity or task. Both of these scenarios can be healing for trauma-affected children, because being shown how to do something by someone who is not that much older than oneself can build bonds between children, and build a sense of community and belonging, and similarly, being asked to teach something to a younger child can build children's self-esteem. These two factors – mixed age groups and peer teaching – are the keys to collaboration between children in Montessori classes. The following vignette illustrates this:

Vignette

Six-and-a-half-year-old Trevor is a newcomer to the 6–9 community at Oakwood Montessori School. For the first three days, he kept his coat on and never looked anyone in the eye, keeping his gaze down at the floor if anyone approached him. He constantly jerked his head around to look behind him as if he suspected that someone was about to jump on him. His mom had not revealed very much about his previous schools except to say that he had attended a Montessori children's house for two years from his third to his fifth birthday which he loved and was thriving at, but for personal reasons, she had to take him out because she had to move to a different state. She said that for the last 18 months, Trevor had attended a public school that did not offer a Montessori program. She stated sadly that she had only recently found out that for most of his time at this public school, Trevor had been bullied both physically and psychologically. For reasons she still did not understand, Trevor concealed the bullying from her. She also said that she and her former husband had divorced just before her move to the new state and Trevor had a lot of new "stuff" in his life to deal with, including his dad's new wife and her three sons, all older than Trevor who were now being blended into his new family. Trevor went on regular visits to his father's house but often did not enjoy the visits. His mom suspected that one of the sons, now Trevor's half-sibling might be bullying Trevor while he was on access visits.

Taking this mixture of fact and supposition into account, the teacher (Amy) in this lower elementary Montessori school was understanding and compassionate and started to build a picture in her head of what life might be like now for Trevor and what things might be triggering for him in this new school. She did a number of things which were ultimately to prove immensely important in helping Trevor to survive and thrive despite the pain and confusion he was experiencing from the recent traumatic events that had changed his life. First, she applied a trauma-informed lens, and so was enabled to understand that the impact of trauma might cause Trevor to act in ways that might seem irrational, ungrateful, and just plain inexplicable at times, until healing started. Second, she understood that if she could identify Trevor's strengths she might be able to help build on them. Third, she understood Trevor would need to know the name of an emotionally attuned adult available to him at all times during school hours so that if he ever wished to talk or confide in someone he would know who to approach and would know that this person (or a designated replacement) was always available to be a non-judgmental listening ear. Fourth, she knew that Trevor needed to be allowed whatever time was necessary for him to feel safe and comfortable enough to speak to and eventually collaborate with other children.

It took a week before Trevor felt safe enough to raise his eyes and look at the teacher and the other children. During this period, the teacher had always made sure to give a gentle smile in Trevor's direction whenever she slowly walked past the small table by the entrance door that Trevor sat at each day. Toward the end of that week, she had "tested the water" by quietly offering a high five to Trevor as she passed, but he acted as though he didn't see her hand. At the very end of the week, she noticed that Trevor seemed to slowly raise his hand as she approached his table, so quietly and gently she raised her hand for a high five, and to her great (but very controlled) delight, Trevor touched her hand. She would have given anything to just hug Trevor, but she did not, because she knew that to do that could spoil everything. She continued her slow, gentle, and measured approach and the next week, Trevor not only raised his hand toward Amy as she walked by his table, but smiled at her. Her heart melted with compassion for this young child. Things got better each day from then on and by the end of the first month, Trevor had started to collaborate with other children first doing activities that did not involve very much speech, such as helping other children to carry tables to different parts of the room, then he slowly but surely moved on to collaborative activities that did involve speech.

These two elements (mixed age groups and peer teaching), which for a long time were unique to Montessori schools, encourage high levels of collaborative activities among the children, which in turn promote a strong sense of community and connectedness to others. This sense of community and connectedness has been shown to be vital in the healing of trauma-affected children (Perry & Szalavitz, 2006/2017; Perry & Winfrey, 2021; Treisman, 2017).

Examining how *empowerment, voice, and choice* are promoted in Montessori schools

Another of the core principles of trauma-informed practice is the concept of empowerment, voice, and choice (Fallot & Harris, 2009). In their 2014 document, SAMHSA explains that in a trauma-informed organization, the experiences and strengths of individuals or groups should be recognized and built on and the organization should foster a belief in the capacity of people, whether they are individuals or groups, to heal from trauma, and to actively promote recovery from traumatic experiences. As such, a trauma-informed organization promotes empowerment for both staff and clients alike. It recognizes that historically both voice and choice in organizations have often been diminished and were frequently replaced by treatment that was essentially authoritarian (SAMHSA, 2014). To mitigate against these practices, a trauma-informed organization should seek to empower the trauma-affected individual by (1) helping them to develop the skills needed to speak up for themselves, (2) ensuring that the voice of the service user is heard, and (3) making sure to offer choice to the service user.

Empowerment

When Montessori set out to help the children with developmental difficulties from the psychiatric hospitals in 1897, and then the children of San Lorenzo in 1907, she was aware that in the schools of her day "empowerment," "voice," and "choice" were ideas that were not just frowned upon but were in fact – anathema, and authoritarian approaches were the norm. Going totally against the grain, Montessori, building on the work of her predecessors (Boyd, 1917), created exercises and activities for children that were essentially skill-building, and therefore they very quickly promoted empowerment in the children. For example, she introduced low sinks, lessons on hand washing, nose-blowing, dressing frames, and lessons on how to fasten buttons, laces, hooks, and eyes, and so gave the children the opportunity to learn how to wash and dress themselves, all of which promoted their independence (and dignity). She introduced Care of the Self and Care of the Environment exercises and activities, all of which, once again, promoted independence and empowerment in the children. She introduced sandpaper letters and numbers that circumvented the children's low levels of sequential memory function (caused by the instability of lifestyle the children were exposed to) which would have prevented them from learning to read, write, and numerate, and instead she introduced mathematical and literacy materials that relied on "muscle memory" rather than sequential memory, which opened the door to the children's precocious "explosion" into writing, followed by reading and mathematical accomplishments (see Chapter 10 for more on sequential memory). She refused to use traditional school desks which she said constrained the child and pinned him down, and replaced them with light tables so that the children could move them around and even take them outside should they decide to work in the outdoors. These practices had a significant impact on the children's sense of empowerment. Eyewitnesses commented frequently on the remarkable level of confidence and empowerment evident in the children (Fisher, 1912; George, 1912; Tozier, 1911; White, 1914). This sense of confidence and empowerment came about through the children's growing mastery of skills, especially Practical Life skills, which led to their subsequent independence (Montessori, 1936). Achieving independence is very important for children who have been traumatized because it enables them to have some level of control over their lives, thereby leading directly to a sense of empowerment. This can have therapeutic benefits for trauma-affected children because it mitigates against the sense of helplessness and powerlessness that often accompanies traumatic experiences (Treisman, 2017).

In contemporary Montessori schools, empowerment in the children is once again promoted by helping the children to gain skills. In the 3–6 classroom (usually called a Primary classroom), this will take the form of giving lessons to the children on Care of the Self – how to wash their hands, comb their hair, do up buttons, zips, fasteners, and laces; Care of their Environment – how to scrub tables, wash bowls plates and cutlery, wash windows, dust shelves, arrange flowers in vases, fold clothes, sweep floors, and use a vacuum cleaner. Academic skills, such as how to write, read, and numerate, are learned by indirect exercises so that the child often is not aware of having being "taught" these skills. In the 6–12 classroom (usually called an Elementary classroom), practical shills may include how to fix a bicycle puncture, how to put up a tent, how to prepare a simple meal, how to cook food in the outdoors, and how to pack a bag for a hike in the forest. Academic skills are now approached in a very practical way so that a child can readily see their purpose, for example, children may use their reading skills to read to older people or people with visual impairments in care facilities. In 12–15 and 15–18 Montessori environments (usually called Erdkinder meaning "children of the land"), empowerment may be promoted through the learning of skills such as how to do a basic service on a car, how to build an outhouse, how to plant, harvest and sell produce, how to prepare, cook and sell foods, how to create small businesses such as a café or craft shop, how to play a musical instrument – guitar, drums, keyboard, or other culturally relevant instrument, how to organize a social event for others, especially those considered to be in some way vulnerable or disadvantaged. All of these activities lead to the development of "empowerment" in children and young people. A sense of empowerment is a vital need for all human beings, but it is crucial for trauma-affected children and young people because the experience of trauma usually leaves people with a profound sense of being disempowered.

Voice and choice

From its inception, the Montessori approach offered "voice" and "choice" to children in matters that affected them. Freedom of choice is fundamental to the Montessori approach at all levels. When Montessori first worked with mentally challenged children in 1897, she recorded how she allowed them to choose what they wanted to work with. She wrote that as soon as they entered the institute (the Orthophrenic School) they were invited to select whatever material they wanted to work with (Montessori, 2008). Montessori later discovered when she began her work with typically developing children in 1907 (through an accident when the teacher forgot to lock the cupboard, and the children selected their own materials) just how important "choice" is for children, and how they have a real need to be allowed to choose their own work (1936). She came to realize that freedom of choice is empowering for children. It is especially empowering for trauma-affected children who are usually placed in positions where there are power imbalances and they have no voice or choice about what happens to them. Montessori schools are unique in the way they have, since their inception, facilitated voice and choice. In a 3–6 classroom, choice is promoted by the orderly layout of the materials on low, open shelves in the classroom. A child (who has been shown how to use a material) is free to take that material off the shelf and work with it. If the child has not been shown how to use the material, teachers may take the opportunity to present the material to the child if they feel that the child is ready for it, or ask the child to defer using it until they have been given a presentation on how to use it. The child is also free to choose where and with whom to work. At all times, a child's freedom to choose an activity, and to choose where and with whom to work, is inseparable from the overarching principle that materials are there to stimulate constructive activity in children. Professor Angeline Lillard, a leading Montessori scholar states that "Dr Montessori believed that the environment had to be prepared to stimulate constructive activity in children" (2005).

In 6–12 classrooms, voice and choice are still very much promoted but there may be a need to comply with Education Departments' requirements to prepare children for state examinations. Here, as Montessorians, we should look back to our roots and remind ourselves that in the late 1890s, it was when Montessori presented the so-called "unteachable" children for the Italian State Examinations (which they passed), that the attention of the world was captured, and set the eyes of educators, both national and international on the newly developing Montessori approach. Although the circumstances were much different, Montessori still faced the task of preparing children for formal examinations. The key point was that she used a unique approach to preparing them that involved giving them the choice to work with materials that interested them. Contemporary Montessori teachers are in a similar situation. Children can be given the choice to work on something that captivates them whether that is sharks, volcanoes, or ballet dancers, and within this, they can be scaffolded to meet the demands of education board writing and numeracy standards. They can also be given the choice of where and with whom to work, and reasonable flexibility with regard to the completion of assigned work.

In Montessori home-schools, voice and choice may be facilitated in the same manner. For example, home-schooled children can talk to a parent or caregiver about what their current interests are, and then choose to work on content that is related to these interests for much of the day, making sure to cover the content required by the school boards. For children who are being home-schooled following a traumatic experience, having freedom of choice in what they work on is crucial because trauma-affected children have often been deprived of freedom of choice and having choice in their lives once more is a step toward empowerment. In Montessori Erdkinder, choice of what, where, and with whom to work or study is an essential part of the program for adolescents.

How cultural, historical, and gender issues can be responded to in Montessori schools

One of the core principles of trauma-informed practice involves an organization's response to cultural, historical, and gender issues (SAMHSA, 2014). How these issues can be responded to in contemporary Montessori schools is discussed below.

Cultural issues

The term culture includes the customs, traditions, beliefs, values, and behaviors of a particular social group. This may be a religious, ethnic, or racial social group. The Montessori approach, since its inception, has always acknowledged and respected diverse cultural traditions and practices, and made them an integral part of the Montessori approach to a history and geography curriculum. Brunold-Conesa states that "One component of the Montessori integrated history/geography curriculum known as the *fundamental needs of humans* helps children recognize that all people on all continents throughout history had and have the same basic needs" (2020, p. 2). Lillard et al. state that the Montessori approach aligns with culturally responsive pedagogy (CRP) (2021). As such, the Montessori approach has always leveraged the healing value of traditional cultural connections (SAMHSA, 2014). In addition, since the original Montessori approach is rooted and grounded in *respect* for every human being, regardless of race, religion, gender, or color, a thoughtful and respectful approach to multi-cultural practices has always been one of its foundational principles. Throughout her life, Maria Montessori worked in many countries, and she embraced them respectfully and regarded herself as a citizen of the world. In contemporary Montessori schools, the diverse cultures of the students and their families are celebrated through art, music, dance, and often the cooking of foods particular to a specific culture followed by the sharing of the meal later on with the children/young people and their families. Books, photographs, and artifacts representing the countries and cultures of the children and families attending the schools are proudly displayed in corridors in order to help the children and families from these countries and cultures to feel welcomed, respected, and above all feel a sense of belonging.

Historical issues

Historically, many people of various races, skin colors, and creeds have been discriminated against and alienated by others who view their own ethnicity as being superior one. Dr. Bruce Perry talks about the toxic stress that can build up in people when people feel a sense that they don't belong, that they have the wrong skin color, religion, gender, culture, or background. He emphasizes that humans are relational beings and inherently social. We are biologically programmed to seek belonging and community. We are directed by our brain to judge whether or not we belong in the environments we find ourselves in. If we get a sense from our peers and from our teachers that we belong, we feel safe. If we do not get this sense that we belong, we feel threatened (Perry, Insights for Educators, ThinkTVPBS, 2020).

Quality contemporary Montessori schools often go to great lengths to make sure children and families of each and every skin color, culture, and creed, are welcomed and are given a sense that they belong to the community they've joined. These simple practices by teachers and other school staff can have hugely positive repercussions. Perry points out that teachers often feel "paralyzed" and helpless when faced with the enormity of the problems associated with race, multi-cultures, diversity and inclusion, yet these small practices, such as helping children and their families to feel that they belong by showing respect for their culture and heritage and welcoming them and their culture into the Montessori community can have huge repercussions and protect those children and their families from the toxic stress associated with feeling that you don't belong (Perry, Insights for Educators, ThinkTVPBS, 2020). Contemporary Montessori teachers have the power to do that, and it costs nothing. We may not share the same language, skin color, culture, or traditions of the people who come to our classrooms, but we share the same need to feel loved, to belong, and to be part of a community. We must never forget what Montessori wrote about the children in her first school, and how she made them feel wanted and welcomed (2008). People remember how you make them feel, and how you make them feel can be a source of healing to them.

Gender issues

Montessori was very conscious of gender issues. She was born at a time and in a country when huge numbers of the population suffered discrimination and prejudice simply because they were born female. Women could not vote, were prevented from entering many professions on the basis of their gender, were deprived of property rights, earned a fraction of the wage a man received for doing the same work, needed their father or husband's permission to go to a doctor, and faced countless other daily humiliations simply because they were born female. Gender issues weighed heavily on Montessori and she took many brave steps even from a young age to bring to the attention of the world, the injustices that women and subsequently children face because of the patriarchal and unjust nature of the structure of societies.

For example, in August, 1896, just a month after her graduation as a medical doctor, Montessori was chosen by the Roman Women's Association to represent the women of Italy at an international women's congress to be held in Berlin in September (Kramer, 1976). There she captivated her audience of over three thousand women (Povell, 2010), carefully avoiding factions by making it clear that she was speaking about injustices against women and not their political parties (Kramer, 1976). She received rapturous applause for her speeches (and pages of media attention on her good looks and femininity, which infuriated her as such comments were not typically written about male speakers) and she returned from the conference determined to fight against the social determinants of physical and mental ill-health which she identified as poverty and discrimination, especially discrimination against women. In keeping with Montessori's passionate concern for the equality of men and women and sensitivity to gender issues, authentic, contemporary Montessori schools should always be careful to follow in Montessori's footsteps and offer a school experience that does not offend any student or their caregivers on the basis of gender.

How the Montessori approach moves past cultural stereotypes and biases (SAMHSA, 2014)

Montessori was one of the first educators to create exercises and activities that are gender neutral and to offer activities to both boys and girls that were traditionally regarded as being gender specific, and this practice continues in contemporary Montessori schools. For example, from the outset, Montessori involved both boys and girls in practical life exercises such as food preparation, laying tables for meals, serving meals, cleaning up after meals, dish washing, clothes washing, clothes folding, sweeping, scrubbing, polishing, and so on. Similarly, she made available to both girls and boys at all ages and levels mathematical and science exercises and materials that allowed for the development of the minds of girls and boys equally. This practice is still in evidence from the Montessori Infant Communities to the Erdkinder settings. In addition, because Montessori laid more emphasis on reality-based activities rather than fantasy-based activities, there is less emphasis in Montessori settings on gender-specific activities such as playing princesses or playing super heroes. In summary, the emphasis on gender-neutral activities, which has been a part of Montessori pedagogy since its inception, is helpful from the point of view of gender issues and takes the pressure off children who may not want to play what they perceive as "boy's games" or "girl's games."

How DEI and ABAR principles can be responded to in Montessori schools

Henfield et al. (2019) state that "It feels dishonest and disingenuous for conversations about trauma and trauma-informed care to occur without considering how racism and other forms of social oppression pervade social systems and institutions" (p. 541). With the exception of Montessori's efforts to set up free trauma-informed programs during the period of WWI, the contemporary trauma-informed movement is relatively young and is far from perfect. One aspect of TIP that has been criticized is its failure to explicitly address systemic or institutionalized trauma. This is a type of trauma caused by the "big" systems most people have to engage with at some point in their lives such as the healthcare system, the educational system, or the justice system. Examples of how the educational system can cause harm abound, for example, research shows that a Black or Latinx child from a low-income family and district will face a higher chance of being excluded from school for behavior issues than a white child (Morris, 2016), and this harsher treatment may well lead them on a well-trodden course from juvenile hall to jail. This research provides a classic example of how some educational systems have tended to criticize the behaviors of children of color rather than provide supports or resources to help them.

In a timely publication entitled, *Equity Examined*, Mira Debs states that "There is a long history of structural racism in the United States and other countries around the world" and that this influences all of us (Wafford & Debs, 2023, p. 20). She goes on to explain that structural racism basically means that powerful structures such as institutions and law-makers, allocate power to one group rather than another. She states that in many countries racial hierarchies have been constructed wherein Indigenous and Black people are placed at the lower echelons of the social system. In addition, she points out that schools, being a major social institution, must be recognized as being part of this pattern of structural racism. She argues that schools have both provided opportunities to individual students, while at the same time created inequalities for some students, by following practices that are inherently discriminatory. Debs addresses the question of how Montessori schools stand in the midst of this, she asks if they have a special status as an anti-bias, anti-racist form of education, as many Montessori educators believe, or is this a myth? Debs sees this view as a myth. She argues that the Montessori approach is not automatically an anti-bias, anti-racist method, but rather "is influenced by teacher and social contexts of racism and other forms of systemic bias" (Wafford & Debs, 2023, p. 20). She asserts that as Montessori educators, we have a duty to educate ourselves about racism both in our own countries and beyond and subsequently change our practices for the better by using this knowledge. She argues that the fact that the majority of Montessori schools charge fees is in itself a significant equity issue, because it favors the children of higher-income families (who in many States, are mostly white children) and excludes those with a lower SES status, (who, in many States, are mostly BIPOC [Black, Indigenous and people of color]). Debs also points out that even when a Montessori school is government funded, that is, a public school, there can still be barriers preventing some families from enrolling, such as the need for families to provide meals and transport to and from the schools at their own expense. She also points out that the desirability of Montessori schools can even be the cause of gentrification and displacement. She quotes one Oklahoma teacher who told her that after a public Montessori school opened in her city, there was a 50% increase in property values around the school. This gentrification of localities obviously makes it difficult, and often impossible, because of high rents, for low-income families to live there (Debs, 2019).

Slade (2021) states that "if we are committed to an education for peace, then we must ensure that we are making the Montessori method available to all children and educators" (p. 28). Slade advises us to ask ourselves questions about our schools such as: "are all the Montessori trained teachers in the school white and all the assistants people of the global majority?" (p. 29). She also urges us to examine our attitudes and policies to see if they are (even inadvertently) promoting structural racism. She states that awareness of racial identity begins in the first plane of development, when children are in the first six years of their lives and that "by the end of the first plane, children of color are aware of their racial group and the negative stereotypes associated with it" (p. 32). She argues that because of this racial awareness in young children, adults' awareness of racial issues and willingness to talk about them in Montessori classrooms is important. She says that honest conversations are needed to examine and turn around the silent beliefs that underlie inequity (Slade, 2021).

Brunold-Conese (2022) writes that although DEI and ABAR are intrinsic to Montessori philosophy, they are not always put into practice in every classroom. She adds that although the terms DEI and ABAR were historically not part of Montessori's lexicon, the principles they embody were part of that lexicon and are still central to Montessori's philosophy of Peace Education and arguably if Montessori were still here, she would advocate for their place in her educational model. With regard to inclusion in Montessori classrooms, Moss and Epstein state that research shows that both typically developing children and children with disabilities in America benefit from Montessori schools that are inclusive and typically developing children who attend inclusive schools see differences among their peers as something completely natural (Moss & Epstein, 2023).

Summary of Chapter 8

1. **Safety:** factors that promote psychological safety in the Montessori classroom are: non-verbal signals such as tone of voice; facial expressions; and body language; and the abolition of awards/punishments; the use of self-correcting materials; and the promotion of positive relational interactions between the teachers and the children.
2. Factors that promote physical safety in the Montessori classroom are the reduction and sometimes elimination of bullying in the indoor and outdoor environments.
3. There is a need for educators to understand that for some children what looks like behavioral challenges are actually survival strategies.
4. **Trustworthiness and transparency:** historically, Montessori promoted transparency, by inviting parents into the classroom and even constructing a glass classroom in 1915. Contemporary schools should emulate this transparency as appropriate to their setting.

5 **Peer support:** peer support can be achieved through the promotion of positive relational interactions between teachers and children, and between children and peers.
6 **Collaboration and mutuality:** these principles are promoted through having mixed age groups, peer teaching, and an absence of the competitive spirit.
7 **Empowerment, voice, and choice:** these principles are promoted through practical skill building, and academic achievement.
8 **Cultural, historical, and gender issues**: the Montessori approach aligns with culturally relevant pedagogy (CRP), and gender issues have traditionally been supported in Montessori schools.
9 **DEI and ABAR** principles in Montessori schools: Montessori educators have a duty to educate ourselves about racism both in our own countries and beyond and then use this knowledge to inform and if necessary, change our practices.

Questions for group discussion

1 How would you promote physical and psychological safety in your Montessori classroom?
2 How would you integrate transparency into your Montessori setting?
3 Discuss her peer support is promoted in contemporary Montessori schools.
4 Give examples of collaboration and mutuality in a Montessori classroom.
5 How are empowerment voice and choice promoted in contemporary Montessori schools?
6 Discuss how cultural, historical, and gender issues are responded to in contemporary Montessori schools.
7 Your opinion how are DEI and ABAR principles responded to in contemporary Montessori schools.

References

Bailey, C. S. (1915). *Montessori children*. Holt
Bomber, L. (2020). *Know me to teach me: Differentiated discipline for those recovering from adverse childhood experiences*. Worth Publishing.
Boyd, W. (1917). *From Locke to Montessori: A critical account of the Montessori point of view*. Harrap & Company.
Brunold-Conesa, C. (2020). Culturally responsive pedagogy: An intersection with Montessori Education. https://www.researchgate.net/publication/339828022

Brunold-Conesa, C. (2022). Montessori with integrity – Part 2. DEI and ABAR practices as essential to quality program implementation. *MontessoriLife*. American Montessori Society. https://amshq.org/Blog/2022-11-14

Craig, S. E. (2016). *Trauma sensitive schools: Learning communities transforming children's lives, K–5* (Illustrated ed.). Teachers College Press.

De Stefano, C. (2022). *The child is the teacher, a life of Maria Montessori*. Other Press.

Debs, M. (2019). *Diverse families, desirable schools: Public Montessori in the era of school of choice*. Harvard Education Press.

Fallot, R. D., & Harris, M. (2009). Creating cultures of trauma-informed care: A self-assessment and planning protocol. *Community Connections*. https://doi.org/10.13140/2.1.4843.6002

Fisher, D. C. (1912). *A Montessori mother*. Henry Holt & Company.

George, A. E. (1912). Dr. Maria Montessori: The achievement and personality of an Italian woman whose discovery is revolutionizing educational methods. *Good Housekeeping*, 55(1), 24–29.

Henfield, M., Washington, A. R., Besirevic, Z., & De La Rue, L. (2019). Introduction to trauma-informed practices for mental health and wellness in urban schools and communities. *Urban Review, 51*, 537–539. https://doi.org/10.1007/s11256-019-00541-2

Holloway, K., Cahill, G., Tieu, T., & Njoroge, W. (2023). Reviewing the literature on the impact of gun violence on early childhood development. *Current Psychiatry Reports, 25*(7), 273–281. https://doi.org/10.1007/s11920-023-01428-6

Hughes, D., & Golding, K. (2012). *Creating loving attachments: Parenting with PACE to nurture confidence and security in the troubled child*. Jessica Kingsley.

Jennings, P. A. (2019). *The trauma-sensitive classroom: Building resilience with compassionate teaching*. W. W. Norton & Company.

Kramer, R. (1976). *Maria Montessori: A biography*. Addison-Wesley.

Lillard, A. (2005). *Montessori: The science behind the genius*. Oxford University Press.

Lillard, P. P. (1996). *Montessori today: A comprehensive approach to education from birth to adulthood*. Doubleday Publishing Group.

Lillard, A. S., & Else-Quest, N. (2006). Evaluating Montessori education. *Science, 313*(5795), 1893–1894. https://doi.org/10.1126/science.1132362

Lillard, A. S., Taggart, J., Yonas, D., & Seale, M. N. (2021). An alternative to "no excuses": Considering Montessori as culturally responsive pedagogy. *Journal of Negro Education*, 1–32.

Ludy-Dobson, C., & Perry, B. D. (2010). The role of healthy relational interactions in buffering the impact of childhood trauma. In E. Gil (Ed.) *Working with children to heal interpersonal trauma: The power of play*. The Guilford Press.

Montessori, M. (1967). *The absorbent mind* (C. A. Claremont, Trans). Dell. (Original work published 1949)

Montessori, M. (1936). *The secret of childhood* (B. B. Carter, Ed. and Trans.). Longmans.

Montessori, M. (1964). *The Montessori method* (A. E. George, Trans.). Schocken Books. (Original work published 1912)

Montessori, M. (2008). *The California lectures of Maria Montessori, 1915: Collected speeches and writings* (R. Buckenmeyer, Ed.). *The Clio Montessori series*. Montessori-Pierson.

Montessori, M. (2013). The house of children, lecture, Kodaikanal, 1944. *NAMTA Journal, 38*(1), 11–19.

Morris, M. (2016). *Pushout: The criminalisation of black girls in schools*. The New Press.

Moss, J. D., & Epstein, A.. (2023). Montessori education and inclusion. In A. Murray, E.-M. T. Ahlquist, M. McKenna, & M. Debs (Eds.) *The Bloomsbury handbook of Montessori education*. (2023). Bloomsbury.

Perry, B. D. (1999). Memories of fear: How the brain stores and retrieves physiological states, feelings, behaviors and thoughts from traumatic events. In J. Goodwin, & R. Attias (Ed.), *Splintered reflections: Images of the body in trauma*. Basic Books.

Perry, B. D., & Szalavitz, M. (2017). *The boy who was raised as a dog and other stories from a child psychiatrist's notebook: What traumatized children can teach us about loss, love and healing*. Basic Books. (Original work published 2006)

Perry, B. D., & Winfrey, O. (2021). *What happened to you? Conversations on trauma, resilience, and healing*. Pan Macmillan.

Porges, S. (2004). Neuroception: A subconscious system for detecting threats and safety. *Zero to Three: Bulletin of the National Centre for Clinical Infant Programs (J), 24*(5), 19–24.

Povell, P. (2010). *Montessori comes to America: The leadership of Maria Montessori and Nancy McCormick Rambusch*. University Press of America.

Preschlack, P. (2023). *The Montessori potential: How to foster independence, respect, and joy in every child*. Chicago Review Press.

Randolph, J. J., Bryson, A., Menon, L., Henderson, D. K., Kureethara Manuel, A., Michaels, S., Rosenstein, D. L. W., McPherson, W., O'Grady, R., & Lillard, A. S. (2023). Montessori education's impact on academic and nonacademic outcomes: A systematic review. *Campbell Systematic Reviews, 19*, e1330.https://doi.org/10.1002/cl2.1330

Substance Abuse and Mental Health Services Administration (SAMHSA), (2014). SAMHSA's concept of trauma and guidance for a trauma-informed approach. https://store.samhsa.gov/shin/content/SMA14-4884/SMA-4884.pdf

Slade, E. (2021). *Montessori in action: Building resilient Montessori schools*. Jossey-Bass.

Sobe, N. W. (2004). Challenging the gaze: The subject of attention and a 1915 Montessori demonstration classroom. *Educational Theory, 54*(3), 281–297.

Standing, E. M. (1957). *Maria Montessori: Her life and work*. Plume.

ThinkTVPBS. (2020, August 25). Stress, trauma, and the brain: Insights for educators-the power of connection [video]. YouTube. https://www.youtube.com/watch?v=_3is_3XHKKs

Tozier, J. (1911). An educational wonder-worker: The methods of Maria Montessori. *McClure's Magazine, 37*(1), 3–19.

Treisman, K. (2017). *Working with relational and developmental trauma in children and adolescents*. Routledge.

van der Kolk, B. A. (2003). The neurobiology of childhood trauma and abuse. *Child and Adolescent Psychiatric Clinics of North America, 12*(2), 293. https://doi.org/10.1016/s1056-4993(03)00003-8

Wafford, M., & Debs, M.. (2023). Countering myths in Montessori education. In *Equity examined: How to design schools and teacher education programs where everyone thrives*. American Montessori Society (AMS). (amshq.org).

White, J. (1914). *Montessori schools: As seen in the early summer of 1913*. H. Milford. Oxford University Press.

Wright, T. (2019). Growing Hope: Developing supportive Montessori classrooms for traumatized children. *Montessori Collaborative World Review, 1*(1), 134–145.

Wright, T. (2023). *Emotionally responsive teaching: Expanding trauma informed practice with young children*. Teachers College Press.

9 How the four TIP assumptions can be incorporated into Montessori schools

Chapter objectives

- To show how Montessori staff can be helped to **realize** the pervasive impact of trauma.
- To provide examples of how to **recognize** the possible signs and symptoms of trauma.
- To show how Montessori schools can **respond** to trauma in policies and practices.
- To examine how Montessori schools can **resist** re-traumatization of students (SAMHSA, 2014).

Learning outcomes

At the end of this chapter, the learner will know why a Montessori-TIP approach should:

- **Realize** the pervasiveness of trauma and comprehend the possible routes to recovery.
- Know how to **Recognize** the signs and symptoms of trauma in their students and others.
- **Respond** by incorporating knowledge about trauma into policies, and practices.
- **Resist** re-traumatization of students, their families, and school staff in an active manner (SAMHSA, 2014).

Considering how Montessori schools can realize the widespread impact of trauma

Quality TIP programs are crucial for Montessori educators to realize the pervasive impact of trauma and understand the possible paths for recovery (SAMHSA, 2014). During the years 1916/1917, Montessori showed a strong understanding of the necessity for teachers and nurses to realize the widespread impact of trauma, especially on children affected by wars and natural disasters, and to understand the potential paths for recovery. It is recorded that she went to extraordinary efforts (even writing to the Pope) to get support for the establishment of an organization (the White Cross), which would, among other things, provide free interdisciplinary TIP programs to help teachers and nurses understand how to support children adversely affected by wars and natural disasters (Montessori, 1917/2013). She clearly saw the necessity of integrating interdisciplinary knowledge on trauma along with Montessori teacher training. She also showed remarkable insight into the risks posed by unaddressed childhood trauma on later adult health and well-being (Phillips, 2023). Moreover, she anticipated research in epigenetics by her statements that the harm caused to children by exposure to trauma had the capacity to be passed on to future generations (Montessori, 1917/2013).

It is incumbent on contemporary Montessori schools to follow in Montessori's footsteps and participate in TIP programs which provide interdisciplinary knowledge about trauma and its potential effects on families and communities, as well as individuals (SAMHSA, 2014). Contemporary Montessori schools should have a basic understanding of why behaviors need to be viewed and understood in the context of coping strategies, which some individuals (both children and adults) may have had to use in order to survive adversity and circumstances that overwhelmed them. This understanding may apply not just to the children who attend the schools, but also to their family members, and members of the school staff. Traumatic events which are impacting the children, their families, or school staff members may relate to the past (e.g., prior neglect or abuse), the present (e.g., ongoing trauma such as domestic violence in the home, racism in the community), or they may be related to secondary traumatic stress (e.g., experienced by someone who is directly involved in the care of a trauma-affected person). This "realization" also includes understanding that exposure to traumatic events can play a role in mental ill-health, as well as substance misuse disorders SAMHSA, 2014). The original ACE study (Felitti et al., 1998) starkly demonstrated this potential connection.

Outlining how Montessori schools can recognize the signs/symptoms of trauma

Once again, quality interdisciplinary TIP programs are crucial for Montessori educators to be able to recognize the signs and symptoms of trauma in children and young people. In Montessori schools, teachers should be alert to certain behaviors which may be important such as:

In the 3–6 classroom

- Reluctance to shake hands or look at the teacher on arrival in the mornings. This could be associated with feelings of shame, especially if the child is experiencing sexual abuse, although it should be recognized that other factors such as introversion may be at play here.
- Sleepiness early in the day, including falling asleep in class or in the playground. This could be associated with inability to sleep if arguments or domestic violence in the home are preventing the child from sleeping at night. Again, however, it should be noted that many other factors may lead to daytime sleepiness such as poor diet, lack of exercise, excessive screen time, chronic illness, or a poor sleep routine. In addition, children may feel sleepy if they go to school without having had any food, but it must also be noted that in some cases, this may be because the child has a poor appetite and will not eat in the mornings, and in other cases, it may be due to poverty or neglect.
- Irritability or anger outbursts for no apparent reason. This may indicate that children are experiencing levels of stress that are overwhelming for them.
- Defiant attitude toward teachers and peers. What looks like defiance in young children is often a cover for fear – so when adults ask them to do something, they may act as if they haven't heard, or they may refuse to comply (Perry et al., 1995). The child may feel a need to be constantly in defense mode and so appears to be uncooperative toward teachers and peers alike. Teachers should avoid a stand-off when children behave like this because what the child most needs is to feel safe and to feel that there is someone they can trust. Teachers should stoop down so that they do not appear threatening to the child and use a quiet tone of voice and positive facial expressions, and body language to help calm the child. In quality Montessori classrooms, this is standard practice.

In the 6–12 classroom

- A lack of concentration, or inability to focus, especially if the child normally has good concentration, could indicate (other factors considered) that the child is experiencing overwhelming stress. This may be coming directly from the child's home, because of exposure to violence or domestic abuse in the home, or it may be coming from outside of the home, e.g., the child may be experiencing bullying and not telling the family about it, or the child may be experiencing abuse at the hands of a family relative or friend. The child may be hypervigilant, which, as explained earlier, can also affect concentration.
- Absorption in academic work with no sign of joy or satisfaction. This could indicate that the child is experiencing stress and is using work to distract themselves from having to think about the stressful situation.
- Looking sad or anxious, biting fingernails, pulling at hair, losing patches of hair. These are often signs of distress and anxiety and suggest that a child needs to have a trusted, emotionally attuned, adult in whom to confide.

- Changes in eating habits – either eating very little, over-eating, or taking other children's lunches. Sudden changes in eating habits may be a sign that a child is experiencing traumatic stress that is overwhelming for them. Once again, these could suggest that the child needs to have a trusted, emotionally attuned, adult in whom to confide.
- Aggressive behavior toward peers or teachers, with no empathy for others. This may indicate that children are experiencing levels of stress that are overwhelming for them or that they are being exposed to violent behavior in their homes, i.e., domestic abuse, or it may indicate that they are being exposed to violent video games, or films.
- Destructive behavior in school, i.e., breaking things. This may stem from pent-up emotions that may or may not be trauma-related. Many common, everyday factors including the arrival of a new baby or sibling rivalry could be at play here. However, children showing these behaviors for no obvious reason need the intervention of an emotionally attuned adult who may be able to identify the source of this behavior.

In the 12–15 classroom

- A young adolescent may show violent mood swings. In her book *From Childhood to Adolescence* (1948/1973), Montessori talked about these types of mood swings which are common in adolescence and are not necessarily associated with trauma. However, if they are perpetual, and the young person is continuously troubled, trauma may well be a factor. Once again, an emotionally attuned adult, who can relate to the adolescent and with whom the adolescent feels safe, may well be able to get to the core of the problem.
- A young adolescent may also show an inability to express his/her feelings. Again, this is not necessarily associated with trauma, although exposure to trauma should be considered if the young person shows distress at not being able to express their feelings.
- A young adolescent may show an inability to concentrate or focus on anything. Once again, this is something that Montessori commented on in her book *From Childhood to Adolescence* (Montessori, 1948/1973). She interpreted it as a characteristic of this Plane of Development, and it does not necessarily have an association with trauma. However, an inability to concentrate or focus on anything is a typical sign and symptom of exposure to trauma. Therefore, a teacher should try to observe the young person, keeping in mind the possibility that they may have had exposure to trauma.
- A young adolescent may show signs of aggressive or bullying behavior especially toward younger or more vulnerable children. This may be related to trauma (among other factors), and observation and vigilance are necessary.

In the 15–18 Erdkinder

- Eating disorders often occur in this age group. Research suggests a link between trauma and eating disorders. They may be (other factors considered) a symptom

of stress. Therefore, teachers should observe young people in this age group who may have/or are known to have an eating disorder, keeping in mind the possibility that they may have had exposure to traumatic events.
- Substance misuse is also very common in this age group. It is not necessarily related to exposure to trauma. It may well emerge as a result of peer group pressure. However, teachers should be vigilant and if they suspect substance misuse, follow the guidelines in their school policies, but be aware that a trauma-informed approach, emphasizing compassion is necessary.
- If a child in this age group is being exposed to trauma, their academic performance may show a decline (although, this can also happen due to other factors). The role of an emotionally attuned, compassionate adult is indispensable here.

Examining how Montessori schools respond to trauma in their policies and practices

SAMHSA states that a "trauma-informed organization *responds* by integrating information and knowledge about trauma into its policies, its procedures, and its practices" (2014). This section looks at how contemporary Montessori schools can do this (many are doing it already).

Policies, procedures, and practices

It is worth re-stating that just a few years after Maria Montessori qualified as a doctor, she returned to the University of Rome to study (for several years) the history of educational approaches and methods (i.e., pedagogical anthropology), experimental psychology and philosophy, and within a relatively short time (1904), became Professor of Pedagogical Anthropology at that University. During this period, she spent a considerable amount of time visiting schools and observing the teaching methods being used. Very soon after (in 1907), when she became educational director (Foschi, 2008) of the Case dei Bambini (Children's Houses), she had already gathered a large body of knowledge about the educational practices being used in schools. She considered many of these practices to be harmful or traumatic to children and she *responded* to them quickly and precisely. First, she made it a "policy" that in her schools the universal practice of giving rewards and punishments was to be totally abolished. Media reports announced that rewards and punishments were completely banished from the Children's Houses (Tozier, 1911). This was a brave and revolutionary step to take at that period in time when the physical punishment of children was the norm, and rewards were frequently given as bribes for compliant behavior. In contemporary Montessori schools, even though physical punishments have never had a place, teachers should always aim to ensure that children are not put into situations where they are being (albeit unintentionally) exposed to potentially stressful situations, such as being humiliated or snubbed in any way (Montessori, 1949/1967). We must be sure to establish psychological, social, and emotional safety in our classrooms. Additionally, teachers must be vigilant to prevent any form of negative behavior among children, which can sometimes enter even a well-run classroom when new children who have not had an earlier Montessori experience join a Montessori elementary classroom, or when Montessori children are suddenly exposed to overwhelming stress stemming from something outside of school which may lead them to behave negatively toward other children. Also, we must make sure that the system of rewards does not enter the school in any well-intentioned but misinformed way, for example, when a kindly but mis-informed parent brings "candies for the best children." Children who have been affected by trauma may well come from (or still live in) homes where some siblings are favored while others are ignored or mistreated. In such circumstances, allowing any type of rewards system to infiltrate a Montessori classroom may be re-traumatizing for some children and must be avoided at all costs.

Second, Montessori made it a policy to remove the competitive element of schooling by having children work at their own pace, with the teacher scaffolding their learning as they followed their own interests. She encouraged collaboration among children rather than competition. At all times, her focus was on preventing sources of stress for children within the school system. Eyewitnesses wrote that Montessori went personally into the classes to show her teachers how to handle the children in a manner that protected them from mental strain and left their brains untaxed (Tozier, 1911). There are numerous references in the historical literature about how she took pre-emptive steps to prevent or reduce mental strain in the children (Tozier, 1911). Stevens (1912) also stated that Montessori as a physician and a teacher demonstrated to her teachers how to protect the children's nervous systems from strain (Stevens, 1912). She made mindfulness activities such as the "silence game" a regular part of the daily activities in her schools (Lillard, 2011; Phillips et al., 2022). She took learning outdoors as much as possible, recognizing the healing power of nature (Montessori, 1912/1964). She encouraged breathing exercises (Montessori, 1912/1964), and regulatory activities (drawn from the practical life and sensorial curriculum), as well as rhythmic activities (drawing from the cultural curriculum) such as music and movement and work with clay (Phillips et al., 2022). All of these practices and procedures represent pre-emptive steps to first preserve the mental health of children who have not experienced trauma and second bring psychological healing to children who have experienced traumatic events.

Quality contemporary Montessori schools continue this practice of preventing the school system itself from negatively affecting children in terms of their physical and psychological safety by (1) using the Montessori self-correcting materials which protect the child from the fear of the potential humiliation of being corrected, (2) using materials that keep no record of the child's mistakes which could be a source of humiliation for the child (e.g., the movable alphabet, the counting rods, the cards and counters), (3) allowing children space to work on individual activities if they want to, because often children, specially trauma-affected children need a quiet "alone" space to process their emotions, (4) using exercises that circumvent the need for a well-developed sequential memory, because this is often insufficiently developed in trauma-affected children, e.g. using exercises that only rely on muscle memory, (5) emphasizing reality-based activities, because these have been shown to counteract irrational fears (Montessori, 1936). These procedures and practices help staff to *respond,* in a very practical way, to the issues that are present in trauma-affected children and young people. Contemporary Montessori schools do not need to change any of these tried and tested practices, they just need the freedom to continue doing them. In addition, contemporary Montessori schools must create policies to address potentially trauma-inducing issues that are not specifically mentioned in the historical literature on Montessori schools, such as racism.

Looking at how Montessori schools can resist re-traumatization of students and families

SAMHSA states that a trauma-informed approach aims to resist *re-traumatization* of clients and staff (2014). Re-traumatization refers to a situation in which an individual (or group) either consciously or unconsciously re-experiences the emotions and fear of a traumatic event or events as if they were happening again. This/these event(s) may be recent or in the distant past, but the person experiences the sensations as if the events were happening in the present. This re-traumatization is usually caused by "triggers" in the environment which may comprise of:

Sights, sounds, or smells that invoke a memory of the traumatic event.

Human interactions that mimic the past traumatic experience.

Anniversaries of the traumatic event(s).

Reports in the media about events similar to the traumatized person's experience.

Films/plays/books that evoke memories of the traumatic event(s).

Conversations (even with loved ones) about the traumatic event(s).

Contemporary Montessori schools should take steps to understand the capacity of "triggers" to re-traumatize students and their families if they are serious about avoiding re-traumatization. Therefore, if students and/or their families have been traumatized by factors (including bullying, racism, discrimination, or inequity), it is incumbent on Montessori schools to be knowledgeable on these issues and face them squarely, making sure that nothing in the Montessori environment leaves a child or their family at risk of re-traumatization (Debs, 2019). As Debs, argues in *Equity Examined*, 2023, the view that Montessori schools are automatically an anti-bias, anti-racism form of education is a myth, and as Montessori educators, we have a duty to educate ourselves about racism both in our own countries and beyond and then use this knowledge to change and improve our practices (Wafford & Debs, 2023). Re-traumatization can happen to any person of any age who has experienced an acute traumatic event (such as a sudden assault, accident, or loss of a loved one), or on-going trauma (such as continuous racial abuse, or continuous exposure to domestic violence). People who are especially vulnerable to both trauma and re-traumatization include children and young people who have experienced street violence such as assaults involving stabbings or shootings; domestic violence in the home especially toward their mother or caregiver; refugees or asylum seekers who have experienced violent conflicts or war from which they were forced to flee (e.g., in the case of refugees and asylum seekers from conflict-affected countries). Symptoms of re-traumatization include:

> Sudden flashbacks
> Strong physical reactions (e.g., lashing out, running away, freezing)
> Anxiousness/panic attacks
> Intense fear often involving shaking, trembling, fainting, sobbing
> Inability to speak, concentrate on anything, or listen to anyone
> Inability to reach out to anyone to ask for help
> Fighting with peers
> Overall inability to control emotions which are usually intense and negative
> Dissociation

How then can contemporary Montessori schools avoid re-traumatization of their students? First, there is a need for a "whole-school" approach, so that teachers, administrators, kitchen staff, bus drivers, and anyone who is in contact with the children or young people at the school are trauma-informed. This means being aware that because of the widespread nature of trauma and the fact that it is found in all socio-economic groups, it is more likely than not that at least some of the students in a school will have been exposed to a traumatic event in the past or are being exposed to on-going traumatic events, and therefore are vulnerable to being "re-triggered." This in turn means that staff need to be knowledgeable about possible trauma triggers and be attuned to the students so that they can quickly recognize shifts in behavior or temperament that could be an indication that a child is being re-triggered. Second, there is a need for an intentional approach to helping children and young people to achieve physical and emotional regulation when a trigger causes them to experience an acute stress response. Staff need to prepare for this knowing that there is a very real likelihood that some children will experience a trauma response to an environmental or non-environmental trigger at some stage and it will most likely occur seemingly "out of the blue." As already shown, in Montessori schools, many exercises and activities have "built-in" regulating features and are available to the child or young person all through the day. For example, a child in a Primary classroom (3–6 years), can be invited to engage in a practical life exercise such as sweeping, scrubbing, polishing, or a cultural activity such as modeling with clay, drawing, painting, or moving to music, in order to use the power of rhythmic movement and repetition to help with their emotional or physical regulation. Third, there is a need for Montessori schools to do all they can do to prevent triggers from occurring in the first place. Since discrimination and racism are often the root causes of trauma triggers for many children and young people, there is a need for culturally relevant pedagogy (CRP) and anti-bias, anti-racism (ABAR) professional training for both experienced and up-coming Montessori teachers (Brunold-Conesa, 2022; Lillard et al., 2021).

Summary of Chapter 9

1. Participation in quality TIP programs is crucial for Montessori educators to realize the widespread impact of trauma and understand what the potential paths for recovery are and what they involve.
2. Participation in quality interdisciplinary TIP programs is important for Montessori educators to be able to recognize the signs and symptoms of trauma in children and young people.
3. Contemporary Montessori schools aspiring to be trauma-informed and trauma-responsive should aim to fully integrate knowledge about trauma into their policies, procedures, and practices (SAMHSA, 2014).
4. Contemporary Montessori school managerial staff who want to avoid the risk of re-traumatizing students and/or their families should take steps to inform all staff about issues that are traumatizing for many people such as racism, and discrimination. Familiarity with contemporary literature on CRP and Montessori schools may be very helpful in this regard and group discussions on these issues should be encouraged among educators and other interested parties.

Questions for group discussion

1. Discuss what steps your school can take in order for all staff to come to a *realization* of the pervasive and often intergenerational impact of trauma on children, families, communities, and groups, and the possible paths to recovery.
2. Discuss the possible signs and symptoms of trauma in children and young people. Reflect on your ability to *recognize* these signs and symptoms of trauma in children, their families, and their communities. What steps could you take to increase your ability to recognize these signs?
3. Reflect on how your school might *respond* in policies, procedures, and practices to the reality of trauma and individuals, families, and communities.
4. Discuss the steps your school might need to take to *resist* the re-traumatization of individuals, families, and groups.

References

Brunold-Conese, C. (2020). Culturally responsive pedagogy: An intersection with Montessori Education. https://www.researchgate.net/publication/339828022

Brunold-Conesa, C. (2022). Montessori with integrity – Part 2. DEI and ABAR practices as essential to quality program implementation. *MontessoriLife*. American Montessori Society.

Debs, M. (2019). *Diverse families, desirable schools: Public Montessori in the era of school of choice*. Harvard Education Press.

Felitti, V. J., Anda, R. F., Nordenberg, D., Williamson, D. F., Spitz, A. M., Edwards, V., Koss, M. P., & Marks, J. S. (1998). Relationship of childhood abuse and household dysfunction to many of the leading causes of death in adults: The adverse childhood experiences (ACE) study. *American Journal of Preventive Medicine, 14*(4), 245–258. https://doi.org/10.1016/s0749-3797(98)00017-8

Foschi, R. (2008). Science and culture around the Montessori's first "Children's Houses" in Rome (1907–1915). *Journal of the History of the Behavioral Sciences, 44*(3), 238–257. https://doi.org/10.1002/jhbs.20313

Lillard, A. (2011). Mindfulness practices in education: Montessori's approach. *Mindfulness, 2*, 78–85. https://doi.org/10.1007/s12671-011-0045-6

Lillard, A. S., Taggart, J., Yonas, D., & Seale, M. N. (2021). An alternative to "no excuses": Considering Montessori as culturally responsive pedagogy. *Journal of Negro Education*, 1–32

Montessori, M. (1936). *The secret of childhood* (B. B. Carter, Ed. and Trans.). Longmans.

Montessori, M. (1964). *The Montessori method* (A. E. George, Trans.). Schocken Books. (Original work published 1912)

Montessori, M. (1967). *The absorbent mind* (C. A. Claremont, Trans). Dell. (Original work published 1949)

Montessori, M. (1973). *From childhood to adolescence*. Schocken Books. (First published in 1948).

Montessori, M. (2013). The white cross. *AMI Journal, 1-2*, 37–41. (Original work published 1917)

Perry, B. D., Pollard, R. A., Blakley, Y. L., Baker, W. L., & Vigilante, D. (1995). Childhood trauma, the neurobiology of adaptation, and use-dependent development of the brain: How states become traits. *Infant Mental Health Journal, 16*(4), 271–291. https://doi.org/10.1002/1097-0355(199524)16:4≤271::AID-IMHJ2280160404≥3.0.CO;2-B

Phillips, B. (2023). Montessori elder and dementia care, and trauma informed approaches: A thematic analysis examining connections between the models. *Journal of Montessori Research, 9*(2), 66–79.

Phillips, B., O'Toole, C., McGilloway, S., & Phillips, S. (2022). Montessori, the white cross, and trauma-informed practice: Lessons for contemporary education. *Journal of Montessori Research.* 8(1).

Stevens, E. Y. (1912). The Montessori method and the American kindergarten. *McClure's Magazine, 40*, 77–82.

Substance Abuse and Mental Health Services Administration (SAMHSA). (2014). *SAMHSA's concept of trauma and guidance for a trauma-informed approach*. SAMHSA's Trauma and Justice Strategic Initiative. https://ncsacw.acf.hhs.gov/userfiles/files/SAMHSA_Trauma.pdf

Tozier, J. (1911). An educational wonder-worker: The methods of Maria Montessori. *McClure's Magazine, 37*(1), 3–19.

Wafford, M., & Debs, M.. (2023). Countering myths in Montessori education. In *Equity examined: How to design schools and teacher education programs where everyone thrives*. American Montessori Society (AMS). (amshq.org).

10 How contemporary Montessori schools can help trauma-affected children

Chapter objectives

- To examine **sequential memory** and how Montessori schools facilitate its development.
- To outline Montessori exercises that have a **regulating effect** on children and young people.
- To examine the factors in Montessori that promote **relationally rich** environments and "belonging."
- To show how Montessori environments promote **deep engagement** – and how "flow" promotes healing from trauma.

Learning outcomes

At the end of this chapter, the learner will have a knowledge of:

- **Sequential memory** and how Montessori schools facilitate its development.
- Exercises and activities that have a **regulating effect** on children and young people.
- Factors in Montessori that promote **relationally rich** environments and a sense of "belonging."
- How Montessori environments promote **deep engagement** – and how "flow" promotes healing from trauma.

DOI: 10.4324/9781003438021-15

Examining sequential memory and how Montessori schools aid its development

Why sequential memory is impaired in adversity or trauma-affected children

In their landmark publication, *Helping Traumatized Children Learn* (2005), Cole et al. state that "Traumatic experiences can inhibit this ability to organize material sequentially, leading to difficulty reading, writing, and communicating verbally" (2005, p. 26). Drawing from Craig (1992), they explain the importance of sequential memory (a type of memory which has the capacity to recall auditory and visual inputs in sequence) in the learning process. They explain that children's ability to complete many academic tasks depends on their ability to bring orderliness to the muddle of daily life experiences (Cole et al., 2005; Craig, 1992). These authors point out that exposure to trauma can impede the development of sequential memory resulting in academic failure. They also explain that in the first few years of life, sequential memory is not yet developed and the brain records events as a string of unrelated episodes or random events (Cole et al., 2005). The cognitive process that takes these random events and crafts them into a coherent story is sequential memory. Because we are born without the benefit of a developed sequential memory, we can only develop it by living in the world, it is entirely experience-dependent. In view of this, Craig (1992) emphasizes the crucial need for stable, predictable, ordered environments, and equally stable caregiving, to support the optimal development of sequential memory in young children. She explains that the passage to sequential semantic memory is best supported by providing young children with consistent, predictable environments where familiar routines are a priority, and time spent with familiar and reliable caregivers is the norm (Craig, 1992). She points out that when these conditions are not available, sequential memory does not develop as it should (Craig, 1992).

Ample evidence indicates that countless numbers of children throughout the world do not grow up in stable environments. This is particularly true of children who are exposed to adversity and or trauma which may include growing up in homes or communities where there are chaotic or challenging conditions arising from such realities as parental mental illness or other family mental health problems, substance abuse issues, domestic abuse, incarceration of family members, or exposure to systemic discrimination or racism. In these circumstances, the threats to the development of sequential memory are significant. Craig also points out that even children who grow up in environments that are not characterized by these serious stressors, but are marked by unpredictability, or where the rules can vary according to the transient inclination of the caregiver, will have difficulty developing sequential memory. She explains that when children grow up in households in which routines and rules vary constantly depending on the whims of the caregiver, children are deprived of the predictability and consistency that they need them to comprehend the concept of sequential order and to see the sequential ordering of the world they find themselves in (Craig, 1992).

This situation has serious consequences for the child's ability to learn and can lead to school difficulties. Cole et al. state that trauma-affected children who have difficulties with sequential organization do well in classrooms in which there are clear rules and expectations, orderly transitions from subject to subject, or classroom to classroom, and where assistance is available to them with the organization of their tasks (2005).

How sequential memory problems are circumvented in the Montessori school

Many of the children who attended the early Montessori schools (1907–1917) would undoubtedly have had problems with sequential memory owing to their exposure to adversity or trauma with its attendant unpredictability of lifestyle. For example, when the author and eyewitness, Caroline Bailey, described the four-year-old orphan, Bruno, who had survived the Messina earthquake and was accommodated at the Montessori school on the Via Guisti, she wrote that Bruno was quite neglected and had grown up in chaotic conditions wherein he sometimes was fed, but frequently was not, sometimes was nurtured, but frequently was not. She recognized the negative effect of this unpredictability on Bruno's developing brain, and she wrote that Bruno's mind appeared to be "dulled" and he had difficulty with comprehension. He could hear the words spoken to him but was unable to cognitively process their meaning, and this left him vulnerable to physical abuse from the adults who misunderstood the root cause of his failure to follow commands (Bailey, 1915).

There would have been many children attending Montessori's early schools (circa 1907–1917) who were just like Bruno, and displayed difficulties with cognition and sequential memory, especially those who had survived the Messina earthquake. For this reason, Montessori relied on another type of memory to help the children to learn while their sequential memory was beginning to develop (with the help of the order and routines in the school). This type of memory is called "muscular memory." In a series of articles published in the San Francisco Call and Post in 1915 and reprinted in the California Lectures of Maria Montessori 1915, Montessori spoke of how she purposely utilized "muscular memory" to support learning in her schools (2008). Muscular memory (also called muscle memory) refers to a type of memory that involves committing a specific motor task into memory through repetition of certain movements, examples include such activities as riding a bicycle, typing, or playing a musical instrument. When these activities have been imprinted into muscular memory by constant repetition of specific movements, they become automatic, and an individual can do them without thinking about the actions involved. This circumvents the learning challenges that arise when a child has an underdeveloped sequential memory.

Montessori first used muscular memory to teach children the shapes of numerals and letters of the alphabet. She said that in order to teach children the outline of the letters of the alphabet, she set out to fix the memory of the shape of each letter into the child's muscular memory (Montessori, 2008). Tozier, an eyewitness to the early schools, alluded to how the children learned to "feel" sounds and to "feel" numerals as the teacher guided their fingers over sandpaper letters and numbers, so that they could develop a "muscular memory" of their shapes (1911). She adds that not only was this a worthwhile goal in itself, but it also had the additional advantage of reducing and in fact minimizing, the potential strain on the brain caused by other methods (Tozier, 1911). Stevens (1912) claimed that Montessori, being both a physician and an educator, shows teachers how to protect the child's nervous system from strain. Tozier said it was one of the most important of Montessori's achievements that she managed to teach young children to write and then to read without putting even the smallest strain on their nervous systems (1911). Likewise, mathematical concepts were learned through "muscular memory," for example, a range of wooden materials were used to teach mathematical principles including, for example, long rods which required the children to stretch out their arms to "feel" a sense of the length of the longest rod. The basic premise underlying these approaches (both in language and mathematical exercises) was that they helped the child to "embody" concepts through the use of "muscular memory" and thus reduced the potential for stress or what Tozier referred to as mental strain on the children's nervous systems (Tozier, 1911). The absorption of academic content via muscular memory was clearly successful in reducing or avoiding academic-related stress as evidenced by the fact that the children (voluntarily) kept repeating the exercises over and over (Fisher, 1912; Tozier, 1911). As the children engaged in exercises that used muscular memory, their sequential memory was developing, owing, in no small part to the order and structure inherent in the materials and arrangement of the Montessori environments.

How sequential memory is developed in contemporary Montessori schools

One of the most remarkable features of a well-run Montessori school is the presence of order. Order pervades the school. It is to be found in every aspect of the environment, the teachers, and the children. It is infused into the layout of the classrooms and garden, the layout and meticulousness of the materials, the demeanor and approach of the teachers, and the behavior of the children. This of course is no accident. Well-run Montessori schools are designed to meet the developmental needs of the children they serve. In the case of 3–6-year-olds, Montessori pointed out that the most fundamental developmental need is for "order" and routines (1936). She called this need a sensitive period in development. Early on in her work with children, Montessori discovered that there are a number of "sensitive periods" in the course of development and that the most crucial sensitive period for young children is between birth and six years. It is the period of life in which nature programs young children to focus on order, patterns, routines, and sequences in their daily lives in order to lead them toward something that is vital for their survival – healthy brain development.

With this conviction of the crucial importance of the sensitive period for order, for the construction of a healthy brain, Montessori embedded order into every aspect of the Montessori environments for children between birth and six years.

It is this emphasis on order which necessarily involves carrying out activities in a sequence that can enhance the development of sequential memory in the Montessori school. For a child who has been exposed to trauma which has subsequently resulted in challenges to the building of sequential memory, the Montessori school could be a game-changer. Every activity the child engages in, whether it is scrubbing a table, washing a window, polishing a mirror, or building a binomial or a trinomial cube, involves a sequence of steps, meticulously planned out, to enable not just the completion of the activity, but, in the long term, to aid the development of a healthy brain. Therefore, the absence of routines and sequences of events in the home can be compensated for, on a daily basis, by the multitude of opportunities made available to the child in a Montessori school (through the materials and the exercises) to organize material sequentially, and to carry out exercises in an ordered, sequence of steps. This simple approach, unique to Montessori schools, is the secret to facilitating the development of sequential memory, a type of memory vital for learning, and crucial for success in future academic tasks.

Prioritizing activities that are *regulating* for children and young people

> **Vignette**
>
> **Tom a 7-year-old boy in a Montessori home-school**
>
> Susan and Gareth fostered Tom when he was seven years old. He had lived with three other foster families since his young mother had lost custody of him when he was two, and she was deemed to be unable to care for him due to drug addiction problems. He is now eight and a half and although he has settled relatively well into his home, he has always had at least one "meltdown" a day over what some people would call minor issues, e.g., the lid of his lunch box will never close back properly when he takes his sandwich out at lunchtime in school, or his books won't fit into his backpack when its hometime even though they fitted when he was coming in to school, another issue is his perception that his classmates, Molly and Richard snigger at him when he is trying to hang up his coat in the school hallway each day. Last month, he reached the point where he so hated going to school that Susan and Gareth decided to take him out of school and try home-schooling instead. Some things have improved because of this, at least Tom doesn't feel that anyone is sniggering at him in the hallway. However, he still has what Susan and Garrett would call "meltdowns" over things that seem to them to be very minor, for example, Susan washed his favorite red pyjamas late one afternoon, and they were not fully dry at bedtime so he refused to go to bed and would not wear the other ones offered to him.

Gareth and Susan are exploring ways of home-schooling and are interested in using Montessori approaches combined with trauma-informed practices. Many years ago, Susan completed a high-quality program of training in Montessori education but never actually worked in Montessori education. In addition, they both attended an introductory course on attachment and trauma awareness before they applied to the foster agency. They are very much aware that Tom has been through a lot of emotional upheaval and have learned about Siegal's concept of "a window of tolerance" and some information on relational trauma. They often nod to each other knowingly when they notice that Tom is moving outside his window of tolerance and therefore is unable to stay calm even over a minor issue. A friend who is a Montessori-trained teacher with a lot of experience suggested they start by offering age-appropriate Practical Life activities to Tom. They decided to offer fence painting because the weather was suitable for this kind of activity and the fence really needed painting! When they suggested this activity to Tom, he did not express any interest in doing it, so Gareth went outside and started painting it himself, hoping Tom might join him. It worked. Within 20 minutes, Tom asked if he could help, and for two hours, with practically no talking, but a lot of concentration on the rhythmic up and down movements of their wrists and arms, Gareth and Tom painted the fence together. When they were finished, they went inside for dinner. Susan noted that Tom was calm, quiet, and peaceful. He also seemed more relational, for example, he smiled and wanted to talk to Susan and Gareth. He chatted about how he was enjoying being home-schooled, and then he brought up the subject of how in school he always felt that Molly and Richard were sniggering at him, but now he wondered if they were just sharing a funny story together and not sniggering at him at all. His foster mum Susan was speechless at these unexpected insights. It was as if Tom had just engaged in something therapeutic. Actually, he had just done exactly that!

Practical life activities that have a calming effect on children

Initially, when Montessori and her teachers worked with children who had experienced traumatic events (e.g., the Messina earthquake, WWI), or less dramatic but still traumatizing events (such as lack of nurturing, poverty, or discrimination), she noted that engagement in practical life activities with repetitive gross or small motor movements seemed to have a calming effect on the children's anxiety (Phillips et al., 2022), and left them appearing emotionally regulated, happy and relational (that is, wanting to relate to others) (Montessori, 1936). A century later, Dr. Bruce Perry, the world-renowned neuroscientist and adjunct professor of psychiatry, who pioneered the Neurosequential Model in Education, with its Sequence of engagement, *Regulate, Relate and Reason,* explained that the first step in helping a child to "regulate," that is, move from high anxiety states to calmer more cognitive states, is through the use of what he calls repetitive and somatosensory activities (Perry, 2009). He explains from neuroscience that these activities are rhythmic and rhythm regulates the dysregulated brain. Perry recommends repetitive, rhythmic activities such as balancing exercises, and music and movement (2009). In

Montessori schools, *regulating* activities can be provided for every age group – the infant community (birth – 3 years), the primary classrooms (3–6 years), lower elementary (6–9 years), upper elementary (9–12 years), and erdkinder (12–15 and 15–18 years). Suggestions for Practical Life *regulating* activities that also promote flow are provided in a later section.

Cultural activities that promote emotional regulation in children

Music and movement

In an article published in 2009, on the power of music to enhance emotional regulation in children who have been negatively affected by traumatic experiences, Lucille Foran points out that research supports the positive role of music in helping trauma-affected children to regulate their emotions, activate brain pathways, and absorb new emotional and academic information (2009). However, she says that teachers, as a rule, are not trained musicians, nor are they typically trained in music therapy. On this note, it is interesting and fortuitous that this was not the case in Montessori's early schools, because one of Montessori's students, Professor Anna Maccheroni (who became a lifelong friend), was a trained musician and her professorship was in music. As stated in Chapter 2, in her early schools, Montessori, with the help of her student and colleague, Professor Anna Maccheroni, developed music and dance exercises for the children. The exercises were rhythmic and repetitive and appeared to function not just as musical education but also as music therapy for the children. Eyewitnesses to the early schools, in particular the writer Carolyn Bailey, commented on the regulating effect these exercises had on the children's emotions (Bailey, 1915). Research in neuroscience confirms the power of music to regulate the brain and improve our mood. Foran (2009) states that music and movement are of great importance in establishing emotional regulation in trauma survivors. Drawing from the work of Levitin (2006), she explains that functional magnetic imaging has been used to analyze the neural pathways involved when an individual is listening to music. She states that Levitin's work revealed that when we listen to music, first, the auditory cortex is activated, then the frontal lobes, followed by the activation of the limbic system. This activates the release of dopamine. Finally, the nucleus accumbens is activated which is the center of the brain's reward system. Levitin's work argues that the act of listening to music is wired to enhance our mood and feelings of happiness based on the brain's neural pathways (Foran, 2009).

Foran also refers to Fran Herman (1991), a music therapist who described the case of a trauma-affected nine-year-old boy who responded positively to music therapy after other therapies had proved to be unsuccessful (Foran, 2009). She explains that the child had been unable to participate properly in school because of his emotional dysregulation, and aggressive behavior which was related to his severe depression (Foran, 2009). However, Foran recounts that after a series of music therapy sessions that initially focused on lengthening the child's attention span, and allowing him to enjoy free self-expression, his ability to take turns increased, along with his ability to restrain his impulsivity. Foran states that Herman was able to report that the boy, completed the series of music therapy sessions and subsequently was able to return to school where he was successful in learning to read.

Research shows that active music-making, such as singing, playing a musical instrument, or even composing music electronically, can lead to the release of neurotransmitters like dopamine, a feel-good chemical that influences concentration, memory, mood, and motivation, and serotonin, a chemical that influences anxiety levels, pain sensitivity, and mood (Ferreri et al., 2019). Singing has been shown to reduce the levels of cortisol, the stress hormone in the body, and produce a feeling of relaxation through the breathing patterns involved in producing song. Moreover, the hormone oxytocin, a hormone associated with social bonding, is released when people sing in a group and helps to make people feel connected to others. This is important for any person, but in particular, it is vital for children and young people who are trauma-affected because it helps to offset the feeling of being disconnected or separate from others frequently felt by children who have been exposed to trauma (Craig, 2016). In contemporary Montessori schools, at all levels, teachers can harness the power of music and movement to help trauma-affected children and young people regulate their emotions, just as Maccheroni and Montessori did in the early schools.

Working with clay

Another cultural exercise that appears to have been instrumental in supporting the regulation of stress responses in trauma-affected children and young people in Montessori's early schools is working with clay. The American philanthropist, Mary Rebecca Cromwell, who helped to rehabilitate the French and Belgian child refugees using the Montessori approach listed work with clay as one of the exercises that brought calm and regulation to the traumatized children in her care (Cromwell, 1916/2006). Research confirms the power of working with clay to regulate trauma-affected children (Sholt & Gavron, 2006). These authors recount the case of a teenage girl (14 years of age) who because of angry outbursts directed against her parents, and difficulties developing peer relationships, was referred to art therapy. They record that in one particular session, she molded the clay with her eyes closed for an unusually long period, stroking the clay in a gentle manner. They say that when she opened her eyes, she examined the clay form that she had created and described what she saw. They say she saw a child and a mother, and the mother, who is crying, is holding her little girl, who is wiping the mother's tears. These authors recount that this work with clay opened the way for this distressed teenager to tell her story which was one of being the child of a seriously depressed mother. The authors write that this contact or work with the clay helped this girl to bring out into the open the hidden and fundamental issues which were vital to understanding how she felt and what her needs were (Sholt & Gavron, 2006).

These authors also point out that this connection between work with clay and the expression of hidden emotions around loss appears in many studies. They refer to Henley (2002) and explain that individuals who are experiencing loss and are in mourning can use clay work to express their emotions such as anger, frustration, or agony, and these emotions can be acted out on the lump of clay. They (drawing from Henley) explain that clay can be used to recreate the image of what or who was lost. They re-tell the story of a teenage girl who having lost her mother to illness was experiencing such deep grief that she could not verbalize it. It is recounted that within a few months of clay therapy, she made a large clay cup which she held lovingly in her hands. She had engraved the word "mother" on the cup, and the process of making this cup with clay had enabled her to verbalize her longing for her mother's touch.

A very poignant story of a seven-year-old boy is also recounted. This boy was abandoned by his biological father and owing to his mother's illness had to be placed in a foster home. During clay therapy, the boy made two heads, one representing his biological father and the other one representing his foster father with whom he had developed a good relationship. The boy used the two heads to make the two fathers "talk" to each other. This creation of a dialogue between the two fathers allowed the boy to work through first, the sense of rejection he felt from being abandoned by his biological father, and second, the new attachment bond he was beginning to establish with his foster father. In these two examples, work with clay facilitated these children's need to create concrete representations of the losses they were suffering.

Heimlich and Mark (1990) describe how working with clay can mitigate the feelings of helplessness frequently felt by trauma-affected children. They explain that when even timid children engage in clay work which involves handling, manipulating, and sculpting a shapeless lump of clay, they immediately experience feeling of how they are not entirely powerless and through this experience, children can quickly come to understand their own efficacy.

Sholt and Gavron (2006) identified several major therapeutic factors that emerged through the use of clay work, including: (1) the expression of emotions, (2) cathartic release, (3) the bringing of repressed memories into consciousness, (4) the facilitation of rich and deep subjective expressions, (5) the facilitation of verbal communication, and (6) the embodying of thoughts, feelings, and conflicts into concrete objects (Sholt & Gavron, 2006). Contemporary Montessori schools may be able to support trauma-affected children to regulate their emotions by allowing them to work (for uninterrupted periods of time), with clay just as teachers in Montessori's early schools did (Phillips et al., 2022).

Drawing

A further cultural exercise that appears to have been beneficial in terms of helping trauma-affected children and young people in Montessori's early schools to better regulate their emotions is drawing. The historian, Paola Trabalzini (2013), wrote about a Montessori school run by the Societa Umanitaria, which played a vital role in assisting the children of soldiers and young refugees in Italy during WWI. This school cared exclusively for refugee children and Trabolzini records some of the reports written by teachers looking after these children. One teacher, speaking of the trauma-affected children, wrote that the children's drawings reflected images of the war. She said they drew weapons, army trucks, planes, soldiers, zeppelins, and more weapons (Trabalzini, 2013). The children clearly felt a psychological need to process their experience of the intrusion of weapons, army trucks, and other war-related machinery into their lives, and they used drawing rather than speech as a means of processing these frightening experiences. Haring et al. (2020) state that young children often are simply not capable of verbalizing their fears, frustrations, or sense of distress, therefore, being able to put these things into their drawings and paintings may be able to help these children to overcome distress and trauma (Haring et al., 2020). In their paper, they seek to develop an understanding of how artmaking works to soothe trauma. This process is examined more fully in the light of "flow theory" in the last section of this chapter. The vignette below tells how a trauma-affected young girl began to heal through the artwork she pursued with the support of her teachers in a Montessori school.

Vignette

A ten-year-old girl in Montessori upper elementary

Beatrice was ten years old when the sexual abuse by her stepfather began. She had been a happy-go-lucky child who loved her Montessori upper elementary school. She had always enjoyed learning new things and had been a real socialite, always wanting to spend time with school friends at weekends and during the holidays. The abuse began just a week into the summer vacation when her mom was away at a residential course and Beatrice was at home with her stepdad, and the abuse soon became a recurring event even when her mom returned. Beatrice felt shock, shame, fear, and confusion. When her mom returned from the course, Beatrice had intended to tell her what had happened, but her mom seemed so happy with her step dad and he seemed to be so kind and attentive to her that Beatrice just couldn't tell her mom and so the abuse continued. In September, when school resumed, Beatrice felt as though she had two identities, the person she used to be and the person she had become in the last few weeks since the abuse began. She began to struggle in school, she couldn't concentrate or take in even the simplest pieces of information, she didn't want to socialize or hang out with anyone and she became either tearful at the tiniest problem or full of aggression if she felt slighted. After just three weeks back in school, her class teacher reached out to her and asked her if she needed to talk. They talked, and within a few minutes Beatrice broke into sobs and told her teacher what was happening at home. What followed was neither easy nor pleasant, nor was it short-lived. However, 12 months later, Beatrice is on the road to recovery and one of the chief factors in that recovery was the art work she pursued with the support of her teachers in her Montessori school.

Creating environments that are *relationally* rich and promote belonging

Contemporary research in neuroscience demonstrates the centrality of attuned relationships in the healing of trauma (Ludy-Dobson & Perry, 2010; Perry & Szalavitz, 2006; Treisman, 2017). According to Perry, following the use of rhythmic activities to promote emotional regulation, the next step is to help the child to relate. Perry and colleagues have documented the crucial role of positive relationships in the healing process for children who have been affected by trauma (Ludy-Dobson & Perry, 2010). As stated in Chapter 2, Perry emphasizes the importance of human connectedness and the power of having a sense of belonging in helping children to recover from traumatic experiences (Perry & Winfrey, 2021). The concept of "relate" always involves having an emotionally attuned adult (someone who recognizes, understands, and engages with another's emotional state) available to the child.

From the outset of her work with children, most of whom had been exposed to some level of adversity and or trauma, Montessori appeared to intuitively grasp the fact that positive relations and rich relational environments buffer stress and therefore are healing for trauma-affected children. As stated in Chapter 2, when Montessori described her approach with the first group of children she worked with, she emphasized her relational approach. She stated that for the first time, the children were made to feel that they were wanted and she helped them to feel that they belonged and were cherished (Montessori, 2008). From the beginning, she utilized a number of specific factors that created and maintained a rich "relational" environment in her schools and promoted a sense of belonging in the children. These factors included – mixed age groups and peer teaching.

Mixed age groups and relational neurobiology

From the outset of her work with children, Montessori had mixed age groups in her classes and she was quick to observe the benefits of this arrangement from the point of view of relational neurobiology. She stated that to segregate children on the basis of age is cruel and inhumane (Montessori, 1967). She added that it is a basic mistake because it creates a barrier to the development of the social sense. She said it is vital to mix the ages, because her schools demonstrate that children of different ages have a natural tendency to help one another (Montessori, 1967). The mixture of ages in Montessori schools promotes a feeling of connectedness and kinship, and this in itself has been shown to be a source of healing for trauma-affected children because it helps to offset the feeling of being disconnected from others frequently felt by children who have been exposed to trauma (Craig, 2016). Montessori, when describing her early classrooms, pointed out that the mixture of ages in some of her schools had the potential to span several years. She wrote that the classrooms for children of three to six years were often not even rigidly separated from those of the seven to nine-year-old children. She said that the dividing walls were merely partitions (waist high), and there was always easy access from one classroom to the next (Montessori, 1967). She added that the children were free to go in and out of these adjoining classrooms. As a consequence, children spent time in an environment that is more like a typical family with siblings of differing ages, different abilities, and preferences, all held together by a sense of belonging and kinship. This arrangement was, according to Montessori (and still is in our opinion), respectful of our biological need as human beings to live in communities and collaborate with others (Montessori, 1967).

Ervin and Sacerdote (2016) explain that up until the beginning of the 20th century, American public schools were predominantly school-houses having just one room where just one teacher taught children of all levels. However, they say that as rural agrarian society shifted to a largely urban, industrialized model, the structure of schools changed also and they moved away from multi-age classrooms and followed the factory model which had transformed the American economy (Ervin & Sacerdote, 2016). However, they point out that in Montessori schools, this trend was not adopted, and multi-age classrooms remained the norm. These authors elucidate the many cognitive, social, and pedagogical advantages of multi-age classrooms (Ervin & Sacerdote, 2016). From the point of view of creating a rich relational environment for children, especially those affected by trauma, the Montessori model is clearly respectful of the biological needs of human beings to be relational.

Peer teaching and relational neurobiology

In a similar fashion, Montessori was quick to recognize the value of peer-teaching from a relational point of view. She wrote that a three-year-old child will be interested in what a five-year-old is doing, because the five-year-old's capabilities are not too far removed from his own capabilities (Montessori, 1967). She describes the positive aspects of this for both the older and the younger child. She says that the older children become like heroes and teachers to the younger children and the younger ones look upon the older children with admiration (Montessori, 1967). She commented on the traditional school's lack of understanding of this phenomenon and how their structure causes them to miss out on opportunities for social development in children. She remarked that in traditional schools, where children are all the same age, the children with advanced intelligence could easily teach the others, but this is rarely allowed (Montessori, 1967). She points out that the outcome of this practice is often a negative one with the result that the less intelligent children develop feelings of envy toward the more intelligent children (Montessori, 1967). By comparison, she points out that in the Montessori schools, positive and uplifting attributes begin to develop and flourish when the ages and intelligence levels are mixed. She said that in her schools, older children see themselves as the protectors of younger children, and she said that this situation leads to real bonding among the classmates, so that they are almost glued together by genuine love and admiration (Montessori, 1967)

Maintaining environments that promote *deep engagement* – how "flow" heals trauma

Early on in her work with the impoverished children of San Lorenzo (1907), Montessori became fascinated by a phenomenon she witnessed again and again in the children. She noticed that when they found a material or exercise/activity that interested them, they frequently became so immersed in the activity that they repeated it over and over again. Sometimes, they went into such a deep state of concentration that they became unaware of anything going on around them. She famously recounted how a little child working with the cylinder blocks repeated the task 42 times and was oblivious to the movements and activities of the children around her. Then she suddenly stopped, as if she was emerging from a dream, and smiled and appeared to be very happy (Montessori, 1936). This phenomenon of deep concentration on a task, to the extent that the child becomes oblivious to the presence of others, followed by an observable state of happiness in the child, was noted by many eyewitnesses to Montessori's early classrooms. Elizabeth Harrison of the National Kindergarten Union, in her report on a 1914 study trip to Rome, where she observed many of the trauma-affected child survivors of the Messina earthquake, recounted, that she had seen as many as 80 visitors in Montessori classrooms where sometimes there were only twelve children, yet the children appeared not to be in the least disturbed or even conscious of these observers (1914). Another eyewitness who observed many groups of impoverished children who were deeply concentrated on sensorial exercises wrote that the happiness and tranquility that the children manifested after just a few weeks of working with the Montessori materials (especially the sensorial materials) was remarkable (George, 1912). A short time later, these levels of intense concentration in children were noted by the media at Montessori's demonstration Glass Classroom, which was erected at the Panama-Pacific International Exposition in 1915. Noah Sobe writes that the children in the glass classroom were oblivious to the crowds who were observing the classroom from the bleachers, and for long periods of time they appeared not to notice the spectators and were certainly not distracted by them because they were so absorbed in the work they were doing (2004).

In her book, *The Absorbent Mind* (1967), Montessori discusses this phenomenon of deep concentration that she observed in most of the children in her schools (many of whom were trauma-affected). She described it as a transition from one state (a perturbed or uneasy state) to another (a calm and peaceful state) following deep engagement in a self-chosen exercise or activity. She stated that this passage from one state to another in children, always follows the same process which is engagement with a piece of work, done by the hands, with real objects, and this work is accompanied by deep mental concentration (Montessori, 1967). She said that she found this phenomenon of concentration on a task, resulting in deep concentration, followed by a sense of calm and happiness in the children, was repeated unfailingly in all her schools, with children from different social and ethnic backgrounds (Montessori, 1967). She added that the discovery of this phenomenon (the transition of the child from a state of being uneasy, perturbed, even chaotic, to a state of being calm and happy) following concentration on a piece of work, done by the hands, was the most important single result of her entire work (Montessori, 1967). This phenomenon was seen by Montessori as a "moment of healing" (1967, p. 206). She frequently uses the words "healing" (pp. 206, 207), and "cure" (pp. 204, 205, 206), when she discusses this phenomenon. She wrote – "This psychological event, which brings to mind the cure of adults by psychoanalysis, we have called by the technical term *normalisation*" (p. 204). Montessori understood normalization to be an "integration" (p. 203) in the child's mind which had a transformative effect on the child such that it was visible to on-lookers. She wrote that the phenomenon she came to call normalization through work comes about through deep engagement with an activity or piece of work that provides just the right amount of challenge to maintain the child's interest, and provoke repetition, which in turn promotes concentration. She saw the normalized child simply as a child who has been given the conditions necessary to get back on track, back to normal, having been pushed off the road of optimal development by life's challenges. Normalization, therefore, is simply allowing a child to re-connect with the conditions normally needed for a child's optimal development. These conditions are primarily the provision of suitable "work" (meaningful activities) and the opportunity to concentrate on that work without interruption, until the combination of "work" and "concentration" has done its job and the child experiences a feeling of calm, happiness, and peace, followed by an observable sociability (Montessori, 1967).

Over the last two decades, the similarities between Montessori's discovery of this phenomenon which she called "normalization" or "normalization through work," and the phenomenon of "Optimal Experience" or "Flow Theory" pioneered by the psychologist Mihály Csíkszentmihályi (1990), have been closely examined (Rathunde, 2015, 2023; Rathunde & Csíkszentmihályi, 2005). According to Rathunde (2023), the word "flow" describes a block of time when an individual is so fully absorbed and concentrated on a task that they become oblivious to the passage of time and are motivated from within to work on the task because of the enjoyment they receive from simply engaging in the activity (Rathunde, 2023). He says that when we compare flow theory with Montessori education it is clear that flow is an essential element of Montessori pedagogy (Rathunde, 2023). According to Rathunde (2023), there are important similarities between flow theory and Montessori philosophy in explicating the connections between optimal development and learning (Rathunde, 2023). He states that essentially the Montessori approach is constructed around the overarching goal of creating environments for deep concentration, and that there are clear similarities between key aspects of the Montessori approach and flow theory (Rathunde, 2015). He also says that both Montessori education and flow theory emphasize the centrality of deep concentration that is intrinsically motivated, not just in the educational process, but also in lifelong development, and both place their focus on how this state of deep concentration might be facilitated to promote optimal development in children and adults (Rathunde, 2015). He adds that Montessori's descriptions of the deep concentration she witnessed in children are very close to the research-based descriptions of the characterizations of the flow experience such as absorbed attention and deep concentration which isolates an individual from all the distractions of their environment (Rathunde, 2015).

According to Rathunde, the main challenge of trying to implement a form of education that is based on deep concentration is trying to figure out how to create environments for children that promote the flow experience rather than stifle it with activities that are really just busywork, or other activities imposed by adults that are barriers to the possibility of flow experiences in the classroom (2015). Rathunde says that this was the key challenge that confronted Montessori but that she determined to make the facilitation and promotion of these episodes of deep, uninterrupted concentration, the priority of her pedagogical approach. He says that for over a century, other educators, inspired by Montessori's discovery of the power of this flow or normalization experience on children, have taken up this challenge. In the light of Montessori's writings on the phenomenon of "normalization," it is arguable that her theory anticipated Csíkszentmihályi's "optimal experience" ("flow") theory by 100 years.

With regard to trauma, the possibility that flow could be healing for trauma-affected individuals is just beginning to be investigated in contemporary research. Despite the fact that (as stated above) Montessori was using the words *healing, cure,* and *integration* of the mind in relation to the normalization phenomenon decades ago, the possibility that deep concentration on a task could be healing for trauma-affected children or adults is a relatively new concept in contemporary literature. Haring et al. state that the very actions involved in creating art appear to be part of the healing process for children as much as it is an expressive practice for them (2020). These authors examine the concept of the state of flow during the drawing process as a medium for supporting children to overcome the negative effects of exposure to trauma (Haring et al., 2020). They refer to the *healing* effect of drawing while in the flow which they claim, supports trauma-affected children. They explain that when trauma-affected children are drawing or painting and enter a flow state, these children experience a loss or an absence of conscious and it is during this state of being outside of consciousness that (what they refer to as) an *integration* of the mind takes place which produces positive feelings, reduces feelings of depression, and ultimately increases feelings of happiness (Haring et al., 2020). Elaborating on this they state that the mechanism behind this process is that when children engage in drawing, they become completely engaged in a non-verbal activity that requires their total concentration and involvement, and they argue that it is during this intense, non-verbal activity that the integrative process which produces the positive reactions just listed takes place (Haring et al., 2020). It is interesting that Montessori also noted that children in a state of deep concentration tend to do their self-chosen task in silence until they emerge from this intense, concentrated state (Montessori, 1936).

Montessori schools, therefore, differ from traditional schools in that they consciously construct environments to promote the phenomenon that Montessori called normalization through work (1912/1964), and which, as we have shown, is very similar to Csíkszentmihályi's concept of "flow" (1990). Examples of exercises and activities that can be offered to children and young adults in Montessori schools and Montessori home schools to promote "flow" are now listed:

Exercises and activities for children 3–6 years

Scrubbing a table
Digging soil
Raking leaves
Shoveling snow
Dancing to music
Work with clay

Exercises and activities for children 6–12

Washing a car
Painting a fence
Music and movement
Work with clay
Theater and drama work

Exercises and activities for children and young people 12–18

Fixing a puncture on a bicycle
Valeting a car
Making a costume or item of clothing
Theater and drama work

Summary of Chapter 10

1 The development of sequential memory (the organization of information into an ordered sequence) is often delayed in trauma-affected children, because these children frequently grow up in households where there is a high degree of disorder.
2 Historically, Montessori by-passed the need for learning through sequential memory by creating activities that relied on "muscular memory" or procedural memory, a type of memory that involves committing motor tasks to memory by the repetition of certain movements. Examples of muscular memory include riding a bike, or typing, where the necessary movements become ingrained.
3 The development of sequential memory is aided in Montessori schools by the ordered environment, for example, the sequential ordering of activities on shelves, and the sequential ordering of steps in an exercise.

4 Montessori schools prioritize the use of practical life activities that are regulating for children and young people.
5 Montessori schools prioritize the use of cultural activities such as music and movement, clay work, and artwork such as free drawing and painting, which have been shown to be therapeutic for trauma-affected children and young people.
6 Montessori schools promote relationally rich environments by the use of mixed age groups, and peer teaching.
7 Montessori schools have, since their inception, prioritized the experience of what Montessori called "normalization through work" which is very similar to Csíkszentmihályi's "Flow" theory. Emerging research shows that the experience of Flow is healing for trauma-affected individuals.

Questions for group discussion

1 Discuss sequential memory and its importance for learning academic tasks such as literacy and numeracy.
2 Consider the use of procedural memory in the Montessori classroom, what would you see as its benefits?
3 How does the Montessori classroom aid the development of sequential memory in children?
4 Discuss practical life activities that would be regulating for children and young people in Montessori classrooms.
5 Consider the use of cultural activities such as music and movement, work with clay, artwork such as drawing and painting, and their role as therapeutic agents for trauma-affected children and young people in the Montessori classroom. Do contemporary Montessori classrooms allow children enough time to engage in these activities?
6 Discuss how Montessori schools promote relationally rich environments by the use of mixed age groups and peer teaching.
7 Reflect on the concept of "Flow" and Montessori's theory of "normalization through work." In your experience, do contemporary Montessori schools create conditions that allow the Flow experience or the "normalization through work" phenomenon to be the hallmark of the school?

References

Bailey, C. S. (1915). *Montessori children*. Holt
Cole, S. F., Greenwald O'Brien, J., Gadd, M. G., Ristuccia, J., Wallace, D. L., & Gregory, M. (2005). Helping traumatized children learn: Supportive school environments for children traumatized by family violence. Massachusetts Advocates for Children,

Trauma and Learning Policy Initiative. https://traumasensitiveschools.org/wp-content/uploads/2013/06/Helping-Traumatized-Children-Learn.pdf

Craig, S. E. (1992). The educational needs of children living with violence. *Phi Delta Kappan, 74*, 67–71.

Craig, S. E. (2016). *Trauma sensitive schools: Learning communities transforming children's lives, K–5* (Illustrated ed.). Teachers College Press.

Cromwell, M. (2006). The Montessori method adapted to the little French and Belgian refugees. *AMI Communications, 2*, 11–13. (Original work published 1916)

Csíkszentmihályi, M. (1990). *Flow*. Harper & Row.

Ervin, B., & Sacerdote, C. (2016). *Examining the literature on authentic Montessori practices: Multi-age groupings*. AMS. Research Committee White Paper. pp 1–4.

Ferreri, L., Mas-Herrero, E., Zatorre, R. J., Ripollés, P., Gomez-Andres, A., Alicart, H., Olivé, G., Marco-Pallarés, J., Antonijoan, R. M., Valle, M., Riba, J., & Rodriguez-Fornells, A. (2019). Dopamine modulates the reward experiences elicited by music. *Proceedings of the National Academy of Sciences of the United States of America, 116*(9), 3793–3798.

Fisher, D. C. (1912). *A Montessori mother*. Henry Holt & Company.

Foran, L. M. (2009). Listening to music: Helping children regulate their emotions and improve learning in the classroom. *Horizons, 88*(1), 51–58.

George, A. E. (1912). Dr. Maria Montessori: The achievement and personality of an Italian woman whose discovery is revolutionizing educational methods. *Good Housekeeping, 55*(1), 24–29.

Haring, U., Sorin, R., & Caltabiano, N. (2020). Exploring the transformative effects of flow on Children's liminality and trauma. *Art/Research/International:/A/Transdisciplinary/Journal, 5*(1), 16–46. https://doi.org/10.18432/ari29492

Harrison, E. (1914). *The Montessori method and the kindergarten. United States Bureau of Education. Bulletin, no. 28. (602)*. Washington Government Printing Office.

Heimlich, E. P., & Mark, A. J. (1990). *Paraverbal communication with children: Not through words alone*. Plenum Press.

Henley, D. (2002). *Clayworks in art therapy: Playing the sacred circle*. Jessica Kingsley.

Herman, F. (1991). The boy that nobody wanted. In K. Bruscia (Ed.), *Case studies in music therapy* (pp. 209–217). Barcelona Publishers LLC.

Levitin, D. (2006). *This is your brain on music*. Plume.

Ludy-Dobson, C., & Perry, B. D. (2010). The role of healthy relational interactions in buffering the impact of childhood trauma. In E. Gil (Ed.) *Working with children to heal interpersonal trauma: The power of play*. The Guilford Press.

Montessori, M. (1936). *The secret of childhood* (B. B. Carter, Ed. and Trans.). Longmans.

Montessori, M. (1964). *The Montessori method* (A. E. George, Trans.). Schocken Books. (Original work published 1912)

Montessori, M. (1967). *The absorbent mind* (C. A. Claremont, Trans). Dell. (Original work published 1949)

Montessori, M. (2008). *The California lectures of Maria Montessori, 1915: Collected speeches and writings*. In R. Buckenmeyer (Ed.), *The Clio Montessori series*. Montessori-Pierson.

Perry, B. D. (2009). Examining child maltreatment through a neurodevelopment lens: Clinical applications of the neurosequential model of therapeutics. *Journal of Loss and Trauma, 14*(4), 240–245. https://doi.org/10.1080/15325020903004350

Perry, B. D., & Szalavitz, M. (2006). *The boy who was raised as a dog: And other stories from a child psychiatrist's notebook—What traumatized children can teach us about loss, love, and healing*. Basic Books.

Perry, B. D., & Winfrey, O. (2021). *What happened to you? Conversations on trauma, resilience, and healing*. Pan Macmillan.

Phillips, B., O'Toole, C., McGilloway, S., & Phillips, S. (2022). Montessori, the white cross, and trauma-informed practice: Lessons for contemporary education. *Journal of Montessori Research*. 8(1).

Rathunde, K. (2015) Creating a context for flow: The importance of personal insight and experience. *The NAMTA Journal. 40* (3), 15–27.

Rathunde, K. (2023). Montessori education, optimal experience, and flow. In A. K. Murray, E. T. M. K. Ahlquist, & M. C. Debs (Eds.), *Chapter 27 –The Bloomsbury handbook of Montessori education* (pp. 271–289). Bloomsbury.

Rathunde, K., & Csikszentmihalyi, M. (2005). Middle school Students' motivation and quality of experience: A comparison of Montessori and traditional school environments. *American Journal of Education, 111*(3), 341–371. https://doi.org/10.1086/428885

Sholt, M., & Gavron, T. (2006). Therapeutic qualities of clay-work in art therapy and psychotherapy: A review. *Art Therapy, 23*(2), 66–72. https://doi.org/10.1080/07421656.2006.10129647.

Sobe, N. W. (2004). Challenging the gaze: The subject of attention and a 1915 Montessori demonstration classroom. *Educational Theory, 15*(1), 166–189. https://www.nsobe.sites.luc.edu/NWS--Challenging%20the%20Gaze%20ED%20THEORY.pdf

Stevens, E. Y. (1912). The Montessori method and the American kindergarten. *McClure's Magazine, 40*, 77–82.

Tozier, J. (1911). An educational wonder-worker: The methods of Maria Montessori. *McClure's Magazine, 37*(1), 3–19.

Trabalzini, P. (2013). Nobody left behind: Montessori's work in defense of children as victims of war. *AMI Journal, 1-2*, 42–45.

Treisman, K. (2017). *Working with relational and developmental trauma in children and adolescents.* Routledge.

Conclusion

Montessori pedagogy began in 1897 with children who were excluded from schools because they could not function like the other children in the classroom. At first glance, they looked like troublesome children, but when the young Dr. Montessori observed them closely, she saw that many of them were children who had mental health or psychological difficulties. Most of these children did not have the social skills to relate to others, nor the verbal skills to express their emotions. In addition to this, they did not have the cognitive skills to comprehend those emotions. Montessori could have looked at these children from a deficit perspective seeing only their shortcomings. Instead, history recounts that she reached out to these children with kindness, love, and compassion. She herself tells us how she first of all greeted them with great cordiality as she welcomed them into her Orthophrenic school. She tells us how she invited them to walk around the institute and freely choose the materials that interested them. She describes the playful, humorous, and trauma-sensitive educational approaches she utilized with these so-called "unteachable" children that led, in a short period of time, to many of them successfully passing the Italian State Examinations.

In 1907, having been immersed for seven years at Rome University, in the study of education, experimental psychology, pedagogical anthropology, and philosophy, she began the educational work for which she is most remembered. To that work, she brought the research and the reflection of these scholarly years, coupled with her years of learning, both practical and academic, to become a physician. Out of this mix of knowledge and practical experience, the approach that came to be called the Montessori method was born. It was during the years, 1907–1917, that the efficacy of Montessori's approach with trauma-affected children was most in evidence. As described in earlier chapters, Montessori's work as an assistant doctor at the Roman Psychiatric Clinic provided her with both experience and expertise in approaching mental health challenges in children. It also contributed to her recognition as an expert in children's mental health. However, it was when she was confronted with the numbed, silent, and traumatized child survivors of the Messina earthquake who clearly were experiencing terrifying flashbacks of the dreadful and sudden event that left them orphaned and homeless, that she began to have a clear understanding of the effects of traumatic experience on the emotional, social, and cognitive functioning and well-being of children. She was haunted by the distress of these children who found it difficult to eat, difficult to sleep, and screamed and cried throughout the night in their distress and despair. She observed them closely and noted how they found comfort in carrying out repetitive activities such as laying placemats and cutlery on elongated tables for meals that they had no appetite to eat. She began to see the power of what Dr. Bruce Perry would later identify as the capacity of repetitive, patterned, rhythmic activities to calm and regulate the brain (Perry, 2009). Then she discovered another phenomenon that (we now know) is vital to the healing of trauma, and that was the power of positive attuned relationships to help trauma-affected children to heal (Ludy-Dobson & Perry, 2010; Perry & Szalavitz, 2017). She promoted these positive relationships by making it a policy to have mixed age groups in the classes, and to encourage peer teaching. She also noted the power of rhythmic activities such as music and movement, work with clay, drawing, and painting to regulate trauma-affected children and help them to become calm. Then, she and hundreds of visitors noted that as the children became regulated and able to relate to their teachers and their peers, they began to show an unexpected, and extraordinary capacity for self-motivated learning, with many starting to write at age four, and read at age 4 ½ or five. It was becoming clear to Montessori that repetition and positive relationships played a key role in helping trauma-affected children to heal and then begin to function optimally at school. In these discoveries, she anticipated the work of Perry and colleagues and the Neurosequential Model in Education (NME) (Perry & Graner, 2018).

A few years later, Montessori's interest in child trauma increased when she became involved with another group of traumatized children – the French and Belgian refugees who attended the schools run by Mary Rebecca Cromwell during World War I. As explained earlier the children presented with what Montessori called serious psychological wounds. Once again, the Montessori method showed itself to be an effective approach for these traumatized children who were described by Cromwell as having symptoms of what we now call hyper and hypo-arousal. As Scocchera noted, this period (1916/1917) represents a particular time when Montessori had a deep interest in psychological trauma in children, especially war-torn children (2002/2013). It was because of her deep concern for trauma-affected children that Montessori attempted to set up the White Cross organization, which would complement the work of the Red Cross, and most importantly offer free interdisciplinary courses to teachers and nurses that aimed to help them to support the recovery of traumatized children. However, as Scocchera tells us, Montessori's proposal did not succeed.

Despite this setback, Montessori's early schools continued to show that they were healing environments and that they were, by their very nature, both trauma-aware and trauma-responsive. Essentially, Montessori had created environments that were therapeutic in and of themselves, and children, especially those affected by trauma, could derive mental health benefits from them. This was achieved by the children's daily engagement in a variety of practical, sensorial, academic, and mindfulness-based activities that included music and movement, dance, clay modeling, artwork, and gardening. Montessori made it a policy that the children were free to engage in these activities at any time, at their own pace, and engagement in these activities appeared to have a remarkably positive impact on the children's emotional, social, and cognitive functioning as well as their general well-being. It was not long until the children in these early classes, including the trauma-affected children, were excelling at academic tasks such as writing, reading, and mathematical work. In terms of non-academic achievements, the children were revealing enhanced social and emotional development, improved self-esteem, and all-round flourishing.

What was really extraordinary was the fact that arguably the children were controlling their own therapy and dosage, a practice that is probably unique in the history of education. Another remarkable fact was that trauma-sensitivity was not an add-on, rather it was woven into the very fabric of the schools. The implication therefore is that contemporary Montessori educators (if they adhere to Montessori's admonitions on the "spiritual" preparation of the teacher) can also be a source of healing for trauma-affected children because they can embody the principle of safety, through their gentle tone of voice, their warm and welcoming facial expressions, and their non-threatening body language. In addition, contemporary Montessori schools can also be places of healing because they promote safety, collaboration, and empowerment, through Montessori's policies, which ban punishments, and eradicate the reward system and its competitive spirit, replacing it with mutuality and collaboration which promotes empowerment. Finally, the Montessori materials can be tools of healing which, by being mostly self-correcting, remove the need for a teacher's constant monitoring, and therefore may eradicate fear in trauma-experienced children and promote a sense of safety. Additionally, Montessori pedagogy trains teachers to be emotionally attuned to children and to promote positive relational interactions in the classroom through the teacher's own respectful and caring manner, and through the inclusion of mixed age groups and peer teaching as part of the pedagogical approach. Also, the order in the classrooms and the materials help the development of sequential memory, which is often slow to mature in many trauma-affected children. In addition, archival photographs from Montessori's early schools show that much of the day was spent in the outdoors, especially the mealtimes, and an abundance of research shows that being in nature is healing for trauma. Ultimately, Montessori's schools became known as Case della Salute or Health Homes (1966), and some prominent psychiatrists acknowledged their potential to help in the promotion of mental health in children (Radice, 1920).

Currently, in view of the pervasiveness of trauma, and the growing body of research recommending trauma-informed practice, it is important for Montessori teachers to understand the potential for Montessori schools to act as healing environments for children. Their efficacy will obviously be affected by the extent to which each school is adhering to the core Montessori principles that contribute to this psychological healing. This is a delicate issue because in some countries, the National curricula may mitigate against full adherence to Montessori principles (e.g., uninterrupted three-hour work periods can be an issue). Therefore, fidelity to what is often referred to as "authentic" Montessori can be something that is outside the control of many Montessori schools. Notwithstanding these fidelity issues, it is arguable that in the context of adversity and trauma research, Montessori's work is even more relevant today than ever before. Her methods, approaches, and principles should not be ignored but rather channeled and used in ways that promote trauma-informed practice in contemporary educational settings.

References

Ludy-Dobson, C., & Perry, B. D. (2010). The role of healthy relational interactions in buffering the impact of childhood trauma. In E. Gil (Ed.) *Working with children to heal interpersonal trauma: The power of play*. The Guilford Press.

Montessori, M. (1966). *The secret of childhood* (M. J. Costelloe, Trans). Ballantine.

Perry, B. D. (2009). Examining child maltreatment through a neurodevelopment lens: Clinical applications of the neurosequential model of therapeutics. *Journal of Loss and Trauma, 14*(4), 240–245. https://doi.org/10.1080/15325020903004350

Perry, B. D., & Graner, S. (2018). *The neurosequential model in education: Introduction to the NME series: Trainer's guide (NME training guide)*. Child Trauma Academy.

Perry, B. D., & Szalavitz, M. (2017). *The boy who was raised as a dog: And other stories from a child psychiatrist's notebook—What traumatized children can teach us about loss, love, and healing*. Basic Books.

Radice, S. (1920). *The new children: Talks with Dr. Maria Montessori*. Frederick A. Stokes Company.

Scocchera, A. (2013). Montessori, the white cross, and Prof. Ferrari. *AMI Journal, 1-2*, 48–50. (Original work published 2002)

Index

Ablon, J. S. 115
abolition of rewards and punishments 26–27
The Absorbent Mind (Montessori) 171
abuse 78; emotional 41, 42, 78, 79, 81; physical 42, 66, 78, 79, 80, 161; sexual 42, 60, 78, 79, 85, 94, 100, 151, 168
ACEs Science 86
acute stress response 44, 73, 156
acute trauma 18, 41
adaptive responses 5, 47–48, 53
adverse childhood experiences (ACE) study 5, 77–88; and adversity 84; common 81; findings of 80–82; interrelated 81; limitations of 82–85; negative behaviors 81–82; on-going influence of 86; purpose of 78; questionnaire 79–80; social determinants of physical and mental ill-health 86–87
adversity 2, 4; and ACE study 84; childhood 85, 87, 110, 125, 127, 133; chronic and acute experiences of 14; sequential memory impaired in 160–161; social determinants of 5
Alexander, J. 63–64, 106–107
Anda, Robert 78, 84, 85
anti-bias, anti-racist (ABAR) principles 6, 143–145, 157
anxiety 54, 62, 100–101, 164, 166; signs of 151; and street drugs 78
asthma 63
attachment 63–64
autonomy 27, 95

Bailey, Caroline 33, 161, 165
behaviors: aggressive 152; destructive 54, 152; externalizing 62; internalizing 62

belonging: creating environments promoting 169–170; mixed age groups 169–170; peer teaching 170; relational neurobiology 169–170
Bernard, D. L. 87
biases 143
Black youth 87
body language with children 127
Bomber, Louise 127
Bonfigli, Clodomiro 13
brain disorganization 64
brain plasticity 32
break and repair experiences 63
Bremner, J. D. 73
British Psychological Society (BPS) 12
Brunold-Conesa, C. 141, 145
Brunzell, T. 109
bullying 28–29; protection from 128

Carver, L. J. 74
Centres for Disease Control (CDC) 77–78, 85
child/caregiver relationship 63
childhood adversity 85, 87, 110, 125, 127, 133
children: body language with 127; bullying 28–29; cognitive functioning 68–74; contemporary Montessori schools helping 159–175; and cultural activities 165–168; difficulties 62–63; effects of trauma on 59–75; emotional functioning 60–64; emotional regulation in 165–168; empowerment 33–34; facial expressions with 124–125; feeling valued and loved 24–25; and individual activity 28; language and tone of voice with 126; mixed age groups and collaboration 135–138; peer teaching

and collaboration 135–138; practical life activities 29–30, 164–165; prioritizing activities regulating for 163–168; and psychological healing 5; and resilience 27; Second Plane of Development 135; social functioning 64–68
choice: as principle of TIP 99; promoted in Montessori schools 140–141
chronic trauma 18, 41–42
cognitive functioning of children 68–74
Cole, S. F. 62, 66–67, 110, 160–161
collaboration: between children 135–138; and mixed age groups 135–138; and peer teaching 135–138; as principle of TIP 98–99; promoted in Montessori schools 132–138; trauma-informed practice (TIP) 98–99, 112–113
complex trauma 41–42, 53, 60, 62, 64
concentration: effect of dissociation on 70–71; effect of hyper-vigilance on 69; poor 68–71
contemporary Montessori schools 4; sequential memory developed in 162–163; and trauma-affected children 159–175
controllable stress 27, 43
Craig, S. E. 68, 83, 114, 160
Cromwell, Mary Rebecca 17–18, 31, 166, 179
Csíkszentmihályi, Mihály 172–173
cultural activities: drawing 167–168; music and movement 165–166; promoting emotional regulation in children 165–168; working with clay 166–167
cultural issues: as principle of TIP 99–102; responded in Montessori schools 141
culturally relevant pedagogy (CRP) 157
culturally responsive pedagogy (CRP) 141
cultural stereotypes 143
culture of safety 112–113
cultures: organizational 94; of trauma-informed care 94

Debs, Mira 144, 155
deep engagement, and environments 171–174
DEI principles responded to in Montessori schools 143–145
Delpierre, C. 85
difficulty making friendships 65–66
discrimination 5, 86, 142, 143, 155, 164; auditory 30; as cause of trauma triggers 157; and disability 83; and ethnicity 83; and gender 83; gustatory 30; olfactory 30; and race 83; and sexual orientation 83; systemic 160; tactile and weight 30; visual 30
dissociation 70–71
distress 127, 168, 178–179; psychological 18–19; signs of 151
drawing 167–168
dysregulated adult 115
dysregulated child 115

eating disorders 152–153
eating habits 152
Else-Quest, N. 128
emotional abuse 41, 42, 78, 79, 81
emotional dysregulation 62, 165
emotional functioning of children 60–64
emotional neglect 79, 81
emotional self-care 116
emotional triggers 62
emotions 2, 5, 28, 45, 54–55, 62, 64–66; recognizing/naming 83; regulating 165–168; uncomfortable/painful 62–63, 74
empowerment: of children 33–34; as principle of TIP 99; promoted in Montessori schools 138–139
environments: promoting deep engagement 171–174; relationally rich and promoting belonging 169–170
Epstein, A. 145
Equity Examined (Debs) 144, 155
Ervin, B. 170
expressive language 71, 72–73
externalizing behaviors 62

facial expressions 124–125
Fallot, R. D. 93–94, 96–97, 102, 133
families: Montessori schools resisting re-traumatization of 155–157; re-traumatization of 155–157
feelings 62
Felitti, Vincent 78, 85
felt safety 124, 129
Ferrari, Giulio 20
fight, flight, or freeze response 44
Finkelhor, D. 84
"flow" 173–174
"flow" healing trauma 171–174
"Flow Theory" 172–173
Foran, Lucille 165
Freud, Sigmund 12
From Childhood to Adolescence (Montessori) 152

Gavron, T. 167
gender: discrimination based on 83; issues, as principle of TIP 99–102; issues responded in Montessori schools 142–143; -neutral activities 143; -specific activities 143
George, Anne 125, 135
Glass Classroom 130, 171
Gregerson, S. F. 83–85, 86

Haring, U. 168, 173
Harris, M. 93–94, 96–97, 102, 133
Harrison, Elizabeth 171
"healing" approach 24–35; children feeling valued and loved 24–25
Heimlich, E. P. 167
Helping Traumatized Children Learn (Cole) 160
Henfield, M. 143
Henley, D. 166–167
Herman, Fran 165–166
Herman, J. L. 60, 112
historical issues: as principle of TIP 99–102; responded in Montessori schools 142
homeostasis 53
household dysfunction 79, 80, 87
household mental illness 79
household substance abuse 79
Hughes, Dan 55, 126
hyper-arousal 47–48
hyper-vigilant children 53, 65, 69, 70
hypo-arousal 47–48

Il Metodo (Montessori) 16
incarcerated household member 79
individual activity, and children 28
individual trauma 40
indoor school environment 129–130
internalizing behavior 62
Itard, Jean-Marc-Gaspard 13–14

Jennings, Patricia 59, 83, 115, 129

Kelly-Irving, M. 85

Lacey, R. E. 84
language/tone of voice with children 126
Levitin, D. 165
Lillard, Angeline 128, 140, 141
linguistic competence 73
Lodi, Olga 132
long-term memory 73

Maccheroni, Anna 33, 165, 166
maladaptive habits 53
Mark, A. J. 167
Mate, G. 64
McClure, S. S. 26
"McClure's Magazine" 26
McEwen, C. A. 83–85, 86
memory: issues 73–74; long-term 73; muscle (*see* muscle memory); sequential (*see* sequential memory); short-term 73
Messina earthquake 171, 178; psychological healing in the orphans 16–17; traumatized child survivors of 15–16
Miller, Hugh Crichton 12
Minnis, H. 84
mixed age groups: promoting collaboration between children 135–138; and relational neurobiology 169–170
Montessano, Guisseppi 13
Montessori, Maria 141–143, 145, 152, 153–154, 161, 165–170, 178; background 2, 11–13; campaigning for trauma-informed care 19–21; early "healing" schools 3–4; expert in child mental health 4, 13–14; "healing" approach 24–35; working with trauma-affected children 14–18
Montessori approach: and biases 143; and cultural stereotypes 143
Montessori Children (Bailey) 33
Montessori Infant Communities 143
Montessori Method 2–3, 16
Montessori schools: ABAR principles 143–145; collaboration/mutuality promoted in 132–138; cultural issues 141; DEI principles 143–145; empowerment 138–139; gender issues 142–143; historical issues 142; peer support 131–132; promoting safety in 124–130; realizing widespread impact of trauma 150; recognizing signs/symptoms of trauma 150–153; resisting re-traumatization of students/families 155–157; respond to trauma in policies/practices 153–155; and sequential memory 160–163; TIP assumptions 6; TIP principles 6; transparency in 130–131; and trauma-affected children 6; trustworthiness in 130–131; voice and choice in 140–141
Moss, J. D. 145
mother treated violently 79

muscle memory 31–32, 139, 161–162; language and math activities 31–32; trauma-affected children 31–32
muscular memory *see* muscle memory
music and movement 165–166
mutuality: as principle of TIP 98–99; promoted in Montessori schools 132–138

National Child Traumatic Stress Network (NCTSN) 62
National Kindergarten Union 171
National Scientific Council on the Developing Child (NSCDC) 42–43, 65, 86
neglect: emotional 79, 81; physical 79
Nelson, C. A. 74
Neufield, G. 64
neural dysregulation 30–31
neurobiological mechanisms of trauma 2
neurobiology: of childhood adversity 85; relational 134, 169–170
neuroception 54–55, 124
Neurosequential Model in Education (NME) 179
non-trauma-affected children 63
non-verbal cues/signals 65–66, 68, 101, 112, 125, 132
normalization 172–173
"normalization through work" 172–173
Norrish, J. 109

"Optimal Experience" 172–173
organizational culture 94
outdoor school environment 129–130
over-stimulated stress response system 61; *see also* stress response system
Oxford Handbook of the History of Psychology 11

PACE (Playfulness, Acceptance, Curiosity, Empathy) model 126
Palma, C. 87
Panama-Pacific International Exposition 171
parental attachment bond 63
parental separation 43, 79
Peace Education 145
peers: aggressive behavior toward 152; defiant attitude toward 151; teaching 170
peer support: as principle of TIP 98; promoted in Montessori schools 131–132

Perry, B. D. 17, 30–31, 33, 43, 52–53, 64–65, 107, 114–115, 127, 142, 164, 169, 179
physical abuse 42, 66, 78, 79, 80, 161
physical neglect 79
physical safety: protection from bullying 128; protection in outdoor/indoor school environment 129–130
physical self-care 115
Playfulness, Acceptance, Curiosity, and Empathy (PACE) model 55–56
polyvagal theory (PVT) 54–55
poor concentration 68–71
poor verbal skills 71–73
Porges, Stephen 54–55
positive childhood experiences (PCEs) 82
positive stress 43
potentially traumatic events (PTEs) 87
practical life activities: care of the outdoor environment 29; care of the self 29; children 29–30; having calming effect on children 164–165; of the indoor environment 29; neural dysregulation 30; synthetic movements 30
predictable stress 27
Preschlack, Paula Lillard 129, 132
protection: from bullying 128; from dangers in outdoor/indoor school environment 129–130
provocation 62
psychological healing 2–3; and children 5; in French and Belgian refugees 18; in the Messina orphans 16–17; in San Lorenzo children 15
psychological safety cues: body language with children 127; facial expressions with children 124–125; language/tone of voice with children 126
psychological self-care 116

racism 155; and Black youth 87; as cause of trauma triggers 157; structural 144–145; systemic 86, 87, 108
Rathunde, K. 172–173
reality-based activities 29
realization 96–97
real safety 124
receptive language 71–72, 73
recognition 97
Red Cross 17–18, 19, 179
relational neurobiology 134; mixed age groups and 169–170; peer teaching and 170
relational self-care 116

relationship-based approach 107–109
resilience: and children 27; self-correcting materials 27
response 97
re-traumatization 97; defined 155; of students and families 155–157; symptoms of 156
Roman Psychiatric Clinic 178
Roman Women's Association 143
The Royal Technical Institute of Rome 128

Sacerdote, C. 170
safety: factors promoting, in Montessori schools 124–130; physical safety 128, 129–130; as principle of TIP 98; psychological safety cues 124–125, 126, 127
safety cues 124–125; psychological 124–127
safety measures 124
SAMHSA's concept of trauma and guidance for a trauma-informed approach 96
San Francisco Panama-Pacific International Exposition 130
school environment: indoor 129–130; outdoor 129–130
Scocchera, A. 20, 179
secondary trauma 114–115
The Secret of Childhood (Montessori) 15–16
Seguin, Edouard 14, 27, 30
self-care 114–117; emotional 116; physical 115; psychological 116; relational 116; spiritual 116
self-correcting materials 27
self-esteem 27
sensorial activities, and trauma-affected children 30–31
sequential memory: developed in contemporary Montessori schools 162–163; impaired in adversity 160–161; impaired in trauma-affected children 160–161; and Montessori schools 160–163
serious behavior issues 100
sexual abuse 42, 60, 78, 79, 85, 94, 100, 151, 168
Sholt, M. 167
short-term memory 73
Siegel, Daniel 53
Slade, E. 145
Sobe, Noah 130, 171
Social/Behavioral Measures 128
social functioning of children 64–68

social medicine 13
social motherhood 16
Societa Umanitaria 167
socioeconomic status (SES) 84, 86
Sorrels, B. 64, 69
spaces for individual activity 28
spiritual preparation of the teacher 124, 127
spiritual self-care 116
Standing, E. M. 15, 132–133, 134–135
state-dependent functioning 52–53
stereotypes: cultural 143; Montessori approach moves past 143
Stevens, E. Y. 32, 154, 162
Stevens, J. E. 68
Streeck-Fisher, A. 70
strengths-based approach 109–111
stress: controllable 27, 43; positive 43; predictable 27; tolerable 43; toxic 43–44; types of 42–44
stress response system 44–47; adaptive responses 47; fight, flight, or freeze response 44; over-stimulated 61; survival strategies 47; triggering of 44–46
structural racism 144–145
Substance Abuse and Mental Health Services Administration (SAMHSA) 40, 96–98, 105, 130, 131, 132, 138, 153, 155
Supervision in Education programs 117
survival strategies 47
Sylvestre, A. 73
systemic racism 86, 87, 108
Szalavitz, M. 107

Talamo, Eduardo 132
teachers: aggressive behavior toward 152; defiant attitude toward 151; spiritual preparation of 124, 127
teaching, peer 135–138, 170
Thomas, M. S. 105
tolerable stress 43
toxic stress 43–44
Tozier, Josephine 26, 31, 162
Trabalzini, Paola 167
transparency: as principle of TIP 98; promoted in Montessori schools 130–131
trauma: 3 Es of 40; acute 18, 41; and children 2; chronic 18, 41–42; chronic and acute experiences of 14; complex 41–42, 53, 60, 62, 64; defined 5, 40–41; effects of 5; "flow" healing 171–174; impact on cognitive functioning 68–74; impact on

emotional functioning 60–64; impact on social functioning 64–68; Montessori schools realizing impact of 150; Montessori schools recognizing signs/symptoms of 150–153; neurobiological mechanisms of 2; prevalence and causes of 5; secondary 114–115; social determinants of 5; types of 41–42

trauma-affected children: attachment problems 63–64; challenges 67–68; contemporary Montessori schools helping 159–175; difficulties with emotional regulation 60–64; difficulty understanding 62–63; emotional triggers 62; impoverished children of San Lorenzo 14–15; mental health 29; Montessori working with 14–18; muscle memory 31–32; non-verbal cues 65–66; non-verbal signals 65; over-stimulated stress response system 61; practical life activities 29–30; psychological healing in French and Belgian refugees 18; psychological healing in Messina orphans 16–17; psychological healing in San Lorenzo children 15; reality-based activities 29; re-wiring the brain 32–33; sensorial activities 30–31; sequential memory impaired in 160–161; strength 110; traumatized child survivors of Messina earthquake 15–16; traumatized French and Belgian war orphans 17–18; unease in social situations 66–67; world as dangerous place 60

trauma-informed approach 94–95

trauma-informed care 19–21; cultures of 94

trauma-informed lens 106; defined 26; observing children through 26

trauma-informed organization 94–97, 98–99, 112, 130, 132, 138, 153

trauma-informed practice (TIP) 4, 5, 93–103; assumptions incorporated into Montessori schools 6; assumptions of 96–97; benefits for children, teachers, and families 113–114; children to feel safe/be safe 26–29; collaboration 98–99, 112–113; cultural, historical, and gender issues 99–102; culture of safety 112–113; in education 6, 104–118; empowerment 112–113; empowerment, voice, and choice 99; overview 93–96; peer support 98; principles are incorporated into Montessori schools 6; principles of 97–102; as relationship-based approach 107–109; safety 98; self-care 114–117; as strengths-based approach 109–111; trauma-informed school 117; trust and transparency 98; as whole-school approach 112

trauma-informed school 6, 112, 117

trauma-informed service 93, 95

traumatic stress: signs and symptoms of 49–52; state-dependent functioning 52–53; window of tolerance 53–56

trust/trustworthiness: establishing/maintaining 98; as principle of TIP 98; promoted in Montessori schools 130–131

unease in social situations 66–67

van der Kolk, B. A. 60, 63, 66, 69, 70
Venet, A. S. 112, 116
verbal skills 62, 73, 110, 178
voice: as principle of TIP 99; promoted in Montessori schools 140–141

White, Jessie 28, 128
White Cross 19–20, 179
whole-school approach 112, 156
window of tolerance 53–56
Wolpow, R. 105
working with clay 166–167
world as dangerous place 60
World Health Organization (WHO) 85
World War I (WWI) 17–18, 21, 144, 164, 167, 179
wound 40; *see also* trauma
Wright, Travis 11, 129–130, 132

For Product Safety Concerns and Information please contact our EU representative GPSR@taylorandfrancis.com
Taylor & Francis Verlag GmbH, Kaufingerstraße 24, 80331 München, Germany

www.ingramcontent.com/pod-product-compliance
Lightning Source LLC
Chambersburg PA
CBHW071410300426
44114CB00016B/2253